International Tourism

INTERNATIONAL TOURISM

Dr. Prateek Agarwal

Reference Press

4831/24, Ansari Road
Darya Ganj
New Delhi-110 002
Phone: 51563444
Fax: 51563334
E-mail: info@essessreference.com
url: http://www.essessreference.com

First Published 2005

ISBN: 81-88583-85-5

Rs.700/-

Published by:
Reference Press
4831/24, Ansari Road, Darya Ganj,
New Delhi-110 002.
Phone: 51563444
Fax: 51563334
E-mail: info@essessreference.com
url: http://www.essessreference.com

Printed in India at:
Mehra Offset Press, New Delhi

Contents

Preface

Tourism is not an indigenous affair, instead it is a global phenomenon. Various countries among themselves have concluded various treaties in the realm of tourism. Gradually, it has become an international matter. Its day-by-day increasing importance has made the governments conscious to develop more and more tourist places in their respective countries as a huge income generating source.

As for the tourism, two or three decades ago and of today, we can distinguish some significant changes. Now, the tourists are provided with required security and various kinds of facilities. Every government is particularly serious about preventing any sort of mishappening with any foreign tourist.

The book 'International Tourism' is an humble effort to shed light on all aspects of international tourism for the benefit of international tourists with details and a comprehensive and meticulous analysis to solve the problems successfully in order to have the way for a smooth movement.

The present book specifically highlights the importance of international tourism, the steps taken and being taken by the governments of respective countries, specific features of particular countries which distinguish one from the other, security arrangements, special ticket facilities, communication facilities and many more facts pertaining to it. The increasing dent on tourism in recent past, such as murder and misbehaviour with international tourists has alerted the governments, for restricting further occurrence of similar mishaps.

The suggestions and fresh ideas would be taken into consideration seriously.

Author

1

Introduction

Addressing the 41st Annual Convention of the Pacific-Asia Travel Association (PATA) in 1992 at Hongkong, Ronald Underwood of AT&T Communications revealed some interesting facts about phone services. He said, "When we first opened the Trans-Atlantic Phone Service between London and New York in 1927, a telephone call between the two cities cost more than US $ 700 of today. Now, the same 3 minute call to London costs $ 1.7 only."

He attributed this drastic reduction in telephone rates due to the amazing world of telephone wires, wrapped in glass. Each year, telephone companies send millions of international calls across the world oceans on beams of light that travel through a few strands of glass, each thinner than the human hair, but capable of carrying tens and thousands of calls at once with great clarity and economy.

Since 1927, when AT&T pioneered international calls, technological revolution in communications has brought travel within the easy reach of a good percentage of population in the world.

Telephone was followed by telex, and telex by fax. Now, fax which stands for facsimile is being further refined. The next generation of machines will bring about more changes. The new machines will transmit images as sharp as photographs taken from a Nikon-35 millimeter camera. They will transmit a page in just five seconds compared to 30 seconds today. And not the least, they will print on regular paper.

Another significant development is a new service which will multiply the strength of fax machines by several powers of ten. Enhanced fax uses the computer intelligence in the network to provide features that are useful to business of every size and type. For example, with automated broadcast feature, one may feed four papers through the machine only once. The enhanced fax service can then broadcast them to tens, hundreds or thousands of destinations on a mailing list at virtually the same time.

For travel industry, it means, we can send our message across all parts of the world in less than a minute.

Mr. Underwood revealed how travellers on the road will be able to move their office along. He said, "We will be seeing more laptop computers and public phones. AT&T's Public Phone 2000 is currently being tested at New York and Kennedy Airports at New York. The public phone is virtually a portable office for travellers on the road. The travellers can plug in their laptops, access electronic mail, or dial any home or business data base. It has speed dial access to travel reservations, voice message and translation service." Interestingly, it is hearing-aid compatible, its keyboard can be used as a telecommunication device for the deaf.

Mr. Underwood also disclosed how AT&T was overcoming the language barrier for the travellers. "AT&T has a great way of helping travel industry's present and future customers break the language barriers. It is called AT&T Language Line, and helps visitors to communicate with everyone from the hotel staff to travel agents to emergency medical personnel. Our Language Line is an interpretation and document translation service that gives any subscribing member, say a resort or an airline, access to interpreters fluent in more than 140 languages. It is open for 24 hours a day and 365 days a year."

There are other developments in the area of communications revolution. The facility given by the telephone departments in many countries to hold international or national tele-conferences with their executives has opened new horizons but, to some extent, reduced the need for business travel. In years of recession, business travel is the first casualty of the economy drive of any company.

However, researchers have discovered that despite these technological developments in communications overall business travel in the world is up. The reason apparently, is that business, trade and industry are growing worldwide, again due to technological revolution provided by fast communications.

Therefore, it is difficult to say what hurts what. In this new environment of global economy, the travel industry can never look back — it is bound to grow faster than other industries.

Computer Reservation System (CRS) : By far the most significant development in automation of travel industry is the emergence of a very powerful, comprehensive and sophisticated Computer Reservation System (CRS).

How CRS Started? Old-timers will recall checking in at the counter of Air India and Indian Airlines only 10 years ago when the check-in staff used to spread on the table large sheets of papers to locate the name of confirmed passenger to allot him a seat. It could take one, two or even more minutes to give a boarding pass to a passenger. But, now, it just takes a few seconds and the boarding pass comes out of a machine, duly printed. No manual writing is involved. The system simply started as an automatic reservation process. In the fifties, a few airlines had begun to use computers to keep track of the number of seats available on some of their busy flights. The travel agents who called those airlines discovered that they could get the seat confirmed promptly. Initially, the computers simply kept track of the number of seats sold on a 'flight'. Later, an important breakthrough came when computers developed the ability to match a seat sold with the passenger's name and thus were able to create a record. However, each airline had a different system. So, when one airline wanted to make reservation on another, their computers could not talk and they had to send teletype messages.

As the airlines industry continued to grow in the 1960s and the 1970s, it was realised that both carriers and travel agents could benefit if agents could communicate directly with the airline's computer than with a reservation agent. Calling in for reservations, changes or cancellations was a time-consuming and costly effort for airlines as well as their agents. Since travel agents sold all airlines tickets, they could not afford to keep the computers of all the airlines in their office. They neither had space nor the resources to do it. Therefore, need arose for a Computer Reservation System which could show the flight availability of all the airlines, or at least many of them. An attempt was made to develop a Central Reservation System (CRS) which could serve the needs of all airlines without having a bias for or against any airlines. But, the efforts could not succeed in the absence of a consensus.

Now, a few major airlines have developed their CRSs on their own or in partnership with others. Travel agencies have also discarded the tele-ticketing machines in favour of airline systems that permit acquisition of more hardware and two-way automated communications. As a result, a travel agency now spends less time calling airlines and waiting on hold and even much less time in typing and writing. Agents put information directly into the system using their keyboards and by entering special formats.

The airlines can communicate with individual travel agents by using a queue format. The reservation systems have printers that produce tickets, invoices, and itineraries. The printers differ from earlier tele-ticketing machines in that an agent and not the airline gives instructions to the computer to print the tickets.

In the USA and Europe, 96 per cent of travel agencies now purchase or lease hardware from one, and occasionally from two carriers. In India. "The 4% of travel agencies that were not linked to a system were 'technological dinosaurs' or focused on niche market that are not well represented on CRS" (Collier D 1993). Air India and Indian Airlines have recently gone into automated computer reservation system and the computer their terminal are available in offices of leading travel agencies. Others are still depending on the telephone system to get reservations which are given by the airlines promptly. In the next 5 years, all IATA approved travel agencies are likely to have their own terminals. It is becoming affordable and small by medium sized travel agencies.

CRS as a Marketing Tool : The development in computing and telecommunication technology have radically changed the way in which multinational organisations like airlines and hotel chains do their business. New methods of storage, organisation, distribution, exploitation and analysis of the product and consumer data have changed the marketing techniques and investment priorities of airlines.

CRS, today, is unmistakably the most important marketing tool of airlines. No need to hire an army of salesmen to talk to travel agents, individually explain to them the product and price and to buy them free lunch to get more business. Now, the objective can be achieved by a fax message.

The CRSs originated in the USA. The first and also the largest is SABRE, owned by USA's leading carrier American Airlines.

American Airlines' Sabre, began operation in early 1960's (Collier, 1989). At this time sale seats on a flight usually involved a transaction between an airline reservation agent who would consult his internal CRS, and a remote travel agent. Travel Agents searched through printed guides and tariff for flights and fare information before calling the airline to determine availability and confirm other pertinent information.

The labour intensive nature of this process did not change till the late 1970s when the CRS began to make the leap from 'in house systems' to remote, networked terminals (Balfet, 1993). The change was driven by several factors like increase in the number of airlines as a result of deregulation of airlines in the USA and resultant increase in the range of fares and flights available to the general public. Another motivating factor was that the travel agencies could use their CRS terminals for several other labour saving purposes like accounting, issuing reminders to customers who had not paid etc.

Presently, Sabre and three others owned by US Airlines dominate the market not only in the USA but also in the rest of the world through alliances. Each member airline pays a fee when the computer makes a reservation for it. The other three leading US CRSs are Apollo (United Airlines), System One owned by Eastern Airlines and Worldspan - jointly owned by TWA, Delta and North-Western Airlines.

A brief description of Sabre's organisation and capabilities will illustrate the sophistication of the modern CRSs. Sabre is one of the largest privately owned computer networks of the world. Its hardware is situated in Tulsa, USA, in a building specifically designed to make it virtually impregnable to terrorist and/or criminal attack and safe from natural disasters. It is difficult not to be impressed by Sabre's size and capacity.

1. It uses six of the largest IBM computers, connected by 70,000 miles of network data circuits to well over 100,000 terminals.
2. It contains flight and fare data on over 35,000 city pairs throughout the world with the schedules of over 700 airlines.
3. Its database has more than 50 million domestic and international fares, with the ability to construct many more, updated every business day at the rate of up to one million per day.
4. It can be used to book rooms in over 17,500 hotels, properties, rental cars from over 50 companies and seats on six railways. It contains detailed information on more than 65,000 vacation and recreation activities.

In July 1994, Air India and Indian Airlines signed an agreement with American Airlines to distribute Sabre Reservation System to travel agents in India.

Air India and Indian Airlines have decided to brand the Sabre product as Sitar or the System Interface for Travel Agents Reservation. Sitar is a customised version of Sabre to be marketed by Air India and Indian Airlines in India.

At present, there are 350 travel agents on the Air India/ Indian Airlines reservation network with terminals of their own. They will have access to Sabre product also.

Sitar provides travel agents with flight schedules, fares, seat availability and instantaneous reservation on 360 airlines in the world. Hitherto, Indian travel agents could only access the reservation system of one airline at a time and not all airlines of the world on a single screen as available through Sitar.

The new Sitar system also gives them access to information on rail journeys, car rentals, 27,000 hotels and 36 tour wholesalers.

It is interesting to note that SABRE system, now Sitar in India, connects 29,000 travel agents in 70 countries and in six continents representing 1,10,000 video terminals. (Canedy - 1996)

Developments in Europe : As the American carriers developed the CRSs, the European and Asian Airlines felt discriminated. The owning airline would naturally have a Trias' in its favour or what is termed as 'HALO EFFECT'. The 'Halo Effect' is the additional business which an airlines may derive from ownership of a CRS. The agents who subscribe to that CRS are likely to be more familiar with the services of the host airline. One way of producing the Trias' is that the owning airline invariably includes its own service on top of the flights available between one city and another. Since the computer screen can accommodate on first screening, only six to eight flights, the flights of the host airline may get a preferential treatment. Although the agent can seek the display of second or third set of flights on his computer screen, researches have confirmed that 75 per cent of the booking are done by travel agents on the first display itself. Agents do not have patience to go for second or third displays unless the client has already given his choice of the airline.

Some systems claim that they do not have bias while others admit and plead that the computerised reservation system is after all, a marketing tool and the Owning airlines have made massive investments in developing these CRSs.

The business from the 'Halo Effect' could be substantial. So, some European and Asian carriers did not want to be sidelined. They developed their own CRSs. British Airways, Swissair, KLM, Alitalia, Austrian Airways, Olympic of Greece and TAP of Portugal now own the GALILEO, and Air France, Lufthansa, Iberia and SAS have jointly developed AMADEUS. The name Amadeus came from the restaurant, where the executives of these airlines met and chalked out a programme to develop their own CRS. Asian Airlines have not remained far behind. And the Cathay Pacific of Hongkong (CPA), and Singapore Airlines (SIA) have their own CRS—ABACUS.

The following chart will give the readers an idea of how the CRSs are being used. The number of agencies using the CRSs is estimated to have gone up by 25 per cent since this information was compiled in 1991.

CRS in Different Regions

Region	Company	Agencies	Terminals
USA	Sabre	14,000	69,000
	Apollo	11,500	44,000
	Worldspan	8,500	38,000
	System One	7,120	30,000
Canada	Gemini	3,500	10,500
	Sabre	1,600	5,400
Source: US Travel Weekly,Oct.91.			
Europe	Amadeus	12,000	60,000
	Galileo	n/a	27,000
	Sabre	2,600	n/a
	Worldspan	3,500	n/a
Source: Companies' Estimates, Nov. 91.			
Asia/Pacific	Sabre 2,900		
	Apollo 1,000 (inc. 900 Japan)		
	Worldspan Abacus 1,600 (SE Asia)		
	Worldspan Infinite 1,500 (Japan)		
	Galileo S. Cross 1,300 (Australia)		
Source: US Travel		Weekly, New York, Oct. 91)	
Rest of the World	GETS	2,000+00,000 Terminals)	
	Sabre	2,000 (750 Latin America/ Caribbean)	
	Apollo	1,300	
	Worldspan	1,200	
	System One	800 (mostly Latin America/ Caribbean)	

Source: US Travel Weekly, New York, Oct. 91 & Companies' Estimates, Nov. 91.

In order to remain competitive, Air India decided to participate in several of them. Beside Sabre they include Apollo, System One, Data II (Delta), Gemini (Air Canada), Galileo, Amadeus and Abacus.

All CRSs are not the same. There are two basic types of CRSs which differ both in terms of operation and information offered.

Single Access : Single CRSs are the most common. The advantage of a single access CRS is that for any given city pair it will show the services of all participating airlines operating on the route, including many who do so by means of connecting services. The passenger is, therefore, able to choose the service he wants.

Multi-access : Multi-access CRSs are different. They provide travel agents/ subscribers with access to the individual CRSs of several airlines, without the need to have more than one computer terminal. Essentially, a multi-access CRS is just a switch which directs an agent's enquiry to the CRS of one of its participating airlines.

For owners of major CRSs, the systems have become an important source of revenue. When asked if it came to a crunch, whether he would sell his airlines or his company's CRS, Sabre, Robert Crandell, Chief Executive of the American Airlines said, "The Airline". He is also reported to have stated that if the company wanted to make more profit on each dollar invested, it should give up flying aeroplanes and just concentrate on CRS.

Computers and Travel Industry : The travel industry needs computers for the following reasons:

1. Direct access to an airline's reservation system (CRS) enables an agent to see the schedules and fares of airlines worldwide and make reservation immediately.
2. The same CRS has access to data on hotels, car rental companies, trains, cruises, buses, destinations, climate, currency, exchange rate, etc. With the push of a button, all arrangements are confirmed.
3. Besides reservation, the computer can perform routine tasks at lightning speed, i.e., changes in reservations, cancellation, etc.

4. When linked to a printer, the computer can print complete airline tickets, itineraries and invoices.
5. A computer with appropriate software can summarise sales and commission income. Such information permits the manager of a travel agency to monitor the performance of his company.
6. Through sophisticated backroom system, an agency can print invoices, record of payments made by clients, keep track of receivable accounts, write cheques on date specified by the agency, keep an inventory of tour and group programmes, track commissions from hotels and car rental companies, maintain the agency's payrolls, produce financial statements, compile employee's productivity reports, store mailing list of special clients, print address labels and undertake many other functions. There is hardly any function of the travel agency which your computer cannot do.

What CRS Can do for Travel Agents : Automation allows the agent to:

(a) Check flight availability on any of the world's major carriers nearly a year in advance.

(b) Display schedules and connecting services between city pairs.

(c) Display the schedules of hundreds of airlines.

(d) Quote domestic fares, international fares, and many specially constructed fares.

(e) Book the reservation and automatically price most itineraries.

(f) Assign reservations to queue for ticketing on the appropriate date.

(g) Print the ticket, provide an invoice, and prepare the passenger's itinerary.

The system also can

(a) Check availability and confirm reservation for hotels.

(b) Confirm car rental reservations.

(c) Make Reservations and book tickets for some railway journeys.

(d) Provide international rail information.

(e) Access cruise information.

(f) Provide such information as weather conditions, theatre offerings, ski conditions, and availability of convention facilities.

(g) Keep files on frequent travellers and their preferences.

CRS and Airlines : An airline reservation can be made in either of the two ways:

(a) By requesting availability display and choosing flights from the display.

(b) By requesting space directly if the flight number and the airline to be booked is already determined.

After choosing the flight, the complete record of the passengers-- Passenger Name Record (PNR)—appears on the display. It contains the following mandatory bits of informations:

(a) Name of the airline

(b) Right number

(c) Class of service

(d) Date of departure

(e) Departure city

(f) Destination city

(g) Desired number of seats

When the necessary segments are confirmed, the following information is added:

(a) Passenger's family name, initials and titles.

(b) Passenger's home/business telephone number.

(c) Travel agency—name, phone and agent's identification code.

(d) Ticketing information, the date by which the passenger must pay for and pick up the ticket or lose the reservation (option data) and the form of payment.

Additional fields (hotels, cars, cruise, etc.) could also become part of the record — if necessary.

To complete the PNR, the user must press a key on his CRT to end the transaction. This key indicates that the transaction is complete, and that the message should now be sent to suppliers concerned. If the booking agent does not press the key, the entire PNR will disappear and no record will be left.

Computers rarely lose messages — that can happen only if the computer is malfunctioning. The message, however, can be delayed as other messages may be waiting in the queue.

Future Trends : Four main trends can be seen in the international CRS world:

Commercial and Regulatory Pressures : Increased competition between CRSs, the rising costs of system maintenance and development, as well as the poor financial position of many airlines and travel agencies are squeezing CRS revenues.

World in a Single Chain

Operationally, there are many inter-CRS marketing and technical agreements. These alliances reflect not only a realistic appraisal by the CRSs that they have to expand to survive, but also an honest attempt to provide a global service for both product vendors and their travel agency subscribers.

Expansion of Travel-Related Sales : To be profitable, the CRSs have to expand their market. An increased focus on travel related or leisure product sales is common to all CRS systems. The development of leisure sales, therefore, has become an essential activity and CRSs are looking to develop leisure-related databases alone or in conjunction with other parties.

Development of New Applications at the Point of Sale This would involve the development of additional services at the point-of-sale or throughout the major CRS systems. Some of these applications are device-related and some are complex PC software applications. Apart from the CRSs themselves other service providers as well as third-party software suppliers are developing new applications.

Marketing of Tourist Places

CRSs provides an excellent tool for tourism marketing. But there are some constraints too.

1. Almost everyone's requirements for information are unique and separate from the decision to travel and process of purchase. It is hard to develop standard replies to different questions.
2. CRSs have only recently started to enhance their range of ancillary services to subscribing agencies. Information technology development now allow organisations to combine a range of their existing assets and activities (products database, customer data base and the reservation system) to offer it to leisure travel organisers.

However, the performance of their new special products is constrained by the archaic basic system architecture from which they have been developed. CRSs as multinational organisations were developed essentially to serve the requirements of the business travel market. Their role in the service of leisure travel market is, at present, limited by both technical and commercial constraints. But, it is likely to expand in the coming years.

Since the existing travel market is virtually saturated, the CRSs need new sources of revenue from tourism marketeers. The National Tourism Administrations, as yet, are not sure as to what their role is in the new technological developments or CRS systems.

A lot of effort is needed to restructure them to serve the needs of leisure travellers. And, it is bound to succeed in course of time.

A possibility is that Airline's CRSs will soon include information on tour packages and permit agents to book directly from an inventory. Instead of using the same brochures as the client, agents may receive diskettes compatible with back-office systems. The diskettes would enable agents to display pages of special version of the brochure on the CRT as well as additional information on hotels, sightseeing and other optional features. In fact, any agent with ability, time and the right backroom system could enter this data from brochure, reference books, guidebooks and the national tourist offices and could write programmes to aid people who do the selling at the counters. The screen may show to the client a 14-day programme of an Indian holiday starting in October or any other month of the year, or, for that matter, any other destination in the world. It may also include comments from clients who have undertaken similar tours earlier.

Frequent Flying Programmes : Another major marketing tool, besides the CRSs described above developed by airlines, is the Frequent Flying Programme.

The intense competition among airlines in the United States led to an innovative concept of marketing to foster brand loyalty among people who travel most frequently. A few years ago, most of the American carriers in North America introduced what they called Frequent Flying Programmes (FFP) directed largely to people who travel often on business. Passengers gained points for travelling, say every 1,000 kilometres. The more they travelled with a particular airline the more points they earned. At various levels, these points could be turned in for upgrading in the plane to a higher class or for a free ticket for the traveller or his spouse, or even a free fly-cruise package. The airlines which could not create their own Frequent Flying Programmes, joined other airlines to keep pace with the competition. For instance, Air India had once a tie-up with TWA on certain sectors in this programme.

Frequent Flying Programmes have tended to create brand loyalty to specific airlines and have acted as disincentives for regular fliers to try different airlines.

To retain or improve their market share, leading airlines of the world are outdoing each other to offer these incentives to people who can surely pay for their or their spouse's travel.

The Frequent Flying Programme has now wider dimensions, since hotel chains and car rental companies have agreements with one or more airlines whereby participants are credited with air mileage for using a particular hotel chain or car rental services.

All plans work about the same way with minor variations. First, a participant has to sign up with an airline offering a Frequent Flying Programme as a participant. Once enrolled, the flyer must make sure the mileage of each flight is recorded. The mechanics vary. With some plans, you put a sticker supplied by the participating airline on each flight coupon, with others you fill in a certificate and submit it at the gate with your ticket. And with some others, you simply show a membership card or provide your number when you check in for a flight. You automatically get the credit for the new mileage.

Again, frequent flying programmes have their origin in Computer Technology. Computers can keep track of the mileage and points earned by a passenger.

Air India and Indian Airlines Frequent Flying Programme: Air India and Indian Airlines which till recently had no such scheme have introduced their own brand of Frequent Flying

Programme in the face of new challenge from international airlines and the private domestic carriers in India. The system was introduced in mid-1994.

Passengers on Air India and Indian Airlines can now look forward to flying free of cost to over 100 destinations in India and abroad if they join this programme.

Branded "FLYING RETURNS", it is the only Frequent Flyer programme from India to offer the facility of accrual and redemption of mileage points on a combination of domestic and international level and that too to the largest number of destinations within India and from this country. It will, therefore, offer to India-based flyers the maximum flight options and the maximum opportunity to accrue mileage.

Members of the joint AI/IA Frequent Flyer Programme, the most attractive FFP for the Indian travellers, can accrue mileage points on either or both the airlines and redeem them for award of free tickets on either Air India or Indian Airlines or on both airlines. The required mileage points for both international or domestic travel can be accrued with international or domestic travel in any class of service on any sector of Air India and Indian Airlines or both airlines.

Tickets bought and paid for in India against all published fares, including excursion, group fare and night fare tickets, will qualify for accrual of mileage points. Members travelling in First Class will accrue higher mileage points than members travelling in the

Executive Class, who in turn will be able to accrue more mileage points than members travelling in the Economy Class. Thus, passengers travelling in Air India's First Class would be able to claim rewards after making a lesser number of trips than if they were to travel in Executive Class (offered on AI/IA Airbus A300/ A310 flights). Similarly, an Executive Class (known as Business Class on Indian Airlines' A320 services) passenger would have to make lesser number of trips than an Economy Class passenger.

Members will be able to redeem the mileage accrued by them in the form of award tickets on condition they complete 30,000 mileage points within 12 months of joining. Redemption award tickets will be freely endorsable between Air India and Indian Airlines.

Private airlines have introduced their own special programme for frequent flyers.

International Networking

A new dimension in information technology has been added by the Internet network which is likely to totally change the travel industry distribution in the world. The system is very simple—anyone owning a personal computer (P.C.) will be in a position to book his entire itinerary from airline booking to hotels at the destination by the touch of a button. He will also be able to see on the screen how his hotel looks like and could also see on the screen the lawns of the Taj Mahal or the banks of the Niagara Falls.

Dr. Negorponte — the 'Guru' of the system—in 1995 at the annual convention of Pacific Area Travel Association at Auckland predicted that direct bookings of travel through internet system will be available in the United States in three years and by the year A.D. 2000, it will be commonplace happening in the country. He predicts that by A.D. 2000 there will be 50 million computers in the US and that the price of computers will tumble down from the current US $ 1,500 to only $ 100. Worldwide the number of personal computers will exceed one billion by A.D. 2000.

The system may be operational in USA in 1997 while it will come a little later in Europe and Japan. India, a technology conscious country, will not be far behind.

This will have a tremendous impact on the travel agency distribution system all over the world. Agents depending entirely on commissions from airlines may be phased out — only those agents will survive who add value to their services. It may be interesting to note that of late there has been a stagnancy in the growth of travel agencies in USA — it may as well be the beginning of the decline.

The internet system will accept payment for travel booking through 'CYBER CASH', making the transaction complete. The airline ticket will be waiting for the passenger at the check-in counter at the airport.

Internet Challenge to CRS : Internet is the largest and the fastest growing information network in the world — and represents an important new challenge to the CRS. Not only is the network registering 25 per cent annual growth in users — it represents also a very lucrative market of potentially high spending travellers with an average annual income of US $ 60,000. Of the users 64 per cent have at least one college degree and are classified among the professional or managerial class (Cyberatlas-1996).

The ease and low cost with which its users (consumers and travel retailers) can access it has forced many CRS operators to establish worldwide Web Sites. *Sabre*, for instance, has introduced on-line *Essy Sabre* for consumers and commercial *Sabre* for corporate use. At present, the cunsumer *Sabre* generates about 2 per cent and commercial *Sabre* only 5 per cent of the Sabre revenue.

Sabre has recently announced that it will launch Internet version of its full CRS system — replacing its traditional hardwared format. By moving its CRS customers to a web-based system, *Sabre* argues that travel agencies will save time and expense of installing *Sabre* hardware, wiring and dedicated phone lines (Rosen - 1997).

It is not yet clear whether *Sabre* and other existing CRS will continue to dominate the on-line reservations in the 21st century.

Automation in Hotel Operations : Computerised Reservation Systems in hotel industry were first centralised by Sheraton Group in 1956. These were further developed and refined by Holiday Inn in 1960s and since then have gone through generations of refinement. Every hotel chain has its own Computerised Reservation System or one based on readily available software.

From computerised check-in to automatic wake-up call systems; electronic locks to closed-circuit TV; fire and security protection systems to tele-conferencing; nothing is more systematised than today's hotels and resorts. One wonders how a modern hotel operates so efficiently.

The various integrated systems that tie several operational requirements together include a reservation system which checks the availability of rooms for individuals or for groups, assigns room types, tracks deposits, and prints management reports.

A front desk system handles registration and checkout; automatically posts guest accounts; provides telephone operators with room directory; updates accounts receivable and tracks housekeeping staff.

An accounting system handles guest accounting, night auditing and all back-office accounting functions. With available, options, the same system supports energy management, monitors life safety systems and controls telecommunication equipment.

Information Related to Processing : An area in which technology has already advanced rapidly is information processing, including the use of company-wide reservation network, and at individual hotels, room management systems, point-of-sale charging, accounting, word-processing and personal computing. The hotel industry has moved dramatically from non-electronic equipment such as cash registers and accounting machines replacing them with computerised and electronic equipment that integrate conventional data-processing application with other hotel systems like energy control and communication systems.

A second major category of information processing is the broad area of property management systems. Over the past decade, according to a survey of American Hotel and Motel Association, as the technology matured, the number of systems that perform a host of management tasks at property level has increased twenty times. They ably and reliably perform not only reservation functions but also room management, front and back office accounting and operational reporting. That includes among others guest reservation, guest registration and folio accounting (the record of guest charges for room, food, beverage and telephone), accounting including night audit, city ledger, accounts payable, and general ledger, travel agency accounting including record of the commission to be paid, guest history and related marketing reports, daily and monthly operating reports, payrolls and the inventory.

Various vendors are now competing to satisfy the needs of each hotel or resorts. They not only satisfy their specific requirements but go out of the way to modify the systems to meet individual needs. In addition, the vendors will integrate their systems with automated and non-automated parts of the hotel.

For example, the more sophisticated systems are able to interconnect with other equipment that monitors telephone calls, energy consumption, restaurant and bar purchases, and fire and security conditions.

Point-of-sale systems have become commonplace in many food outlets, restaurants, clubs as well as hotels. A restaurant system allows the waiter to place order at a console located in the dining room, which prints it out in the kitchen. The restaurant systems reduce errors in calculating and totalling the final check, immediately post charges to guest's room account and provide a variety of analysis including daily reports and food inventory.

Automation has changed the complexion of travel industry especially airlines industry in less than two decades.

Computer Reservation Systems (CRSs) were perfected during the decade of the eighties. At present, some of the leading airlines own major computer Reservation Systems which can store information on flight schedules of hundreds of airlines and if requested, can confirm the seats on any airline in a matter of seconds. This is not the only thing they do. They store information on thousands of hotels and accommodation establishment, car rental companies, tour packages available and can promptly confirm their availability.

CRSs have, therefore, become a major marketing tool for the airlines, with the owning airline getting some advantage in the matter of display of their flights. The advantage is called 'bias' or 'Halo Effect'.

The Computer Reservation System were first developed in USA in early sixties — their performance improved in the seventies and in the eighties they expanded globally. Since European and Asian airlines did not want to be disadvantaged by the 'bias' of American carriers, some of them joined hands and developed their own CRSs. Airlines like Air India and Indian Airlines who do not have their own CRS, have joined several of the leading CRSs. Their flights are displayed on all of them. They pay a fee to the owning airline for each reservation they receive through them.

The process of airline automation led to travel agency automation. The airline owning the CRSs leased or rented their computer terminals to the agencies. These terminals can do the reservation and printing of tickets instantly as well as perform additional functions through sophisticated backrooms system. Among these functions are printing invoices, keeping track of receivable accounts, tracking commission payments, maintaining agency payroll, accounts, writing cheques, etc.

Another marketing tool used by several leading airlines is the Frequent Flying Programme. It is a way of developing brand loyalty—clients who travel on the same airline again and again earn points which could get them a free ticket, upgradation to a higher class when one buys an economy ticket, etc. It is a bait which airlines give to business travellers to frequently use their service.

The new technology has similarly changed hotel operations. Most hotel chains have devised their own reservation systems. Others buy the programmes from vendors. Hotel chains also use Airlines CRSs for international and national reservations.

National Tourism Administration of India

The tourist organisation of India had its beginning in the report of the Sargent Committee in 1946. Sir John Sargent, the then Educational Adviser to the Government of India, was the Chairman of a committee set up to survey the potential of developing tourist traffic to this country. The committee recommended that it would be in the interest of India to develop tourist traffic, both internal and external. An ad-hoc Tourist Traffic Committee was appointed in 1948 to suggest ways and means to promote tourist traffic. On its recommendations, a tourist traffic branch was set up in 1949 with regional offices in Bombay and Delhi. In 1951, similar regional offices were opened in Calcutta and Madras. These offices were assigned the following tasks: to survey tourist resources available in the country, to advise the government regarding measures whereby resources in the form of accommodation and transport could be enlarged and improved, to keep in touch with the State Governments, travel trade and finally to disseminate tourist information and tourist literature on their respective areas.

The first overseas office was opened in New York in 1952 to carry out promotional programmes for India followed by offices in London, Paris, Colombo, Melbourne and San Francisco. The Colombo office was later closed because the local government imposed restrictions on travel of its citizens abroad. A tourist office was opened in Frankfurt in 1957. At the headquarters, the Tourist Traffic Branch was further expanded in 1955-56 from one branch to four branches.

On March 1, 1958, a separate Department of Tourism was created in place of a Tourist Traffic Branch under the Ministry of Transport and Communications. It was headed by a Director General in the rank of Joint Secretary to the Government of India who was assigned the task of dealing with all matters concerning development and promotion of tourism. He was assisted by one Deputy Director General and a few Directors-in-charge of different sections. Simultaneously, an Advisory Council, called the Tourist Development Council, was constituted which was chaired by the minister in charge of tourism. Its membership included select Members of Parliament, Ministers of Tourism from states, leading publicmen, representatives of the travel industry and senior government officials dealing with tourism.

In 1962, for the first time, there was a decline in tourist traffic to India — from 1,39,804 in 1961 to 1,34,036 in 1962. This prompted the government to appoint an ad hoc committee on tourism in March 1963, under the chairmanship of L.K. Jha, the then Secretary, Department of Economic Affairs, Ministry of Finance. S.N. Chib, then Director General of Tourism, was the Member Secretary. The committee examined the problems of tourism in depth and came to the conclusion that the declining trend was due to causes other than the Chinese aggression in 1962 and there was need for some organisational changes to meet the new situation.

The Jha Committee made several recommendations to improve tourism flow to India, specially in regard to facilitation. Visitors were allowed 7-day entry into India without visa on application at the airport. The committee recommended establishment of three tourist corporations in the public sector to develop hotels, transport and entertainment. To make immigration and customs staff friendly and polite, training programmes were suggested. It was recommended that a standing committee of the main departments of government dealing with tourism be set up to streamline tourism procedures.

As a follow-up to the Jha Committee recommendations, three new corporations were set up but they did not work well and were, therefore, merged to make a single India Tourism Development Corporation (ITDC) on October 1,1966. The purpose of setting up this corporation was to give the Department of Tourism an agency which could perform some functions on its behalf as an autonomous body. The importance of tourism was further underlined when the Prime Minister of India, the late Smt. Indira Gandhi, convened a Round Table Conference on October 28, 1966 to discuss matters pertaining to the development of tourism. The deliberations resulted in the creation of a separate Ministry of Tourism and Civil Aviation with Dr. Karan Singh as Cabinet Minister. This was a significant step as it brought tourism and civil aviation together under one administration.

Since the formation of the Ministry of Tourism and Civil Aviation, Indian tourism has been developing in spite of constraint on resources and relatively low priority given to this important economic activity. India Tourism Development Corporation has shaped into a large public sector organisation implementing programmes and policies laid down by the government. In 1985, the late Prime Minister Rajiv Gandhi retained the charge of Ministry of Tourism and Civil Aviation, with a Minister of State working under him. It gave tourism a good boost.

The Department of Tourism, at present, is under the charge of a Director General who is also an Additional Secretary to the

Government of India and reports directly to the Minister. Under him, there are divisions of planning, administration, publicity, hotels, marketing research, wildlife tourism, supplementary accommodation, etc.

Activities of the Department of Tourism: The activities of the department of tourism or for that matter any National Tourist Administration of a country include:

(a) compilation, collection and dissemination of tourist information in India and abroad and attending to enquiries from international tourists, tour-operators and travel industry sectors such as airlines, steamship companies and hotels, production of tourist literature, posters, brochures, information directories and, tourist maps, for wide distribution;

(b) cooperation at international level with tourism organisations at government and non-government levels;

(c) facilitation work such as simplification of frontier formalities in respect of international tourists;

(d) development of tourist facilities of interest to international and domestic tourists;

(e) publicity at home and abroad with the object of creating an overall awareness of the importance of tourism;

(f) regulation of the activities of various segments of the travel trade, such as hotels, youth hostels, travel agents, wildlife outfitters, guides, tourist car operators and shopkeepers catering to tourist needs; and

(g) compilation of statistics and market research on international tourist traffic to India and their utilisation for more effective tourist marketing.

Operation Europe

In 1968, a new scheme for overseas publicity called 'Operation Europe' was launched. The object of the scheme was to closely involve Air India with the Department of Tourism towards national efforts for promotion of tourism overseas. Besides tourist offices, Air India offices were given targets for inbound tourism. Air India agreed to participate financially in the promotional budget of the Department of Tourism as this arrangement was mutually beneficial. As a result of this collaboration, new tourist offices were opened in Geneva, Milan, Brussels, Vienna and Stockholm, in addition to the then existing two offices at Paris and Frankfurt in Europe. The new tourist offices had greater flexibility in their marketing efforts because of the involvement of Air India. The result was a spectacular growth from Europe in 1969 followed by steady improvement every year.

Encouraged by the success of 'Operation Europe', the scheme was extended to the United Kingdom, the USA and Canada in 1972. Presently, the scheme covers the whole world. There are six regions from the point of view of tourism development and each works under a Regional Director. The regions are North America, Europe, UK, West Asia, East Asia, and Australasia including Singapore and Malaysia.

The initial honeymoon between Air India and Tourist Offices is over now. Presently, Air India's contribution is limited to providing some funds for overseas publicity to tourist offices of the Government of India. Cooperation has led to confrontation in some cases due to ego problems of the officers on both sides.

The functions of India tourist offices overseas are not different from functions of the tourist offices of other National Tourist Administrations abroad. The tourist offices in India, however, work on a different pattern. The aims and objectives of Indian offices are to service the tourist on arrival at the airport, to facilitate him through formalities, to service him with literature and information, to keep a close liaison with the state government, travel trade and hotels to ensure smooth movement of overseas visitors.

Tourist offices in India have lists of approved shops and approved guides. They compile tourist information on areas under their charge and disseminate this information to visitors. Tourist offices have a 'Home Visit' scheme to enable visitors to India to meet their professional counterparts over a cup of tea without any cost to the visitors. Tourist offices maintain a list of Indian families willing to socially meet visitors from overseas.

There are four regional offices in India located at Mumbai,

Kolkata, Delhi and Chennai. Besides, there are several other offices at focal points of international tourist interest: Agra, Aurangabad, Cochin, Jaipur, Jammu, Khajuraho, Varanasi, Bangalore, Hyderabad, Patna, Lucknow and Guwahati, etc.

Tourism Set-up in States : Most states of India have a Tourism Administration consisting of a Department of Tourism dealing with policy and regulatory matters and a Tourism Development Corporation running hotels, motels and tourist transport. The states have followed the central pattern and established top heavy corporations. A majority of their corporations are running under losses. State governments, however, cannot easily dismantle or privatise the tourism corporations as jobs of thousands of people working in these corporations are at stake and they have formidable unions.

The Government of India have taken a policy decision that tourism services must go back to the private sector but implementation of the policy is slow. At the centre, India Tourism Development Corporation (ITDC) invited tenders for the sale of some of its hotels—decision has been pending for three years.

Rajasthan and Himachal Pradesh State Governments also invited tenders for the sale of their hotels, but the decision was reversed by the new governments which came to power in 1994.

Tourism in India is a state subject. The centre does not even have concurrent jurisdiction in tourism matters. The centre has the power to advise the state governments in matters of tourism policy but it cannot enforce its advice. It cannot enact a uniform legislation which may apply to the entire country without the consent of the states. Sometimes, the states and the centre appear to be working at cross purposes. Take, for instance, road tourism. For three decades, the central department of tourism has been working on schemes that there should be a single-point taxation for the inter-state movement of tourist cars and coaches, but states have been resisting. Instead, they have defiantly increased taxes on tourist cars and coaches coming from other states, bringing them at prohibitive levels. The foreign visitors to India are irked by the checks and delays at the state borders. According to India Today (June 30, 1994):

In August 1993, Government of India issued a notification allowing tourist coaches with All India permits to pass through different states without paying separate tolls. No state recognises this permit.

A few years ago, the centre imposed an expenditure tax of 20 per cent on five-star hotels all over India without realising that it would make Indian tourism packages uncompetitive with neighbouring destinations. The states did not want to be left behind. Some of them imposed their own 10 to 15 per cent taxes which they termed as 'Luxury Tax'. Now the centre has reduced this tax to 10 per cent, expecting the states to do the same. But, the states have not obliged.

As mentioned earlier, each state has its own department of tourism — and these departments would not like their respective governments to impose unnecessary restrictions or unwarranted taxes which could hurt tourism. But tourism departments are often not consulted or are overruled by the Ministry of Finance.

Tourism, therefore, becomes a victim of the whims of a complicated bureaucratic system.

Like India, USA also has a federal system and tourism falls within the jurisdiction of the states. But, there are no road blocks at the state borders to check tourist cars and coaches and to collect taxes. The Indian system has only led to corruption and bribery. Police has a developed vested interest in retaining the restrictions and extracting money from transport operations.

In the EEC countries of Europe, there are no restrictions on the entry of tourist coaches from one country to another. But in India, the states seem to act more like foreign countries checking the movement of tourist vehicles. The checks may be minor, but the delays are long.

All the 52 States of USA have their own tourism set-up. The budget of the State Offices of Tourism (SOTs) are larger than that of the Federal Organisation, USTTA, which has an annual budget of only US $ 14 million. But, they all work harmoniously to promote tourism to their country. Some of the leading tourist states of USA like California, New York, Hawaii and Florida spend huge amounts of money on overseas advertising. For instance, the State of Hawaii, which had a budget of US $ 23. million in 1991-92, spent US $ 10 million on advertising Hawaii in Japan. The Japanese constituted 40 per cent of the 6.8 million arrivals in 1991—more than the US citizens visiting Hawaii. Often the advertisements are placed by the Hawaii Visitors Bureau (HVB) jointly with travel industry enterprises. For instance, a hotel chain or a resort in Hawaii would certainly like to collaborate with HVB — the State Office of Tourism for joint advertising. Both gain from such advertising, and the advertising money goes very far.

The total budget of the 52 State Tourism Offices in the United States in 1992 was US $ 342 million — with Texas State having the largest budget—US $ 27 million. State Offices of Tourism are active marketing organisations and they spend 90 per cent of their money on marketing, promotions, information or research, using very small staff. For instance, the share of administrative budget to total budget is only 6.9 per cent in Illinois and 12 per cent in New York States. The share of administrative budget to total tourism budget in the Indian states often exceeds 50 per cent. Similarly, at the central government level the ratio of the administrative budget of India's overseas tourist offices is far too high in relation to the promotional budget.

Commenting on centre-state relations, in the matter of tourism, the National Committee on Tourism (NCT), set up by the late Prime Minister Rajiv Gandhi, had the following comments:

Tourism is a national product that is not limited by a particular state or regional boundaries. It has been seen that a typical foreign tourist who visits India has a minimum itinerary covering two or three states and sometimes even more.... It would perhaps be appropriate to bring tourism under the concurrent list of the Indian Constitution.

The tourism structure, both at the centre and in the states, has to be changed. Attempts were made in the past but any new effort at restructuring is killed by procrastination and delays by *bureaucrats who have vested interest in the* status quo. And, as the decision appears imminent, either the minister is changed or the government falls.

Thoughts on Restructuring of India's Department of Tourism : The question of making the Department of Tourism a more effective wing of government has been considered by the Government of India from time to time. It was with this objective that in 1970 the government invited a UNDP team led by Dr. Timothy O' Driscoll, former head of National Tourism Organisation of Ireland, to study the present tourist set-up of India. The study team recommended the establishment of a single tourist authority to deal with tourism matters. The task of making detailed recommendations on organisation was assigned to the Indian Institute of Public Administration in 1972. The main recommendation of the Institute was the setting up of a 'National Tourist Authority' with a marketing approach to 'sell' the Indian tourist product in the world markets and provide encouragement through vigorous incentives such as tax rebates, loans and grants, etc., to travel trade and travel agencies. The Institute supported the idea of a single tourism authority, suggesting that it continue as part of the government with operational autonomy. The government did not accept the need for creating a tourism authority. Instead, they set up a National Tourism Board under the chairmanship of the Minister of Tourism and Civil Aviation to advise him on tourism matters. It was the brainchild of the minister, Dr. Karan Singh, who introduced among its members some of his close intellectual friends. The Board became a debating society and died a natural death when the minister gave up the tourism portfolio. The author of the book was witness to the debates of the board which produced little.

It will, therefore, be seen that no major change had taken place in the tourist organisation of India since its emergence as a separate department in 1958 except minor expansions here or there.

Another exercise in restructuring was indicated in 1986 when Prime Minister Rajiv Gandhi set up a National Committee on Tourism (NCT) under the chairmanship of his trusted friend and Member of Parliament, Mohammad Yunus. The National Committee included some of the most experienced bureaucrats as well as experts from travel industry like P.N. Haksar, former Chairman of ITC, Gautam Khanna, Senior Vice-President, Oberoi Hotels, Inder Sharma, Chairman of the SITA World Travels and S.K. Misra, Secretary, Ministry of Tourism and Civil Aviation. R. K. Puri, who was then a Senior Vice-President of India Tourism Development Corporation, was its Member Secretary.

NCT unanimously recommended establishment of an autonomous tourism authority, like the one recommended by Dr. O' Driscoll to replace the Department of Tourism. The committee got comprehensive research done on all aspects of Indian travel industry and had hired the services of some of Indian's top management experts to suggest a new organisational set-up. A summary of recommendation of NCT on reorganisation is reproduced below:

1. The existing organisational structure of the Department of Tourism is inadequate to cater to the emerging role of tourism as an important stimulant of economic growth and social integration. It is also not capable of moulding itself into a marketing and developmental institution with well defined targets.
2. The secretariat and operational wings of the Ministry of Tourism should be organised on the pattern of the Railway Board. In the new set-up, there is no need to maintain the present segregated identities of the Ministry and Director General's office.
3. The newly established apex body called the National Tourism Board, will be responsible among other things, for formulating a tourism policy, drawing up perspective plans, monitoring and coordinating tourism projects and schemes.
4. A specialised management cadre for tourism called the Indian Tourism Service should be constituted. Such a cadre would have the advantage of equipping the personnel with an in-depth knowledge and experience of dealing with tourism as a national activity. Lateral induction of personnel should be made at appropriate levels to impart dynamism to the system.
5. The role of India Tourism Development Corporation should be redefined as an umbrella body for the tourism industry in the country. This autonomous body to be called the 'National Tourism Development Corporation' should have 50 per cent joint venture interests in all states. For a

developmental role, it should continue to pave the way for tourism in the areas where the private sector is wary to invest.

6. The Hotel Corporation of India should be merged with the India Tourism Development Corporation. Such a set-up would ensure coordinated accommodation network. At the same time, the loss-making HCI, functioning on the economies of scale, would start making profits.
7. A Standing Committee of Tourism Ministers should be constituted to provide an integrated approach to tourism development and also effectively associate the state governments in this process.

When the report was published, Prime Minister Rajiv Gandhi was no longer in power. The report is still gathering dust in the archives of the Department of Tourism.

The two-year-long labour of some of the top brains of the country and millions of rupees spent on research were wasted due to government apathy or call it ignorance of bureaucrats and politicians'.

India Tourism Development Corporation (ITDC) : India Tourism Development Corporation (ITDC) is a public sector corporation created by the government to undertake major responsibilities in areas where the government, due to its own limitations, could not participate actively. It came into existence in the mid-sixties when the private sector was not that active in tourism development and entrepreneurs were not willing to go to areas where profitability was not guaranteed. Besides, the government needed an independent agency to run and operate many small hotels and motels which had been built by the government in different parts of India to cater to the needs of foreign tourists and the newly emerging class of upper income domestic tourists.

ITDC undertook responsibilities of tourism seriously in areas when profit was not easy. To compensate it, ITDC was given monopoly in some businesses where loss was not possible. For instance, monopoly of duty-free shops at all international airports and the responsibility of producing literature for the Department of Tourism where 10 per cent profit was guaranteed to ITDC over and above its cost of production.

ITDC in its present form was set up on October 1,1966, with an authorised capital of five crore rupees. The amount was increased to thirty crores in 1973-74 and to sixty crores in 1981-82. The paid-up equity capital of the corporation is Rs. 31.94 Crores. The corporation is a Government of India undertaking. Funds are provided by the government in the shape of equity and loan capital.

Presently, the government is not funding ITDC. It has been asked to create its own resources and to meet its expansion plans. There is also a move to sell some of its hotels — presently operated by the ITDC.

It is interesting to note that since its inception on October 1, 1966, ITDC is one of the few public sector corporations which has been profitable, though profit margins have been very small. The returns in the massive government investments over the years is minimal. All its properties, however, have appreciated.

The corporation, as its name suggests, was aimed at setting up a sound base for the development of tourism infrastructure. It is perhaps the only undertaking of its kind in the world, offering almost a complete package of tourist services: accommodation, transport, shopping, entertainment and publicity. It offers all this in a spirit of healthy competition with the private sector. And, in a short span of less than three decades, it has emerged as a pioneer, opening up new tourist destinations popularising Indian cuisine and providing entertainment.

With four thousand rooms in ITDCs 35 hotels, motels and resorts, Ashok Chain is the largest in India and the only one to provide tourist services in all parts of the country. Hotels have been divided into three categories: Elite, Classic and Comfort Hotels. The first two categories consist of deluxe as well as three to five-star properties, while Comfort are the budget hotels. The following list shows their geographical spread:

Ashok Elite Hotels

1. Ashok Hotel, New Delhi
2. Hotel Samrat, New Delhi

3. Hotel Ashok, Bangalore,
4. Hotel Airport Ashok, Calcutta
5. Kovalam Ashok Beach Resort, Kovalam
6. Lalitha Mahal Palace Hotel, Mysore

Ashok Classic Hotels

1. Hotel Kanishka, New Delhi
2. Qutab Hotel, New Delhi
3. Hotel Janpath, New Delhi
4. Hotel Agra Ashok, Agra
5. Bharatpur Forest Lodge, Bharatpur
6. Hotel Kalinga Ashok, Bhubaneswar
7. Hotel Bodh Gaya Ashok, Bodh Gaya
8. Hotel Jaipur Ashok, Jaipur
9. Hotel Jammu Ashok, Jammu
10. Hotel Khajuraho Ashok, Khajuraho
11. Hotel Madurai Ashok, Madurai
12. Temple Bay Ashok Beach Resort, Mahabalipuram
13. Hotel Manali Ashok, Manali.
14. Hotel Patliputra Ashok, Patna
15. Laxmi Vilas Palace Hotel, Udaipur
16. Hotel Varanasi Ashok, Varanasi

Ashok Comfort Hotels

1. Hotel Ranjit, New Delhi
2. Lodhi Hotel, New Delhi
3. Ashok Yatri Niwas, New Delhi
4. Hotel Lake View Ashok, Bhopal
5. Hotel Brahmaputra Ashok, Guwahati
6. Hotel Hassan Ashok, Hassan
7. Hotel Donyi Polo Ashok, Itanagar
8. Hotel Japfu Ashok, Kohima
9. Hotel Pondicherry Ashok, Pondicherry
10. Hotel Nilanchal Ashok, Puri

11. Hotel Ranchi Ashok, Ranchi
12. Hotel Pinewood Ashok, Shillong
13. Hotel Aurangabad Ashok, Aurangabad

ITDC runs fourteen independent restaurants, six of them at airports. The organisation is backed by a nationwide transport system from 12 centres operating with a fleet of about 400 vehicles, including cars and coaches. It produces a vast variety of publicity material, both for central and state departments of tourism as well as for its own use.

The corporation runs duty-free shops at five international airports of Kolkata, Mumbai, Chennai, Delhi and Tiruvananthapuram. It has added one more shop in Ashok Hotel, New Delhi, to enable tourists to order their goods in the hotel itself to be delivered at the airport. There is, however, a proposal to deprive ITDC of its monopoly of duty-free shops. In the sphere of entertainment, ITDC runs "Sound and Light" shows at Red Fort, Delhi; Shalimar, Srinagar; and at Sabarmati Ashram, Ahmedabad. The show at Red Fort is considered to be one of the best in Asia.

ITDC's most significant success has come from the growth it stimulated all over the country. Today, Khajuraho, Kovalam and Mahabalipuram feature in many tourist itineraries which once did not go beyond the beaten tracks of Delhi, Agra and Jaipur. The entire subcontinent has been opened up to visitors.

ITDC is, at present, a giant organisation. It has diversified into new areas like consultancy in hotel development as well as doing pioneering work in the production of tourist literature. Its travel agency, called Ashok Travels and Tours (ATT), is a full service travel service offering services to both foreign and domestic travellers. ATT has introduced exciting tour packages like Shopping Tours of India, Honeymoon Heaven, Temples and Shrine Tours, Mountain Tours, South India Bonanza and special packages for senior citizens.

Another major contribution of ITDC has been in the area of development and popularisation of Indian cuisine with all its regional varieties. Ashok Group offers Indian cuisine in all its diversity at its chain of hotels and restaurants — over 125 restaurants located in 35 hotels. It participates in Food Festivals all over the world to popularise Indian food.

In the coming years, ITDC will undergo many structural changes. It is difficult to predict ITDCs future in current environments of liberalisation. But, the travel industry of India cannot forget the debt it owes to ITDC for its pioneering efforts and dynamic approach to tourism development at a time when the private sector was not interested in tourism projects.

World Tourism Organisation (WTO) : India is one of the founding members of the World Tourism Organisation (WTO). India's second Director General of Tourism, S.K. Roy, who succeeded the late S.N. Chib, played a key role in shaping WTO as a UN body, working closely with the late Robert C. Lonali, the first Secretary General. Another distinguished Indian tourism official, Rajesh Rawat, served WTO as Deputy Secretary General for over a decade till he retired. He, too, played an important role in shaping WTO as an inter-governmental organisation.

The World Tourism Organisation (WTO), an inter-governmental technical body dealing with all aspects of tourism, started work on January 2,1975. It was born of the International Union of Official Travel Organisations (IUOTO), a non-government technical body first set up at The Hague, Netherlands, in 1925 to promote tourism for economic, social and cultural advancement of all nations. This work was interrupted by World War II. In 1946, the organisation was reconstituted in London. Its headquarters were later moved to Geneva where they remained for twenty-five years.

In 1963, a United Nations Conference on International Travel and Tourism was convened at the instance of IUOTO in Rome. The conference recommended that "the United Nations should consider IUOTO as its main instrument for promotion of tourism."

During the intervening years, the swift expansion of travel created the need for the world body which would be able to deal with tourism problems at the government level. This led to the transformation of IUOTO into WTO, an inter-governmental organisation providing an adequate framework for governmental level consultations, and effective cooperation between member states. The first general assembly of WTO in May 1975 decided that the headquarters of WTO should be located at Madrid. It has now an imposing ten-storey office donated by the Government of Spain.

Membership : WTO membership consists of 120 full members— sovereign states and about 250 Affiliate and Associate Members. While the Government of India is a full member, both Air India and Indian Airlines are its affiliate members. SITA World Travel of India, a travel agency, is also an Associate Member.

Functions : The WTO works in cooperation with all international organisations, the United Nations in particular, as well as with commercial and non-commercial bodies like IATA, ICAO, ILO, UNDP, etc., involved with tourism. There are three categories of WTO membership—Full members, Associate members and Affiliate members.

The WTO keeps tourism trends and developments under constant review, and exercises vigilance over changes in world economic and social conditions affecting tourism.

The organisation functions as a world clearing house for available information on international and domestic tourism including statistical data, legislation and regulations, facilitation and special events. Members are supplied with regular special studies, surveys, reports and handbooks as well as updated information on the latest developments in various fields of tourism.

In cooperation with other competent specialised bodies, WTO fosters the adoption of measures making travel easier by reducing and simplifying frontier formalities and removing barriers to the free movement of tourists.

To help national tourism authorities organise, administer and manage their tourism programmes better, WTO organises and convenes international conferences, seminars, round table conferences and technical meetings on all aspects of tourism. It helps members get technical assistance through UN organisations. WTO itself is involved in training programmes to maintain an adequate supply of trained personnel for various branches of tourism. Its regular activities include the collection and updating of available information on training needs. Special activities include participation in technical cooperation projects for vocational training through its International Centre for Advanced Tourism Studies (CIEST), Mexico. It provides a comprehensive range of vocational training and educational programmes through correspondence and residential courses.

The supreme organ and sovereign body of WTO is the General Assembly composed of delegates representing full members, associate members and affiliate members. It meets every two years and may consider any question and make recommendations on any matter within the competence of WTO. The General Assembly has created six regional commissions. The regions covered are: Africa, the Americas, Europe, West Asia, the Pacific and East Asia, and South Asia.

The executive council of WTO consists of full members elected by the Assembly in the ratio of one member for every five full members of the organisation for achieving fair and equitable geographic distribution. The council meets at least twice a year.

The WTO secretariat consists of the Secretary General and such staff as the organisation may require.

Among WTO regular publications are the World Travel and Tourism Mondial, Tourism Compendium, International Travel Statistics, Economic Review of World Tourism, Technical Bulletins and Travel Research Journal.

Address—WTO, Captain Haya 42, Madrid, Spain-28020.

Pacific Asia Travel Association (PATA) : Another international travel organisation where the Government of India plays an important role is the Pacific Asia Travel Association (PATA). Although, geographically, India is only on the fringe of the Pacific ocean, its interest in PATA is due to the Associations' marketing strength.

The Pacific Asia Travel Association is the world's largest travel promotion organisation with thirty-seven governments, 52 carriers, airlines, railway and steamship companies and over 1,850 Allied and Associate members. It covers the vast area bounded by the USA in the East, Pakistan in the West, Alaska in the North and New Zealand in the South. The control of the organisation is vested in active government, carrier and industry members. A forty-six member Board of Directors is elected every year from among PATA's over two thousand members. Among the new entrants to PATA are China and Vietnam.

PATA was set up in Hawaii in 1951 as a non-profit organisation to stimulate interest in the Pacific and adjoining areas as a vacation land and to develop, promote and facilitate travel to and among the many Pacific destinations. The organisation's headquarters is in San Francisco, California.

The underlying philosophy of PATA is that the entire travel industry must work together to develop an ever-increasing flow of travel from which each member will derive a fair share of the total business. Membership of PATA is granted only to government agencies, private travel firms and trade associations having direct interest in some area of travel.

Commenting on PATA's role in tourism promotion, Ian Verchere told the annual conference of PATA in Honolulu in 1992:

> One has only to look at industry cooperatives like the Pacific Asia Travel Association (PATA) to see how successful, sustained, joint-venture marketing can be in advancing the tourism fortunes of a specific region to grasp this point. There is absolutely no way that an amorphous, multi-cultural geography like that of the Pacific Asia could ever have acquired the worldwide understanding and awareness it now enjoys without a collective endeavour. This is because no one country or company—no matter how large, influential or wealthy—would have unilaterally had the will or resources to take on such a task or make it work.

...It is for this reason that so many competing airlines, hotels, NTOS, tour-operators, cruise lines and other industry principals continue to merge their resources and influence rather than dissipate them on sole effort.

PATA is a source of accurate and up-to-date information on travel to its member countries.

Although PATA has an elected Chairman who is the head of the tourist administration of the country where the next PATA conference is scheduled, there is a President who looks after the day-to-day affairs of PATA organisation and presides over the meetings of the Board of Directors. The Executive President is the administrative head with his office in San Francisco. The first Asian to become the executive head of PATA is Lakshman Ratnapala of Sri Lanka. PATA has three other regional offices: Frankfurt for Europe, Singapore for Asia and Sydney for the South Pacific region.

An innovative marketing idea of PATA is its PATA chapters, 78 of them with 20,000 members scattered all over the world. They hold meetings, seminars and conferences to promote Pacific destinations. While there is no provision for membership of PATA for individual members, an individual engaged in the business of travel could become a member of the local PATA chapter on payment of a small fee.

The chapters located within the PATA region are called "Area Chapters" while the chapters outside the PATA region are termed as "Promotional Chapters". Thus, the two chapters in India at New Delhi and Bangalore would be Area Chapters, the Chapter in Frankfurt would be a Promotional Chapter. This novel method of making new members has extended the reach of PATA's promotional activities to all major travel markets of the world without any significant cost to PATA organisation.

PATA annual conventions are great marketing events. A Travel Mart goes with each annual conferences bringing buyers and sellers together. The annual conferences are attended by almost 1,500 delegates. Most PATA member countries vie with each other to host a PATA Conference and Travel Mart for the promotional advantage they get from its hosting. Every Conference and Travel Mart brings some 1,500 travel promoters to the host destination. Each conference is preceded by an annual Chapter Conference in the same country.

Recently, PATA decided that annual Travel Marts will, in future, be held annually at a permanent location—Singapore. PATA develops a range of marketing programmes to create an impact on consumers in key travel markets of the world.

News releases, special feature stories and photographs are provided to newspapers, wire services, magazines, radio and television networks focussing on holiday opportunities in the PATA region.

PATA has a Research Division which carries out researches designed to provide members with marketing information needed to formulate their marketing policies. It publishes an annual statistical report on tourism to PATA countries—a useful publication.

PATA Travel News : Two well produced travel industry

magazines, PTN, are brought out separately for Asia and American regions. PATA programmes are financed by membership dues and marketing fees paid by member countries.

Address: 1, Montgomery Street, Telesis Towers, Suite 1750, San Francisco - CA- 94104 USA.

International Conferences and Conventions Association (ICCA) : With headquarters in Amsterdam (Netherlands), ICCA is an international organisation set up with the objectives of promoting international congresses, conventions, meetings and exhibitions through its membership in 75 countries. These members include National Tourism Administrations, travel agents, airlines, professional conference organisers, hotels, transport companies, etc.

International congresses and conventions, today, constitute a big business, generating an annual revenue of US $ 110 billion.

Every country is eager to get a share of conventions and congresses segment of travel as the conventioneers generally spend in the host destination more than the normal visitors.

Many countries have, therefore, set up their own Convention Promotion Bureaus to solicit convention business.

The most popular countries in the world for hosting of international convention were USA, France, and UK—in that order—in 1992 according to the Union of International Association, AMK, Berlin.

Among the Asian countries Japan ranked 11 and Singapore 18 in the world in terms of popularity as convention destinations. India was not among the top "25 most popular convention destinations".

The cities that attracted most conventions were Paris, London and Geneva — first, second and third, in that order. In Asia, Singapore/Hong Kong and Tokyo — ranking 9,13 and 17 respectively.

Convention Business

In order to get its legitimate share in the convention business, India has become a member of the International Conference and Conventions Association (ICCA). It opened its own India Convention Promotion Bureau (ICBP) in 1988. Financing for the ICPB comes from the Department of Tourism, Government of India, but the travel industry also contributes its share.

ICPB has a small office headed by an Executive Director. The office compiles information about the likely international events where India could bid for hosting. On the basis of this information, the Department of Tourism and travel industry jointly try to put forward the case of India to the organisers of an international conference who are looking for a new venue for their annual conference.

It is estimated that approximately 25,000 conventioneers visit India annually to attend one or the other international meeting, conference, seminar or an exhibition. And at least 20,000 Indians travel abroad every year to attend conferences or meetings in other countries.

To create awareness among Indian businessmen and professionals who travel abroad for participation in such international conferences, ICPB has been issuing advertisements in national magazines suggesting that they act as India's ambassador to such conferences and try to persuade the organisers to hold their next meeting in India.

One of their advertisements had the following title:

"Wanted—Ambassadors for India."

The advertisement appeals to estimated 20,000 Indians visiting overseas every year for participation in international conferences to put ICPB in touch with the conference organisers. ICPB has films, literature and other promotional material to back India's claim for hosting an international conference.

More popular convention cities in the world like Singapore, Manila or Hong Kong have specially designed and constructed convention complexes capable of seating 5,000 or more delegates. India too has convention facilities, but only in big hotels. The maximum capacity is 2,000 delegates each in Ashok or Taj Palace Hotels in New Delhi. Even for a convention of 2,000 in Delhi, there is sometimes total chaos as the organisers cannot rally adequate coach transportation to move delegates from one hotel to the other.

India needs a new convention centre designed specially for holding international conventions and conferences with an attached hotel to accommodate at least 500 or more delegates. There has been a plan to build one at the Trade Fairs Authority Complex in New Delhi.

To summarise, the agency that performs the coordinating role in matters pertaining to tourism in a government is often designated as the National Tourism Administration, or NTA for short. The most visible activity of an NTA is promotion and marketing though they undertake numerous other responsibilities.

Today's NTAs have many duties besides tourism promotion. These comprise planning, development, regulation of tourism activities and, above all, building necessary superstructures like highways, bridges, communications net-wash for the smooth growth of tourism. Some governments like India participate in building infrastructure also, i.e., hotels, resorts, etc.

NTAs are generally funded by the governments. A few governments contribute most funds but contributions are also received from private enterprises benefitting from tourism promotion. There are also a few privately funded tourism administrations in the world.

All National Tourism Administrations have similar functions and goals. But, some like the US Travel and Tourism Administration (USTTA) are devoted only to the marketing of the travel product. In France, the NTA is part of the Ministry of Free Time and has been entrusted with many responsibilities of development. So is the case with Spain and Italy.

USTTA was axed by US Government in 1996.

In India, the Department of Tourism which is India's NTA, is totally funded by the government and works under the Ministry of Tourism. It has both promotional and developmental responsibilities.

Among NTAs important marketing functions is the operation of the tourist offices overseas to attract visitors to the country they represent. The overseas tourist offices undertake marketing activities like advertising, public relations, holding of sales seminars for travel agents, participation in trade fairs, exhibitions and promotion of their country on television networks. In fact, overseas tourist offices try to use every conceivable mass media to let the prospective visitors know about the destination they seek to promote.

India's Department of Tourism (established in 1958) is the National Tourism Administration of the country. ITDC is its public sector wing which has worked as an agency of the government to undertake responsibilities of providing infrastructure in areas where the private sector was shy to invest.

ITDC's role is now changing. They have been directed to find their own resources to run the organisation or expand. Government no longer puts in its own money.

The Department of Tourism has many functions including the running of tourist information offices in major tourist cities in India and overseas. But, a more important function in India is to liaise with the state governments to ensure that there are no hurdles to the smooth growth of tourism. Each state of India has its own tourist set-up. They try to promote domestic tourism.

In India, tourism is the responsibility of the states and the centre cannot impose its will on the states. That poses problems. It has been suggested that tourism should be brought on the concurrent list of the Constitution so that laws pertaining to tourism can be made both by states and the centre.

At the international level, the Department of Tourism is a member of three major international tourism organisations involved in tourism development and promotion. The World Tourism Organisation (WTO) based in Madrid is a UN body which is the main forum for governments to discuss matters relating to tourism. The Pacific Asia Travel Association (PATA), based in San Francisco, is a marketing organisation which promotes Asia Pacific region including India. India is its active member. The International Congresses and Conventions Association (ICCA) is yet another organisation promoting international convention and meetings. The delegates to conventions and congresses spend on an average more money in the host country, than the normal tourists.

To get its legitimate share in conventions business, India has set up an India Conventions Promotion Bureau (ICPB) in New Delhi. It is a joint venture of the Government of India and the travel industry. Its primary function is to promote India as an important convention venue.

2

Global Aspects

Geographers study the spatial expression of tourism as a human activity, focussing on tourist-generating and tourist-receiving areas, and the link between the two. The study can be taken at a variety of scales, ranging from the distribution of climate-zones in the world, through the regional assessment of tourist resources to local landscapes, resorts, etc.

From the geographical point of view, tourism has three main components:

1. The countries of origin of tourists. They are called the generating areas.
2. The destination areas — tourist-receiving countries.
3. The route travelled between these two locations.

The following diagram explains the relationship:

Tourism-	Departing Tourists	Destination
generating	→ →	Country/
Areas	← ←	Region
	Returning Tourists	
	← ← Transit ← ←	

The 10 Biggest States of the World

In Area

Country	Area (sq. km.)	Location
Russia	17,075,000	Europe-Asia
Canada	9,976,139	North America
China	9,561,000	Asia
USA	9,372,614	North America
Brazil	8,511,965	South America
Australia	7,682,300	South Pacific
India	3,287,263	Asia
Argentina	2,776,654	South America
Kazakhistan	2,717,300	Europe-Asia
Sudan	2,505,813	Africa

In Population

Country	Population (in millions)	Location
China	1,280.7	Asia
India	1,049.5	Asia
USA	287.4	North America
Indonesia	217.0	Asia
Brazil	173.8	South America
Russia	143.5	Europe-Asia
Japan	127.4	Asia
Pakistan	143.5	Asia
Bangladesh	133.6	Asia
Nigeria	129.9	Africa

Population of World's 10 Largest Metropolitan Areas

City	*1990 (millions)*	*City*	*2000 (millions)*
Mexico City	20.2	Mexico City	25.6
Tokyo	18.1	Sao Paulo	22.1
Sao Paulo	17.4	Tokyo	19.0
New York	16.2	Shanghai	17.0
Shanghai	13.7	New York	16.8
Los Angeles	11.9	Calcutta	15.7
Calcutta	11.8	Bombay	15.4
Buenos Aires	11.5	Beijing	14.0
Bombay	11.2	Los Angeles	13.9
Seoul	11.0	Jakarta	13.7

The tourist-generating areas comprise the home of the tourists where they start their journeys and where they end it.

We have already examined how demand is created in generating areas for travel to a holiday destination. Among the factors that stimulate demand for travel are geographical location as well as socio-economic and demographic characteristics of tourist-generating areas.

Often tourist destinations — countries or regions — have features and climate which the generating areas may not have. For instance, the sunny beaches of Spain, Sri Lanka, India and Thailand have a great attraction for the residents of Germany and Scandinavian countries where winters are harsh and dreary.

Tourist routes which link the two areas constitute a key element in the system. The efficiency shapes the flow and direction of the traffic, i.e., air, sea and land transportation, etc. The frequency of scheduled or charter air services shapes the traffic pattern. The inexpensive charter air services have made it possible for Europeans to travel all the way to Sri Lanka or India on a price less than that of their trips to nearby crowded Mediterranean resorts despite longer distances. The frequency and efficiency of air services have turned the Atlantic almost into a 'ditch' to be crossed in a matter of a few hours. Every few minutes, a plane takes off from either side of the Atlantic carrying thousands of people at a price which most Americans and Europeans can afford.

Tourism flows as a result of interaction between the two areas. The destination areas have a surplus of a commodity, i.e., tourist attractions. The generating areas have a paucity of similar attractions. Tourism organisers convert those needs into demand by organising packages.

However, the tourist flow does not occur randomly. There is a regular pattern in the movement. It is influenced by a variety of 'Pull' and 'Push' factors.

Push factors depend on the stage of economic development in the generating markets — general level of affluence, prosperity and availability of disposable income. It also depends upon the number of holidays available to the people in the generating areas.

The affluence provides them the means to indulge in a holiday but the pressure of living in crowded urban areas 'pushes' them to take a holiday. Availability of frequent charter air services to beach resorts of Asia have enabled coal miners and labourers in factories of Europe to take a two-week vacation on the sunny beaches of Goa, Sri Lanka or Greece.

Pull factor includes accessibility of a destination and the relative costs; The Japanese, for instance, find it cheaper to have a holiday in the American Island Guam and Hawaii in the Pacific than a domestic holiday in their own country because of rising local costs. Appreciation of yen in relation to US dollar has helped the Japanese travel overseas. Half the foreign visitors to Hawai are the Japanese.

Marketing and advertising done by a destination in a tourism-generating area also helps 'pull' visitors to that destination. Extensive promotion done by Mexico and Canada in the USA has 'pulled' millions of Americans to these two countries. Americans are 'bombarded' with television commercials telling them how nice it is to travel to these two countries — and how affordable.

Researchers have also tried to explain the factors which govern the tourist flows, for instance, distance between the countries. On long distance the volume of traffic is small. The shorter the distance, the larger the traffic. Examples: USA and India—volume is small due to long distance. USA - Mexico— volume is very large. Hong Kong - China—the volume is very, very, large.

Shared cultural, ethnic and business ties make a difference in the volume of tourism. Example: United Kingdom is the tourist Mecca for Australians. So is UK for New Zealanders despite the long distance. A majority of immigrants to Australia and New Zealand have been from the United Kingdom and they want to discover their roots.

An alternate way of explaining the tourist flow is offered by the Gravity Model, based on Newton's Law of Gravity.

Broadly it implies:

(a) The larger the 'mass' of 'pushing' and 'pulling' region, the greater is the flow between two regions. Examples: USA-Europe/USA-Canada. There are very close cultural and economic ties which lead to massive flow of tourists between the two regions.

(b) There is a restraining factor too, based on the distance between the two. Distance, time and cost will determine the volume of traffic. Examples: Despite New Zealanders' keenness to visit UK, the number may not be very large due to distance and cost. The other example is Fiji and India. Although Fiji Indians would love to visit India, not many can afford that because of distance. Half the population of Fiji is of Indian origin.

Climatic Conditions

Climate plays an important role in tourism flow. Geographers divide the world into ten different regions on the basis of climate.

Climatic Region	***Physical Characters***	***Significance for Tourism***	***Areas***
1. Tropical Equatorial Regions	Temperatures Moderately high; humidity; cool onshore winds; lush green.	Good for Beach tourism, Discourages Strenuous activity.	Caribbean South Pacific, Indian Ocean and Amazon basin.

Contd....

Climatic Region	***Physical Characters***	***Significance for Tourism***	***Areas***
2. Tropical Wet-Dry Regions	Great seasonal differences; long dry season with warm days cool nights; long rainy season—usually June to November in Northern hemisphere and Dec-May in Southern hemisphere.	Good for sightseeing, safaris & Beach activities.	Northern India, Zambia, Northern Australia, Centre - West Brazil, etc.
3. Dry Climate Regions	Little or no rainfall; high temperature; nights could be very cold in winter.	Abundant sunshine favours outdoor recreation-but discourages strenuous activities Problems—low water supply, extreme heat, dust storms.	Egypt, Central Australia, South-West USA.
4. Mediterranean Climate Regions.	Warm-hot but pleasant and dry summer; moderate rainfall and abundant sunshine.	Favours beach tourism most of the year.	Majorda, Spain, California, USA, Cape Town South Africa, Central Chile, etc.
5. Warm Temperate Humid Region.	Hot and humid summers; plenty of rains in summer; cool winters.	Good for water sports most of the year; humidity deters strenuous recreation.	South China, Georgia (USA) Georgia (Russia), New South Wales (Australia).

Contd....

Climatic Region	***Physical Characters***	***Significance for Tourism***	***Areas***
6. Cool Temperate Regions.	Cool summers; highly variable weather; mild winters; abundant rains.	Encourages strenuous outdoor recreations—pleasant summer for beach activities.	British Isles—Vancouver Island, South Island of New Zealand, South Chile.
7. Mid-latitude Continental Climate.	Warm, humid summers; moderate rainfall; pronounced seasonal changes; cold winters with snow for several months.	Summer good for outdoor activities—Winter for skiing and other snow based activities.	Sweden, Ontario (Canada) and Hokkaido (Japan).
8. Cold Marine Climate.	Cold and damp; no real summers; overcast skies and strong winds.	Not good for recreation. Rich bird and marine animal life.	Aleutian Islands, South Georgia.
9. Sub-Arctic Polar Climate	Very cold and dry summer; warmth absent despite long hours of dry light; some areas permanently covered with ice; frequent blizzards.	Recreation not possible-only adven-ture.	Northern Alaska, Baffin Island, Spitzberger, etc.

Contd....

Climatic Region	*Physical Characters*	*Significance for Tourism*	*Areas*
10. Highlands (Mountains and Plateaus above 1500 metres).	Altitude makes life difficult; great difference between temperatures in shade and sunlit areas. Intense ultra-violet radiation, low humidity, no dust, interesting plant and animal life.	Attracts trekkers, climbers and naturalists; good for skiing.	Tibet, Colorodo (USA), Alps, Bolivia, Ethiopia.

Having identified different climatic regions, we can now discuss different tourist regions of the world. Climate, undoubtedly, is a major draw for tourists.

By far the most tourist movements take place in Europe and North America followed by Asia and Africa. Over 50 per cent of international trips originate and end in Europe. One-fourth of the total international travel originates in North America.

Section-1

Europe on the Scene

With its rich supply of natural resources and its wealth of cultural heritage, the continent of Europe is the world's principal destination for international tourism. Western Europe alone currently accounts for well over half of all international tourist arrivals. The majority of these trips, at present, comprise visits made by Europeans themselves to countries other than their own. But, an economically significant segment consists of visitors from other continents. The visitors from outside Europe often consider Europe as a single destination and visit 2 to 5 countries in one trip. By 1994, some 300 million international tourist trips were made to or within Europe of a total of over more than 575 million worldwide.

Outbound travel from entire Europe in 1994 has been estimated at 340 million trips, despite recession. Out of this, West Europeans took 201 million trips.

A significant new trend from the point of view of Asian destinations is that Europeans are taking more long-haul holidays. It ranges from 25 per cent in UK, 22 per cent in Germany, 13 per cent in France to 9 per cent in Italy.

Charter airlines have played an important role in Europe's long-haul holiday market. The important charter destinations from Europe are Thailand, Sri Lanka, Malaysia and the Maldives, though India's Goa is also emerging as a significant destination.

Although Europe had tremendous edge in tourism in the past decades, it is facing competition from several other emerging destinations—many of them claiming unspoiled environments. Europe's share in world tourism has declined by 8 per cent during the past one decade from over 60 per cent to 52 per cent.

Two major trading blocks dominate economic activity in Europe. EEC—the European Economic Community—consists of the following countries: Belgium, Luxembourg, Denmark, France, Germany, Greece, Ireland, Italy, the Netherlands, Portugal, Spain and the United Kingdom — the "Europe of 12".

The economic and political destiny of these countries is firmly linked, though they are experiencing problems relating to currency, national pride and egos.

The second trading block is the European Free Trade Association (EFTA). It is EC's major trading partner and comprises Austria, Norway, Iceland, Finland, Switzerland and Sweden.

In October 1991, the EFTA countries joined hands with the ECC to create the European Economic Area, a common market of 380 million people.

East and West Europe : Since World War II, the Iron Curtain had divided Europe into two ideologically competing blocks: East and West.

The curtain fell with the fall of the Berlin Wall in 1989. As the new free nations emerged in Eastern Europe, the mighty erstwhile USSR transformed itself into the Commonwealth of Independent

Nations (CIS) with an uncertain future. Europe's political map has yet to be re-drawn.

Europe has great cultural heritage and some of its monuments attract millions of people every year. The following is a list of some cultural heritages which attract more than one million visitors annually:

Cultural Heritages	***Millions***
1. The Pompido Heritages Centre, Paris	7.9
2. The Louvre, Paris.	4.0
3. The British Museum, London.	3.0
4. The Eiffel Tower, Paris.	3.6
5. The National Gallery, London.	2.8
6. The Chateau of Versailles, Paris.	2.6
7. The Science Museum, London.	2.4
8. Charlottenbury Museum, Berlin.	2.2
9. The Tower of London.	2.2
10. Les Invalides, Paris.	1.4
11. The Uffizi, Florence.	1.2
12. The Prado, Madrid.	1.2
13. The Tale Gate, London.	1.1
14. The Rembrandt Museum, Amsterdam.	1.1

Let us now turn to major tourist nations of Europe. It is a very brief introduction to enable the readers to have knowledge about the tourist geography of each country.

British Isles : The British can certainly lay claim to 'inventing' modern holidays, with Thomas Cook being the father of modern tourism who first gave us the taste of organised travel.

Great Britain, a nation of 58 million, area 244,066 kms, is both a tourist-generating country as well as a popular tourist destination. Ninety-two per cent of its population lives in urban areas. Its outbound tourism far exceeds the inbound, virtually double—35 million against 19 million in 1993. The Britons love inclusive tours. In 1993, some 10 million Britons took inclusive overseas tours.

Holiday propensity is very high in the United Kingdom—60 per cent of the British population take a holiday at least once in a year, domestic or international.

Among visitors to Great Britain, 60 per cent arrived by air and 40 per cent by sea. Within the British Isles, the distribution of overseas tourists is concentrated in England, especially in London. Half of them visit UK during the third quarter of the year.

British economy is at present (1996) suffering from deep recession—unemployment is high. In economic terms, it is only ahead of Portugal and Greece. Germany, France and Italy are ahead of it.

Ireland : The small Republic of Ireland, or Ire for short—population 3.5 million, area 70,280 kms—is a popular tourist destination for the neighbouring Britons who comprise 70 per cent of its visitors. Total number of overseas visitors in 1994 was about 4 million, more than the population of Ireland.

Its capital Dublin contains one-third of the total population of the country—over 1 million.

The British-ruled Northern Ireland (Ulster), with its capital Balfast, offers attractive scenery, fishing and water sports.

When Ireland became independent of Britain in 1932, Northern Ireland (Ulster) opted to remain with the United Kingdom. Since then Irish Catholics have been fighting against the Protestants who form a majority in Northern Ireland. It is an endless strife.

Scandinavia : Strictly speaking, Scandinavia is a peninsula comprising Norway and Sweden. For convenience, we can extend it to include Denmark, Finland and Iceland. The region has similar cultural heritage. Scandinavian countries have achieved tremendous economic prosperity during the last century.

The most important tourist resources of Scandinavia are: uncrowded, unpolluted countryside, the spectacular scenery of mountain and coastal regions, islands and holiday villages, and typical Scandinavian culture.

With the exception of Denmark and the Atlantic coastlands of Norway, the region experiences severe cold winters with long hours of darkness, icy winds and frozen seas. In summer, the region warms up a little with nearly 2,100 sunshine hours in a year.

Together, these countries have a population of 22.5 million, mainly concentrated in the southern region.

They received over ten million visitors in 1993—half of them to Denmark alone. Germany is the most important tourist-generating market for Scandinavia.

Denmark : Denmark, with an area of 93,069 sq kms and a population of 5.2 million, is the smallest but one of the most popular tourist destination of the area. Its capital, Copenhagen, has a strategic location between the North Sea and the Baltic. It is also a major entrepot handling a large volume of international cargo. Its airport, Kastrup, is the busiest in Scandinavia. Greenland, the world's largest island, forms part of the kingdom of Denmark.

Norway : A remarkably elongated country, Norway extends 2,000 km from Kristiansand to the North Cape. It has a population of 4 million and an area of 324,000 sq kms.

Although the population is small, 75 per cent of them take one holiday in a year and about 50 per cent of them to foreign countries.

Norway contains some of the most spectacular sceneries in Scandinavia and is, therefore, an important tourist destination.

Oslo, the capital, is served by two airports which provide connections to all parts of Europe. Tourists can also use the country's excellent coastal shipping services to the "Land of the Midnight Sun" beyond the Arctic Circle as far as the Russian border. It is called the "Land of the Midnight Sun" because the sun does not set from the middle of May until the end of July nor does it rise above the horizon from the end of November to the end of January.

Sweden : Sweden is the largest Scandinavian country—area 450,000 sq kms and population 8 million. In terms of area, it is the fourth largest country in Europe. Most Swedes live in urban areas. Its economy is good.

Swedes have the highest propensity in holiday making—90 per cent of those between 16 and 65 take a holiday. Thirty per cent of Swedish holidays are to other Scandinavian countries, 4 per cent to other European destinations. Some 7,000 Swedes travel annually to India.

Its capital, the island city of Stockholm, is a well planned, beautiful, and picturesque modern city. Swedish tourist resources include its large, unspoiled forests and lakes, beautiful countryside setting, varied coastline, their folk customs and dances.

The central lake region contains many lakes; the two largest ones, Venner and Veter, are linked by a 190-km-long Gota Canal. The southern Baltic coast of Sweden enjoys exceptionally long sunshine hours.

Facing the North Sea, is the 'golden coast'— 1,400 kms of white 'midnight sun' coast along the Gulf of Bothnia. It is also the gateway to Lappland—the largest unspoiled wilderness in Europe. Sweden is a constitutional monarchy.

Finland : The Republic of Finland, a Baltic state, is a vast country—377,000 sq kms, population 5 million only. Its more than 20,000 lakes and rivers are major tourist attractions. Lakes and rivers take 10 per cent of their country's surface area. Sixty per cent of Finland is under forest cover. The country, once formed part of the Russian Empire, became independent on December 6,1917.

Finland is Europe's last wilderness area and has capitalised on its emergence as a new eco-tourism destination. Other holiday opportunities include cross-country skiing, hiking, climbing, sailing and spa-tourism.

Finns are not great travellers to foreign lands. No wonder, Finland is the only country in Scandinavia with a favourable balance in its tourism account. Its capital, Helsinki, is air-linked to all parts of Europe.

Iceland : Despite its vast area of 103,000 sq kms, Iceland has a population of only 250,000. Less than 1 per cent of the surface area is cultivable. Iceland's active volcanic activity causes hot springs and geysers. The abundant geothermal energy is harnessed to heat swimming pools, buildings and greenhouses. There are over 200 volcanoes in the country with periodic eruptions.

Iceland is an island close to the Arctic Circle in North Atlantic. The warm Gulf Stream makes its winter mild. During short cool summers, there is perpetual daylight for several weeks, making it an Island of the Midnight Sun.

Although Iceland has been trying to promote inbound tourism, annual arrivals in 1994 were less than 75,000.

Iceland's international airport, Keflavik, is connected with the rest of Europe by the national carrier, Iceland Air, and Scandinavian Airlines System (SAS). Its airport, built on rolling hills surrounded by mountains, is often used as a stopover on the Atlantic flights. The 9,000 kms of road network provides easy movement within the country.

Central Europe : Apart from the short German coast, Austria, Switzerland and Germany are three landlocked countries. Physically, the region can be divided into three parts: the coastal lowlands, the central uplands and the Alps. The combined population of the three countries is 95 million with highly developed economies and high standards of living. The demand for tourism and recreation is equally high. Germany is the second largest generator of international tourism after USA. Austria and Switzerland are the major international tourist destinations.

The three countries have a federal structure with considerable devolution of power to the states in Germany, provinces in Austria and the cantons in Switzerland.

Austria : Tourism is Austria's major industry. Foreign tourists contribute about 20 per cent to the country's gross national product.

The Republic of Austria's tourist resources are immense. It contains 35 per cent of the Alpine area compared to only 15 per cent in Switzerland. Between 15 and 16 million visitors arrive in Austria every year. The seasonality element is not so significant—forty per cent of the visitors come to Austria during winter to enjoy skiing and other winter sports. Two-thirds of visitors to Austria come from the neighbouring Germany, followed by the Netherlands and UK.

The country has over one million beds to accommodate the visitors. Most visitors come to Austria by car using its excellent 18,000 kms highway network.

Lately, Austria has developed convention facilities in its major towns like the capital Vienna, Linz, Salzburg, Innsbruck, etc., attracting business travellers. Vienna, the former capital of the great Hapsburg Europe and a port on the Danube, attracts over 5 million visitors annually. Salzburg is known for its castles, cathedrals, baroque architecture and an International Music Festival.

Switzerland : The Swiss are one of the world's great holiday lovers — 75 per cent of the population take a holiday for at least 4 nights in a year. The favoured destinations of Swiss outbound travellers are Italy and France. Over 15,000 Swiss visit India annually despite its small population of about 7 million.

Switzerland is a very popular tourist destination — 10 million visitors annually spending over seven billion US dollars. Tourist earnings make 8 per cent of the gross national product of the country. Tourism provides jobs to 3,60,000 people.

Switzerland is a confederation with an area of 41,293 sq kms. Its capital is Berne. The Alps mountains cover over 60 per cent of the land area.

Private cars dominate the 66,000 kms of its road network. The Swiss government collects enormous sums of money from toll taxes on roads. Swiss National Railways operate 1,400 kms long excellent railway network and their punctuality can be checked with the tick of this clock.

During the past 100 years, Switzerland has transformed itself from a poor country subsisting on agriculture and handicrafts into one of the wealthiest countries of Western Europe. Much of the Swiss success can be attributed to tourism and the country's ability to offer to the world a haven from political and financial storms that engulf the world from time to time.

Geneva and Zurich are two major financial and business centres where dictators, prime ministers and smugglers keep their money. In 1993, it offered another tourist attraction—by legalising casinos.

Germany : Despite its teething troubles due to its merger with the erstwhile East Germany, the unified State of Federal Republic of Germany (80.6 million people) is the largest and the richest State in Europe. It maintains a high profile of being the biggest producer of international tourism—62 million trips in 1994. The Germans spent 37 billion US dollars on foreign travels in the same year. Foreign visitors to Germany spent only 11 billion US dollars.

The country, at present, is facing a major challenge to find ways and means to finance the cost of unification of Germany. A flood of foreign 'asylum seekers' from former East European countries has shaken the peace of Germany with protests from right-wing German demonstrators who do not want them.

Germany has great tourist attractions. Its Baltic coast includes the yachting centre of Kiel, the picturesque old seaport of Lubeck and the resort of Travemunde. Rhineland is a major attraction for foreign visitors with Cologne, Aachen, Bonn and Trier as its principal tourist cities.

To the east of Rhine are uplands of Black Forests which contain Germany's most popular spa—Baden-Baden. There are good opportunities for skiing in winter and hiking in summer. Heidelburg in Neckar Valley is the famous old University Town.

Bavaria is an equally popular State, known for its attractive scenery and well-preserved ancient cities like Rothenburg and Bayreuth.

Unlike most European countries, Germany is not dominated by one capital city, though Berlin, the new political capital, undoubtedly is of great historial interest. Among other German towns, Bonn, the erstwhile federal capital, is relatively small. In the north, Hamburg is Germany's major port, also famous for its uninhibited night-life. Hanover is known for its Trade Fairs, Dusseldorf is the centre of Ruhr industrial region while Frankfurt is the commercial and banking capital. Of the former East Germany, major attractions are East Berlin, Dresden and a cruise on the Elbe River.

Benelux Countries : The Benelux countries comprise the Netherlands, Belgium and Luxembourg. The region can be divided into 3 parts—the low-lands of the coast, the intermediate plateau zone and the uplands. The climate is not very favourable to tourism.

The Benelux countries were joined by a customs union in 1947 and they are now closely integrated. Demand for tourism and recreation is high.

With a combined population of 25 million and a total area of 74,000 sq kms the Benelux countries are not only some of the smallest in Europe but also the most densely populated.

The Netherlands : Holland is the name commonly used for this country. It was once a major colonial power with its empire extending to Indonesia. It is a constitutional monarchy.

The Dutch, the people of the Netherlands, have one of the highest holiday propensities in Europe. Most international tourism is confined to the neighbouring countries. The Dutch like to travel to India. In 1994, there were 31,000 Dutch visitors to India.

The Netherlands received some 5 million foreign visitors in 1993, though their stay was only for one or two days. Foreign exchange earnings exceed 4 billion US $.

Tourists can enter the Netherlands through Schiphol, Amsterdam's international airport. KLM, the country's national airline, has been promoting Amsterdam as a gateway to Europe by offering a free overnight stay to all those who travel to Europe via Amsterdam and with KLM. It ranks high among the world's top tourist cities. It is famous for its canals, art galleries and uninhibited night-life. Other important tourist centres are the Hague, the political capital, and Rotterdam, Netherland's major port at the mouth of the Rhine.

Much of the Netherlands and the north-west of Belgium comprise flat plains and polderlands reclaimed from the sea. The average height is 10 metres above sea level. The story of reclamation and constant battle against the sea is proudly told to visitors in exhibitions and museums of the country. The Dutch coast is well protected against inundation by sea but dunes are vulnerable to tourist pressure.

Area: 41,181 sq kms and population 15 million.

Belgium : Belgium (area 30,573 sq kms, population 10 million) is an important generator of holidays to foreign countries, over 60 per cent of holidays are taken abroad primarily within Europe.

Belgium is culturally divided between the Dutch-speaking Flemings and the French-speaking Walloos of the south.

Belgium's appeal to tourists is derived from its astonishingly diverse cultural scene. For centuries, this region of Europe has been gathering the cultures left by the invaders—Romans, French, Spanish, Austrians, Dutch and Germans.

Today, Brussels, the capital of Belgium, is the home-base of the European Economic Community (EEC). On the crossroads of the common market, this nation of ten million has attracted wealth and investment out of all proportions to its modest size.

With about 10,000 hotel rooms, Brussels receives 3 million foreign visitors annually—90 per cent on business trips. Other important areas of Belgium are the art city of Flanders, Bruges—a well-preserved medieval city with canals, picturesque bridges and quays, museums and churches, and Antwerp which is the business travel centre.

Luxembourg : The tiny Grand Dutchy of Luxembourg (area 2580 kms, population 0.38 million) is Belgium's partner in a monetary and commercial union. They use the same currency. It is home to hordes of Eurocrats working for the European Economic Community (EEC) and foreign banks. Over 27 per cent of the resident population of the country is foreign—the highest in the world. About 30,000 Belgians, French and Germans cross the border every day to work in the Grand Dutchy of Luxembourg. This tiny State of Europe has one of the highest standards of living in the world—and one of the lowest crime rates.

Tourists who stay for a couple of days in Luxembourg are in a position to have breakfast in France, lunch in Belgium and dinner in Germany before coming back to their hotel in Luxembourg. Isn't it exciting for visitors.

France : France (area 547,026 sq kms and population 57 million) by far, is one of the most popular tourist destinations in the world with over 60 million visitor arrivals in 1995—15 million more than USA which ranked third. Tourist earnings amounted to US $ 27 billion.

France is also a major tourist-generating country. The French took 16.6 million international trips in 1995 spending US $ 14 billion in foreign countries.

In recent years, agriculture in France has overtaken tourism in export earnings. The government, therefore, is taking steps to promote tourism more aggressively. The cabinet has a minister responsible exclusively for tourism. He is called the Secretary of State for Tourism and his ministry is called the Ministry of Free Time.

France has about 2,200 travel agents and tour operators. Of these 18 per cent specialise in inbound travel.

The fact that France is one of the world's most popular tourist destinations is not surprising. Within its half million sq km area, a vast diversity of tourist resources are scattered. These range from historical and cultural attractions of Paris or the Loire Chateaux, to Mediterranean resorts of Nice, Cannes and St. Tropez or winter sports centres of the Alps and the Pyrenees. Of course, the popular French cuisine is another attraction.

France has climatic advantages. Here, summer sunshine hours are at their highest and continue through autumn and winter to provide a prolonged tourist season.

Paris, the French capital, receives 10 million visitors annually. Apart from its own attractions, it offers excursions to nearby Versailles and Fountainbleau, or the historic towns of Orleans, Chartres, or Beauvais.

Paris has another man-made attraction—US $ 4 billion Euro-Disney extending over an area of 4,800 acres on the lines of the American Disneyland.

Iberian Peninsula : The Iberian Peninsula and the Spanish and Portuguese holiday islands are among the major tourist destination areas in the world. This was due to Spain's early entry (in the sixties) in the mass tourism inclusive group market. But, Portugal was a late entrant. By the early nineties, arrivals in the two countries were 55 million: Spain 45 million and Portugal 10 million (1995). Mass tourism was possible due to the proximity of Spain to Northern Europe. The warm waters of the Mediterranean coast provided relief to visitors from the cold north. Charter flights made it easier and inexpensive.

Spain : Spain is slightly smaller than France (area 505,000 sq kms, population 39 million). The entire country is contained in the Iberian Peninsula, stretching 800 kms from north to south.

Outside the Peninsula are the Balearic and Canary Islands as well as Ceuta and Melilla on the North African coast near, Morocco.

Spain has a distinctive culture due to its relative isolation from the mainland of Europe. From the north, one can cross into Spain from France by rail and by road through the Pyrenees. In the south, Spain is separated only by a narrow stretch of water from North Africa and its Islamic culture.

Few countries in the world have undergone more profound transformation in a single generation than Spain. Until the mid-1960s, Spain was one of the poorest countries in Western Europe, ruled by a dictator. Tourism and Spain's entry into the European Economic Community in 1986 have spurred economic growth which has created its own social problems. Streets of the capital Madrid are crowded with new cars, and apartments are selling at New York prices. Imports have soared to an extent where tourism receipts can no longer make up for the trade deficit. The Spaniards are buying a million cars every year crowding their roads. In 1992, Spain celebrated its 500th anniversary of discovery of America by Columbus. Tourism covered only about 50 per cent of the trade deficit.

Geographically, most tourist development is concentrated into a few coastal areas and on the outlying islands. In fact, Balearics alone have as many hotel rooms as Greece and twice as many as the neighbouring Portugal. The only other areas besides the coast where development has taken place are the capital Madrid and in the Pyrenees.

The Spanish islands fall into two groups: the Balearics in Western Mediterranean, and the Canaries in the Atlantic. The Balearic Islands of Majorda, Canaries, Minorca and Ibiz are formed by limestone. Water, therefore, has to be obtained from wells and windmills—a characteristic feature of the landscape. Palma, the capital of Balearics, is one of the main seaports of the Mediterranean. Its airport handles the maximum holiday traffic to Spain—perhaps, in the world.

Uncontrolled resort development in Spain has caused environmental damages, exacerbated regional imbalance and affected Spanish lifestyle.

Gibraltar : The British crown colony, the Rock of Gibraltar, commands the entrance to the Mediterranean. It towers 400 metres over the harbour with the town on its western side. It is only 6.5 sq kms in area and has a population of 24,000.

It has a strategic location. Spain claims the Rock and had, therefore, closed its border. The border was re-opened recently. It has enabled people to go to Spain from Gibraltar and vice versa.

Excursions to Morocco are possible from the Rock of Gibraltar using hydrofoil or ferry links.

Portugal : A small country, Portugal has a population of 10 million and an area of 91,985 sq kms.

Due to its long Atlantic coastline, Portugal's climate is milder and more humid. The landscape is greener than Spain.

The Portuguese, a seafaring nation, built a vast empire in the 16th century. That is why Portuguese is spoken in Brazil, in some African countries and in small pockets of Asia. India's Goa is one of their old colonies.

Portugal has shown remarkable economic recovery since joining the European Economic Community (EEC). The new prosperity has caused imports to soar. Portugal imports half of its food, four-fifths of its energy, and most of its capital goods. Booming inbound tourist business receipts of US$ 16 billion in 1995 and massive foreign investments have kept the economy moving within manageable limits.

The main tourist destinations for foreign visitors are Algrave, a region in the south; Lisbon, the capital; Oporto, and Madeira Island, located 700 kms west of Morocco. Madeira offers 15,000 beds. Lisbon has been called Europe's San Francisco. Its steep streets leading down to the water front are lined with ancient pastel-coloured homes with extensive tilework. The waterfront, too, is similar to San Francisco.

Meditteranean Coast : Both Italy and Greece have a very long tradition of tourism. Malta has been only a recent entrant in tourism.

Italy : The 300,000 sq km peninsula of Italy is separated from

Northern Europe by the high mountain barriers of the Alps. It has a long coastline facing both the Adriatic and Western Mediterranean. Its population is 58 million.

Italy has been a focal point for international tourism since the Victorian age and has a well-established tourist industry. In 1995, it attracted 30 million foreign visitors and the receipts from tourism exceeded US $ 27 billion—as much as that of Spain.

Italy was a tourist country even in the Roman times. With Renaissance, Italy again became the centre of European civilisation. At that time, the country was politically divided into several states. Venice, Florence and Genoa had grown rich on the profits of banking and trade. Their rulers used this enormous wealth to decorate churches, palaces and public buildings with art treasures which have become the mainstay of Italian tourism.

The rich British elite never thought that their education was complete till they did the grand tour of Italy. Even today a lot of people are drawn to Italy because of its rich culture and religious appeal as the home of the Pope. Till the sixties, Italy was the most visited tourist destination in Europe before it was overtaken by France, Spain and even USA.

The Italians themselves are great travellers. Their economy has done well and today it is next only to Germany in Europe. They spent US $ 13 billion on foreign travel in 1993, ranking fifth in the world. The Italians have a soft corner for India. In 1994, their arrivals in India exceeded 55,000.

The Italians were pioneers in building highways (Autostradas) in Europe—the first one was built in as early as 1925. There are 6,000 kms of autostradas in Italy and users pay toll. The Italian State Railways run an efficient railway system. The country is served by hotels, pension and inns of all grades. Major luxury hotels have been built in principal tourist cities of Rome, Venice and Florence.

The Italian Alps are becoming increasingly popular for winter sports.

In southern Italy, the best known holiday region is around the

Gulf of Naples, including Sorrento and Islands of Capri and Ischia. The island of Sicily has a great deal to offer with good beaches and cultural attractions.

Malta : A group of islands (area 184 sq kms), Malta is an independent country with a small population of 200,000. Strategically located in central Mediterranean, it has a good coastline. A former British colony, it became free in 1964. Its capital, Valletta, is a fine national harbour.

Despite its low profile as a tourist country, about half a million international travellers visit it annually.

Greece : Greece, a nation of 10 million people and 2,000 islands, is the birthplace of Western civilisation. Travellers through all ages have been fascinated by its philosophy, art, literature and legends.

Greece is on the Mediterranean sea and occupies the southern end of the Balkan peninsula.

Arrivals in Greece from all countries were estimated to be 11 million in 1995 and receipts were about US $ 4 billion.

Most holiday visitors fly into Athens, the capital, Thessaloniki in the north or into the airports of the islands of Corfu, Rhodes, Crete, Mykonos, Zakynthos, Kafalonia and Kos. Greeks have excellent shipping services linking coastal towns. Their national carrier, Olympic, has frequent domestic and international flights.

In Greece, the sea and mountains are seldom far away. Islands constitute 20 per cent of the surface area of the country. The largest island is Crete.

Turkey : Turkey is increasingly becoming popular tourist destination. On the crossroads of Asia and Europe, Turkey's tourism climbed to a record 6 million visitors in 1995, with receipts at US $ 3.5 billion. The rapid increase of tourism in the eighties ignited a hotel boom which has produced an over-supply of rooms in the Aegean and Mediterranean coastal resorts. Istanbul, the old Turkish capital, attracts one-third of the visitors from abroad. Turkey has an area of 779,452 sq kms and a population of 57 million.

Cyprus : It has been 18 years since the Turkish invasion resulted in the division of the Greek Islands of Cyprus. Cyprus is now divided between the Republic of Cyprus in the south and the Turkish Republic of Northern Cyprus. The latter is not yet internationally recognised.

Greek Cypriots have successfully developed tourism in their part of the country — foreign arrivals in 1995 were 2.5 million. With trouble in erstwhile Yugoslavia, tourism to Cyprus is at present booming. Cyprus is a small Island with an area of 9,251 sq kms and a population of 7,000,000. The capital is Nicosia.

Eastern Europe : Before the demolition of the Berlin wall in 1989, Eastern Europe consisted of USSR, East Germany, Poland, Czechoslovakia (now two independent nations called Czech and Slovak), Hungary, Romania, Bulgaria and Albania. Together, they constituted what was called the Eastern Bloc. Yugoslavia, a non-aligned country, was not exactly in the Eastern Bloc but was considered part of Eastern Europe.

The rapid overturn of control by Communist Parties throughout the Eastern Bloc countries and the USSR has brought about political transformation in the entire region. The region had a population of 420 million compared to only 324 million in the European Economic Community. They had a socialist economy which meant that everything was in the hands of the government and none in the private sector.

After about 5 years of economic adjustments, there are signs of economic revival in some of the Eastern Bloc countries. Many new small businesses have come up in the private sector and some people now have money to travel and buy new cars. Poland, Czech, Slovak and Hungary have better prospects of recovery than Bulgaria, Romania and Russia. Tito's Yugoslavia lies wounded, broken up. The Serbs and Bosnian Muslims are at each other's throat.

Following the break-up of the Soviet Empire, there are now 15 new Republics including the Russian Federation, three Baltic States and Georgia.

Ex-Russian Independent States

State	Capital	Population	1991 GDP Per Capita	Major Resources
Armenia	Yerevan	3,504,000 (A-29,800 sq.kms.)	$2,150	Highly industrialised. Skilled and educated workforce. Exports machine tools.
Azerbaijan	Baku	7,146,600 (A-86,600 sq. kms)	$1,670	Fertile land, ample oil. Exports chemicals, textiles, machines.
Belarus	Minsk	10,263,000 (A-207,600 sq. kms)	$3,110	Heavily industrialised. Exports machinery, chemicals, textiles, electric equipment.
Estonia	Tillinn	1,581,000 (A: 45,100 sq. kms)	$3,830	Highly industrialised skilled and educated work force. Exports agricultural products, machinery, electronic equipment.
Georgia	Tbilisi	5,476,000, (A: 69700 sq. kms)	$1640	Tourist industry based on warm climate and cultural history. Exports wine and citrus products.
Kazakhistan	Almaty	16,947,000 (A: 2,717,300 sq. kms)	$2,470	Fertile farm land, minerals, vast oil deposits.
Kyrgyzstan	Bishkek	4,506,000 (A: 198,500 sq. kms)	$1,550	Minerals, arable land. Exports agricultural products, consumer goods machinery.
Latvia	Riga	2,702,000 (A: 98,859 sq. kms)	$3,470	Tradition of foreign trade. Advanced industrial base.
Lithuania	Vilnius	3,736,000 (A: 65,200 sq. kms)	$2,710	Electricity produced by atomic reactors. Exports agricultural products, consumer goods, machinery.

Contd...

State	Capital	1991 GDP Population	Per Capita	Major Resources
Moldova	Chisinau	4,372,000 (A: 33,700 sq. kms)	$2,170	Was the fruit-basket of USSR. Exports wine, consumer goods.
Tajikistan	Dushanbe	5,272,000 (A: 143,100 sq. kms)	$1,050	Hydropower fuels, aluminum industry, supplies most electricity. Exports cotton and agricultural products.
Turkme-	Ashkha-bad	3,856,000 (A: 487,100 sq. kms)	$1,700	Cotton and natural gas. Exports Nistan machinery and textiles.
Ukraine	Kiev	52,103,000 (A: 603,700 sq. kms)	$2,340	Endowed with a wide variety of resources. Vast tracts of fertile soil.
Uzbekistan	Tashkent	21,301,000 (A: 447,400 sq. kms)	$1,350	Major exporter of grain. Cotton is the major resource. Huge reserves of natural gas.

Most of these states have joined together to form what is called Commonwealth of Independent States (CIS) under the leadership of Russia. Their economy is dependent on each other. Visa free entry is allowed to citizens of all the new Republics.

3

Global Chain

Travel had created a demand for home away from home. There is a close link between the growth of accommodation facilities and development of modes of transport. Till the middle of the nineteenth century, journeys were normally confined to roads within the boundaries of a country — both for business and for vacation. To meet the demand of these travellers, inns and hostelieries developed in Europe along the highways and near the main towns. In India, commercial hospitality was virtually unknown. The travellers found shelter in Serais and Dharamshalas built by the State or by charitable people and institutions. Selling accommodation and food was looked down by the Indian people; a visitor was to be welcomed and honoured — it was a pious act to serve him.

Inn-keeping has been around for centuries in Europe. By the time Rome conquered the then known world, inns and taverns were well-established. These provided food, drink and entertainment to travellers against payment. With the decline of Roman Empire by about A.D.500, travellers' inns known to civilisation for a thousand years disappeared due to lack of business. During this period, it was the Church which housed people who travelled for pilgrimage. This was also the system that prevailed in the Indian sub-continent since the dawn of civilisation. The weary travellers got shelter in temples.

By the fifteenth century, inns developed again in several countries of Europe, especially in England and France. Gradually, in the seventeenth and eighteenth centuries, the inns expanded their facilities and some of these had thirty to fifty rooms, stables and quarters for post-boys who carried mail. English common law declared the inn to be a public house and imposed social responsibilities on the innkeeper for the well-being of the travellers. About 200 old coaching and posting inns are still operating in England as hotels, as part of Trust House Forte Limited — a major hotel chain of the United Kingdom. Some of these inns date back four hundred years.

As the railways appeared on the scene in 1825 in England, the fate of inns was sealed. Travel time was drastically reduced, with the result that a majority of stage-coach inns went out of business till these were rediscovered in the early twentieth century by the cyclists and the motorists.

The first Tavern in what is now the United States of America was opened by a man called Samuel Coles in 1634. He had come to the New World with the first shipload of Puritians in 1630. By 1780, Taverns were popular meeting places. In 1783, George Washington said farewell to his top-ranking officers at the Fraunces Tavern in New York City. Patric Henry has described taverns of the colonial America, as "The cradles of liberty". These were the meeting places of the people who brought about the American Revolution. The Boston Tea Party was planned in a Tavern called Green Dragon.

Origin and Growth

Hotels emerged from taverns by the simple expedient of a change in name. The world hotel had a more glamorous ring to it. In France, hotel was the city residence of the rich or prominent persons. Public buildings were also called hotels such as the town hall, mint, etc. By about 1800, the terms 'Tavern', 'Hotel' and 'Coffee House' were used to describe the same thing. By 1820, 'Hotel' became the accepted term to describe a place where people stayed for the night and took their meals on payment. Hotel-keeping over the years has developed a distinctly American flavour all over the world. The American Hotel served a different purpose than the Inn or Railway Hotel in England. Here, the hotel was a place for businessmen to be together. The class system was not rooted in American society and people of all classes landed in hotels to mingle. Daniel J. Boorstern describes American Hotels in the following words: "Americans live in a realm of uncertain boundaries, in an affable, commercial world which strictly speaking, is neither public nor private, a world of first names, open doors, front porches and front lawns and naturally too of lunch counters, restaurants and hotel lobbies."

The 'American Plan', the arrangement by which one charge covers both room and meals, is purely American. It started in the 1830's and 1840's when the Americans were churning around the West and new cities were developing. Even in the early nineteenth century, Americans gathered in hotels to hold their conventions. Henry Clay was nominated for presidency in Baltimore Hotel as early as 1830. This hotel had two hundred apartments. The system of conventions and meetings is a big business in USA today, contributing one-third of the revenue of the American Hotels.

International Networking

Until the late forties, the small international hotel business was managed mainly by the Swiss or the English. American hoteliers were reluctant to invest abroad. In 1948, the US government asked several hotel companies whether they would be willing to build hotel properties in Latin America to improve the economy of these countries. Only Pan American Airways agreed to do so. Intercontinental Hotel Corporation was thus set up as a completely owned subsidiary of Pan American Airways — now sold. New properties were built in several countries and management leases were taken on some. It was only after World War II that America got involved in setting up hotels internationally, thanks to the vision of a great American called Conrad Hilton. He perceived that there was a pent-up demand for hotel rooms. First, he acquired properties in the US and then moved over to foreign countries. In 1948, Conrad Hilton started his first international hotel in San Juan — after that there was no looking back. By 1991, Hilton International, which is now headquartered in UK, had 50,799 rooms in 151 hotels outside the USA. Earnest Handerson was another pioneer in hotel business— he founded the Sheraton Chain. These two modern hotel chains ruled the hotel-market till Hyatt and its atriums came along in the sixties. The air travel led to millions of Americans travelling abroad and the demand for standardised comforts Americans were used to. The host countries across the Atlantic and the developing nations elsewhere wanted Hiltons and Sheratons to build new hotels in their countries or manage the existing ones they already had. Wherever these hotels were built, American traffic followed.

The other major development was the evolvement of standardised roadside and suburban motels by Kemmons Wilson, founder of the Holiday Inn chain, now the largest hotel chain in the world.

He conceived the idea of comfortable, clean and economical accommodations without frills, with a lot of parking space. He followed the highways that were fast coming up in the USA. The new concept of motels spread all over the world, with building of highways and availability of cheap personal cars.

There are two basic reasons which explain the American success in operating hotels abroad: first, Americans are the largest travellers overseas; and second, they travel first class and feel comfortable and reassured in American-managed properties. The appendix to this chapter gives the position of the top fifty international hotel chains in 1991 — a majority of them are American.

The following chart shows the amenities that are provided in the US hotels and motels. Today, all these are the most essential features of international hotels all over the world. The five-star hotels in India are expected to provide all these facilities to earn their stars.

Guest Amenities and Services in US Hotels

01.	Personal Bathroom	75.2%
02.	Free Parking	73.4%
03.	Overnight Dry-Cleaning	72.6%
04.	Audio-Visual Equipment	64.1%
05.	Outdoor Pool	61.4%

06.	Airport Transportation	51.3%
07.	Newstand	50.7%
08.	Gift Shop	45.4%
09.	Multilingual staff	40.6%
10.	Auto-rental	40.6%
11.	Game Room	37.6%
12.	Health Club	34.6%
13.	Concierge Services	29.2%
14.	Indoor Pool	29.2%
15.	Secretarial Services	23.6%
16.	Retail Outlets	21.5%
17.	24-hour Doorman	21.5%
18.	Barber/Beauty Saloon Shop	21.2%
19.	Executive Floors	20.3%
20.	24-Hour Room Service	12.4%
21.	Golf	11.2%
22.	Travel Agent on Premises	9.2%

It may be interesting to note that there are 13 hotel/motel rooms with private bath per thousand population in the United States—the highest in the world.

The accommodation sector in travel industry can be conveniently categorised into;

Extra Space : Hotels and motels often offer similar facilities except that a motel may be more on the highway with a large parking area so that a traveller can move into the room for a night's rest after parking his car. However, hotels and motels, today, offer almost similar facilities and it depends upon the traveller to choose what suits him most.

The ultimate low cost accommodation in large cities has appeared in the form of "capsule hotels" in Japan. Guests are housed in bunks of plastic sleeping capsules measuring five feet high, five feet wide and six feet, seven inches deep. They rent for about 25 dollars a night in Tokyo and are often fully booked. Each capsule is equipped with television, radio, air-conditioner and an alarm clock. A single hotel may contain over four hundred capsules. An increasing number of these establishments are appearing in major Japanese cities.

Webster defines hotel as a "building or institution providing lodging, meals and service to public." From the point of view of users, a hotel is an institution of commercial hospitality. It offers its facilities and services for sale, individually or in various combinations.

Motel is an abbreviation of the phrase Automatic Hotel. As a product for sale, a hotel/motel consists of the following elements. Together, they determine its saleability and price:

(a) *Location:* implies accessibility and convenience to clients.

(b) *Facilities:* refer to the quality of bedrooms, function rooms, restaurants, bars, shopping arcade, transport, taxi facilities, etc.

(c) *Service:* comprises speed, efficiency, degree of personal attention.

(d) *Image:* is the way in which a hotel portrays itself and emerges from the above factors. It is, however, enhanced by factors like atmosphere, name of the hotel and its association, appearance and the type of people who patronise it.

(e) *Price:* is determined by all the elements mentioned above. It is the value given by the hotel/motel through its service, reputation, and general satisfaction of its patrons.

Within the framework of above factors, a hotel becomes marketable. While a hotel fixes its own tariff, patrons determine the price at which it will actually sell.

Supplementary accommodation may be described as premises which offer accommodation but not necessarily hotel services. In the Indian context, this form of accommodation consists of tourist bungalows, government rest houses, canal rest houses, youth hostels, etc. Government rest houses were originally built during the British Raj to house government officials on tour. In the post-independence period, the government built travellers', lodges, tourist lodges, youth hostels, and camping sites to give a boost to domestic tourism. Youth hostels, of which there are about 200 in the country, are a new phenomenon in India. Worldwide, there are more than five thousand youth hostels operating in fifty countries. The prices of youth hostel accommodation in India vary from one rupee in a college building to ten to twenty five rupees per person in the youth hostels constructed by the Government of India. The rates in the USA are 5 to 10 dollars per day, 5 to 10 pounds in UK and 10 to 25 marks in West Germany. The current membership of youth hostels worldwide, according to Youth Hostels Association of India, is 4 million and in India it is 30,000.

In India, the rentable accommodation is supplemented by free accommodation provided in temples, dharamshalas and sarais. No wonder that in India a large population is always on the move. Indian Railways move some 12 million people every day equal to the population of Australia, and another 20 million move in buses.

By far, the largest accommodation in any country is provided by the organised sector of hotels and motels.

Modern Concepts : Condominium hotels are a recent innovation. An American concept, these are hotels with apartments (condominiums) instead of basic rooms. The condominium units are sold by a developer to individual owners, who in turn contract them to the developer or a management company to operate the hotel and rent the space to visiting tourists. The owner may, however, retain the right to stay in his apartment at a specified time of the year or at reduced rate payment. The developer or the management company receives fees for renting and managing the property. At the end of the year, they share profit or loss with the owners of the condominiums. This type of accommodation is preferred by the families as they provide adequate space required by them and are also economical. The apartments have also facilities to cook.

Time Sharing : Time sharing is a special form of condominium ownership. It began in Europe at about the same time as the first condominium hotel was built. But the two are not linked.

The system started when people experienced difficulties in obtaining reservations at a resort of their choice at their preferred time. In order to guarantee space for a week or two, people started prepaying for their accommodation for certain number of years. For instance, if a person wants to go to Miami for 2 weeks in a year, he need hot buy a condominium which may cost US $ 200,000. He could have guaranteed accommodation for 2 weeks for the next 25 years by paying only $ 10,000. The time-sharers can also exchange or sell their time to their friends, in case they don't want to use it in a given year.

The concept has already arrived in India. Dalmia Resorts, Sterling Resorts and other similar organisations are offering this facility. Punjab Tourism Development Corporation has also successfully pioneered a similar scheme. All-suite hotel is the newest concept in Hotel-keeping. Such hotels do hot have single rooms, they only have suites which they offer for the price of a single room in a deluxe hotel.

In the past, only the chief executives or directors could rent a suite in a hotel. The new concept has brought suites within the range of junior executives. It has become possible because all-suite hotels have been built like private properties, providing only the basic services. If a 24-hour restaurant is there, it is operated by a private caterer and not by the management of the hotel.

The sales pitch is that the all-suite hotels offer good value for money — two rooms for the price of one room in a normal hotel. To attract more customers sometimes breakfast is included in the price of the room or 2 hours of free cocktails.

Hundreds of all-suite hotels have been built in the USA and Europe. The concept is also catching up in India. A few all-suite hotels have already been constructed. Several chains like Sheraton, Hilton, Hyatt and Raddison have joined the bandwagon. Interestingly, all-suite hotels have given better yield and shown greater profitability.

Pensions are mostly in Continental Europe. These are accommodation units owned and run by a family that usually lives in the same building. Pensions have only a handful of rental units. Since there are so many pensions in European cities, they play an important role in accommodating the tourists, especially visitors looking for budget accommodation. In German-speaking parts of Europe, the pensions are known as Gasthaus Pensions. Only bed and breakfast is provided in a pension.

Paradors are uniquely Spanish. They are old castles, convents and monasteries converted by the government into hotels. These are operated by the Spanish government.

Paradors are similar to the castles (havelis) of feudal lords in Rajasthan now being converted into Heritage' hotels by owners with the help of the government. Camping is a popular form of overnight accommodation in North America and Europe.

In North America, there are an estimated 20,000 camping grounds; some of these are owned by leading hotel chains. You can park your vehicles and sleep in the tents provided by the operators and enjoy the natural environments.

Closely allied to the camping business are the Recreational Vehicles (RVs) — the fastest growing tourist business in North America. RVs have adjustable sleeping berths and could accommodate a family.

Camping Grounds and RVs stopping spots are earmarked in the national parks and forests in the USA. In the sixties when overland traffic from Europe to India via the Asian Highway was considerable. Government of India had set up camping sites in major cities. Now, these sites are often used by domestic travellers.

Farm Holidays have become increasingly popular in UK and the Continent in recent years. Farm-based accommodation is preferred by holiday makers whose life-style orientation is towards healthy food and natural outdoor life. Tourist authorities in several countries assisted the farmers to develop such accommodation units within their living quarters or on a piece of land earlier used for cultivation. On the European Continent, Denmark has been particularly successful in packaging farms holidays through travel agents for international market. A British innovation, the paying guest accommodation system has become popular in different parts of the world. The system has also been introduced in India. Many foreign visitors love it because it gives them an opportunity to interact with Indian families.

The advantage of this initiative is that it is capable of quickly responding to the seasonal demands. The ski-resorts of Europe and Japan offer a fantastic range of paying guest accommodation to young skiers at very reasonable rates.

In India, it is especially popular in Rajasthan and Goa.

The following chart shows the types of commercial accommodations available worldwide.

All these types are not necessarily available in India.

Commercial Accommodation

Serviced	Self-catered
Hotels	Condominiums
Motels	Time Sharing
Unlicensed and Guest Houses	Hotels, Motels Apartments
Farm Houses	Villas
Paying Guest Accommodation	Hired RVs
Cruise Ships	Youth Hostels
	Hired Yachts

According to Gerald W. Lattin, the four major classifications of American hotels are: (1) The commercial or transient hotel; (2) The resort hotel; (3) The residential hotel; and (4) The motor-motel hotel.

The American classification holds good in most parts of the world.

Administrative Procedures : The traditional pattern of hotel management made up of individually owned and operated hotels, though surviving, has many problems to face. The system has its advantages. Decisions are quick and service personalised. But in today's environment, owners of one or two units of hotels cannot get the economy of scale and are handicapped in marketing their properties. So, more and more individually owned hotels are opting out for new systems of management.

The commonest form of new management is to join a larger hotel chain or a group and become part of a franchise. The purpose of franchise is to offer to the owner the benefit of being part of a large chain while keeping the management control to himself.

The franchise allows the owner of a hotel or motel, the right to use the name of a chain—national or international. In return, the owner agrees to abide by the management policies of the chain including the standards prescribed by them. He has also to remit franchise fee. The hotels share with the chain contains percentage of gross sales.

With the franchise, the hotel becomes part of the chain's national and international reservation system, gets managerial assistance to standardise hotel facilities and procedures, has rights to purchase supplies through the chains suppliers, getting advantage in price and quality.

The franchise concept is also used in other sectors of hospitality industry i.e., restaurants, etc. It has percolated to sweet shops in India.

The other way of managing a hotel is that owners sign a contract with a major hotel chain to manage their property on their behalf. The management terms vary from chain to chain and property to property. Normally, the chains demand management fee as well as share in the gross sales.

There are advantages in signing management contract with a professional hotel chain.

Banks are willing to loan money to the owners if they know that a successful chain is taking over the management of the hotel. Hotel chains too are happy to work under this system as they can enforce their corporate policies, plans and standards without any interference from the owners.

Some chains prefer to design, build and operate the hotel on behalf of the owners who are investors and primarily remain uninvolved. This is called Turnkey operation.

The hotel owners who do not wish to lose their independence, can benefit by joining a Referral Group which has a marketing clout. Referral Groups offer international marketing, reservation and advertising services to its members. They undertake large-scale advertising on behalf of members.

A very well-known Referral Group in North America is Best Western with 3,000 properties worldwide and an inventory of 200,000 rooms. Before accepting a hotel as member, they make sure that it comes up to their standards.

In the early days of railways, hotels were built by railway companies near the Railway Stations.

When airlines came, they did not need to build hotels as the private sector set up a large number of hotels wherever the demand was.

It was Pan Am which started building its own hotels — Inter-continental Hotels—in the late forties. Subsequently, Pan Am sold its properties to Trust House Forte, the British Hotel Company.

Today, there are several airlines linked to hotel chains. KLM owns Hilton International, Air France—Meridien Hotels, Aer Lingns of Ireland—Dunfy Hotels and Air India—Centaur Hotels.

Presently, most airlines think that they should not be in hotel business and attempts are being made to get rid of hotel subsidiaries.

The Merits : The following are the advantages of joining groups or chains of hotels.

(a) Financial economies resulting from the ability of the group to marshal resources from its cash flow or external sources. This is important for expansion and modernisation.

(b) Marketing economies of the group tend to project an image which goes for all its members. There are natural savings in the area of sales and marketing.

(c) The size of the group enables it to attract better staff as prospects of individual growth are tempting.

(d) Risk spreading by a group is achieved with a variety of hotels catering to the requirements of different consumers.

Hence, the advantages of the groups are those of economy of scale. But group operations have their problems too — the problems of size, communications, control on costs, etc. The advantages of group operations must outweigh cost involved in additional expenses incurred by the group to keep everything in place.

Organisational Setup : A modern hotel is a major establishment. Gone are the days when an owner/manager looked after the entire hotel with a lot of staff. He met every guest and gave personal attention. Today, hotel operation is a sophisticated job manned by trained personnel from hotel schools. Public relations is conducted through computers which tell the preferences, likes and dislikes of repeat clients or VIPs.

Some hotels are automated to an extent that if the resident of a hotel orders an omelette of two eggs, inventory notes that two eggs are less in stock and the cost of the omelette is added to the bill of the customer.

The following are the various departments of a modern hotel:

Hotel operation	Primary	1. Rooms
		2. Food
		3. Beverages
	Ancillary	1. Guest laundry and valeting
		2. Guest telephones
		3. Other guest services
Support services (Undistributed overheads)	1. Marketing	
	2. Property operations	
	3. Maintenance of energy	
	4. Administration/General/Accounting	

The accommodation functions of a hotel are often given the name Rooms. These include reception, uniformed services and housekeeping. Uniformed services include bell boys who handle the luggage of arriving and departing guests, parking of cars, or provide information to guests. Reception or the Front Office deals with checking in, mail and guest services, guest accounts, cash, etc. In many hotels advance reservations form part of the Reception while in other hotels advance reservation are dealt within the Sales Departments.

Accounting and Control is also part of the Rooms Department.

They prepare Rooms Department operating statements which show revenue, pay-roll and other expenses of the department for a given period.

According to a UK survey, hotel employees per bedroom in first class hotel are 1.17, economy 1.02 and medium 1.09. In most Indian first class and deluxe hotels, the room ratio is two to three persons per room. In newly constructed hotels, the ratio is less.

The Food and Beverage Departments are the key to success of a hotel. Leading hotels have a Banquet Manager who organises dinners for hundreds of guests at conventions, meetings, marriage parties and other social functions. Food Departments are headed by Executive Chefs. Each restaurant has a separate manager. Bars fall within the purview of the Food and Beverage Department.

Room Sales as a Proportion of Revenue Worldwide

Room Sales	52.6
Food and Beverage Sales	38.8
Misc. sales	8.6
	100.0

Source: Worldwide Hotel Industry.

In developed countries, successful hotels have larger revenue from their food and beverage department than from the rooms. In India, revenue from rooms is higher as food services have several restrictions on service of liquor and taxes, etc. The up-market hotels are subjected to an additional levy of expenditure tax imposed by the central Government which was reduced in 1994 from 20 per cent to 10 per cent.

Housekeeping functions include the servicing of guest rooms—cleaning of bedrooms, staircases, public areas, public cultural rooms, floral arrangements, first-aid to guests, lost property, etc. Several hotels have laundries run by the housekeeping department. In other hotels, laundry is a separate department.

Marketing and Sales can be a separate department of a hotel because profits of a hotel depend on good marketing.

Basically, it is a process by which customers' needs are met by the management to their satisfaction.

Marketing is often confused with sales. Marketing is more like planting the seeds while sales are like harvesting.

Hotel marketing is no different from product marketing, except that a hotel room is a very perishable commodity and cannot be held back. A successful marketing manager has, therefore, to keep this factor in mind while planning his strategy. He may take a clue from product marketing and work on similar lines:

(a) Research and analysis — this also includes an indepth study of what the competition is doing.

(b) Establish unique selling propositions — consumer-oriented propositions to fulfil needs of the customers.

(c) Determine objectives and strategies.

(d) Advertise a promise which is genuine and credible and in which a consumer can easily discern his own benefit.

(e) Keep the promise simple.

(f) Continuous market research and monitoring of the progress.

The above plan of action is applicable to all hotels, big or small. Although potential markets for a hotel are worldwide, yet a hotel manager cannot afford to ignore his own backyard. If he concentrates his efforts on close-at-hand markets, half the efforts in terms of investment and follow-up may double the business.

A hotel manager should look at the following potential prospects for prime sources of business in his own country:

(a) An assortment of prosperous industries and their sales offices,

(b) Major commercial companies,

(c) Government corporations,

(d) Travel agents, both foreign and local, airlines,

(e) Universities,

(f) Sports clubs, and

(g) Chambers of commerce.

A successful marketing manager develops long-lasting contacts. Secretaries and women's executive clubs could meet in the hotel at discounted rates. Secretaries to senior executives could come and eat in the hotel with their escort or spouse, two for the price of one. These are some ways of making lasting contacts. Similarly, packages have to be developed for weekend holidays when the hotel is half full.

Offering attractive honeymoon packages is an interesting marketing idea. Organisation of seminars or workshops for continuing education with the help of local or foreign universities is a good way to develop new traffic. The Taj Group of Hotels in India have been marketing such programmes successfully. When a major hotel, Keo Plaza, opened its doors in Tokyo, they invited top business executives and travel trade for a weekend stay free, all meals included. At the time of departure, the guests were given gifts. Overnight, people who mattered in travel industry got to know how good the new property was.

It is essential for the marketing manager to be acquainted with the local press corps for effective public relations. An occasional press briefing on VIP visits or on special functions in the hotel brings windfall publicity. To achieve better results, press releases must be professionally written. A well-written press release is more likely to find a place in the business or travel columns of the local newspaper.

Consumer needs are the cornerstone of marketing analysis. An hotel manager must learn to view his activities from consumers' perspective. He can thus respond with action which is consumer-oriented rather than management oriented.

Let us take the case of a motoring family of four driving to Florida for a vacation from, say, New York. It starts raining heavily and the husband decides to stop at a motel en route. They have a look at the motel which looks like an expensive property. The husband tells the wife, "Looks very fancy. I wonder how much it costs?" The wife is already drenched and says to herself, "I hope they have a room. Children are tired and would not like to spend another minute on the road."

As they approach the reception, the lady at the counter welcomes them with a smile and gives them the good news that 'We have just the right kind of room for this family.' She immediately produces two umbrellas to enable the couple to bring their baggage. The wife is told that the hotel has games which could be checked out for children to get them busy in the room. She also tells them about other facilities like swimming, golfing, etc. The family is visibly pleased.

Their holiday had already begun. They do not even ask the price. The credit, in this case, goes to the manager who has anticipated the consumer needs and catered to them. And the receptionist at the counter has done an excellent sales job. That should be part of training.

We will discuss principles of marketing in greater detail in a comprehensive chapter on Marketing for Tourism.

Typical Hotel Organisation Chart

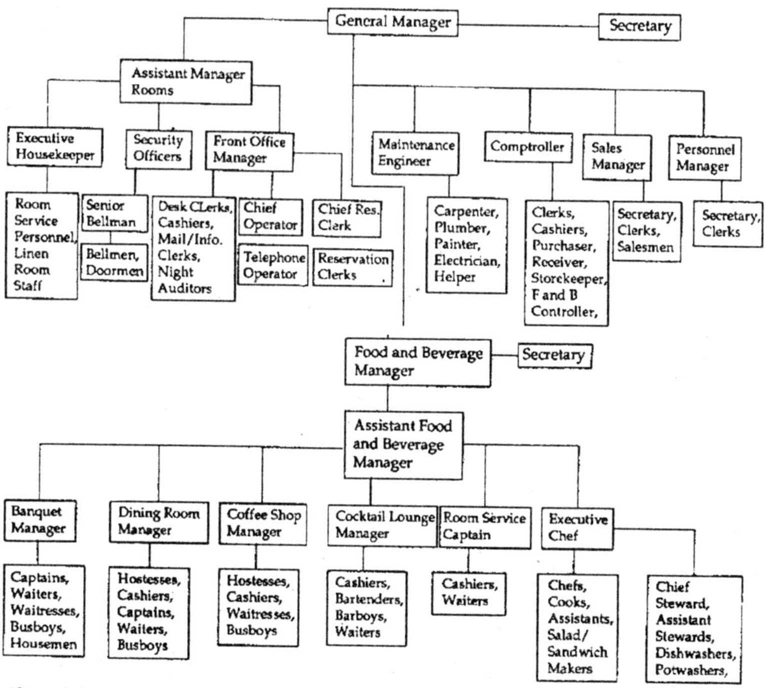

(*Source: Cost Control for the Hospitality Industry*, New York)

The role of the hotel manager has totally changed during the last few decades. The following verse explains the changes in the nature of the responsibilities of a hotel manager over the years and the varied demands on a professional hotel manager.

The following are some common phrases used in the day-to-day working of hotels.

The break-even point for a hotel is when the total cost equals the total revenue. Hotel managers are well aware of the importance of the break-even point. It demonstrates the percentage of occupancy which a hotel must have to sustain itself.

Over-booking refers to the practice of pre-selling more hotel rooms than the hotel can offer, assuming that several of the guests will not turn up. Sometimes, all guests turn up causing problems as well as loss of goodwill.

If a guest with confirmed accommodation turns up, the host hotel has the moral obligation to accommodate him in comparable hotel. The process of turning the guest away and sending him to the competition is called 'Running'.

Flat rate is a discounted rate offered to a group or groups at certain times of the year.

To keep a full house, the management often sell at concessional rate blocks of rooms to tour wholesalers for the whole year or for the slack season.

Room rates at hotels are sometimes quoted in terms that explains what meals, if any, are included in the price of the room.

European Plan means that no meals are included in the price of the room. This is the most commonly quoted rate in the USA and in India.

American Plan implies that all meals are included in the price of the room—a very un-American phenomenon in today's America.

Like airlines, hotels too have a system of tiered or discounted rates.

Revenue not received for unsold rooms is lost for ever. Therefore, hotels may offer discounts in favour of a certain category of guests to attract more customers.

Airline employees get a special rate of 50 per cent discount. They are considered promoters of hotel business.

Travel agents too are similarly treated. Fifty per cent discount is common but select productive agents of a hotel may get complimentary room as well as meals.

Some hotels have special arrangements with business companies and corporations offering a special rate to their employees. It is called Corporate Rate.

It is good marketing idea because business travel is quite inelastic. A special rate may persuade a company to use your a property most of the time.

Many hotels offer family plans. They allow 2 children under 14 to stay in their parent's room without extra charges.

Since conventions are a good business, hotels offer special rates to convention participants, especially during off-season.

Special rates are offered to guests during weekends. The purpose is to encourage guests to extend their stay, or to attract city dwellers to the hotel for a relaxed weekend.

Some hotels/hotel chains have a special rate for senior citizens over 60. Ashok Group in India extensively advertises its regard for senior citizens. Students, too, get a special rate in ITDC hotels. The loss due to cut rates mentioned above is often made up by larger food and beverage sale in a hotel.

A simple method of measuring the profitability of a hotel is to work out its room occupancy and find out the break-even point mentioned above.

This can be done by dividing the number of rooms occupied on a given night by the number of rooms a hotel has to offer. That will give us the occupancy ratio. For instance, if a 200 room hotel has 150 rooms occupied on a given night, the occupancy will be 150/200 x 100 = 75 per cent. Similarly, occupancy can be worked out for weeks, months or on yearly basis. However, to work out foolproof profitability of a hotel one has to take into consideration the number of rooms with double or triple occupancies. The yield of double and triple occupancy rooms is always higher.

Not all the rooms in a hotel are of the same price—some are priced higher. The average rate will increase if a hotel can sell more high-priced rooms and/or if more rooms have double or triple occupancy.

Another useful information is to work out the average daily rate per guest. This is calculated by dividing the total room revenue for a particular period by the total number of guests accommodated during that time.

Many large hotels and even smaller ones affiliated to a major chain have their Computer Reservation System (CRS). Some hotel chains are also listed in the CRSs of airlines and booking can be done through these CRSs.

Several hotel chains/hotels have toll-free customer access. A customer or travel agent can call the hotel reservation system for a booking in the hotel — the hotel foots the bill for the phone call, even if it is an outstation call. Toll-free means that the company which advertises toll-free member, pays and not the caller.

Indian View : The hotel is a Western concept planted in India. Hotels were introduced by the British mainly for their own use, or for the use of visiting foreigners. Sixty years ago, except for the Taj Mahal Hotel built by Jamshedji Nasarwanju Tata in Bombay, almost all hotels in India were owned and operated by British or Swiss families. In the early fifties, the Government of India realised the economic importance of tourism and decided to encourage its development. It was realised that there was an acute shortage of hotel accommodation and that there was a need to build more hotels to accommodate tourists in the country. A decision was taken to build hotels in the public sector, where necessary. The first result of this decision was the construction of Ashok Hotel in 1956, to accommodate delegates to UNESCO international conference in New Delhi. The hotel was constructed in a record time of less than one year due to personal interest taken by the late Prime Minister, Jawaharlal Nehru.

In 1956, the government set up a Hotel Standards and Rate Structure Committee under the chairmanship of a prominent member of the Rajya Sabha, Diwan Chaman Lal. M.S. Oberoi, the then president, Federation of Hotel and Restaurant Association of

India, was one of its members. The committee set before itself the following objectives:

(a) To lay down criteria for the purpose of classification of hotels in India, keeping in view international standards that apply to similar establishments elsewhere;

(b) to suggest ways and means for promoting tourist traffic to and in India;

(c) to suggest arrangements or improvements on existing arrangements desirable for promoting international and external tourism;

(d) whether legislation, and if so, of what type and/or assistance, and if so, what type are necessary for the purpose of hotel industry generally; and

(e) keeping in view the price level prevailing in India, to suggest a suitable rate structure for the hotel industry.

The most important finding of the committee was that in order to improve standards of the hotels, a universally accepted system of classification based on star rating may be adopted. The top classification would be a five-star hotel with deluxe amenities followed by other star gradings with lesser facilities. The committee also recommended that the classification be done by an organisation like the Department of Tourism which can be objective in its assessment. For the rate structure, the committee recommended Hubbart Formula as accepted and recommended by the American Hotel Association, with appropriate modifications taking the Indian conditions into consideration.

The Categories : The recommendations of the Diwan Chaman Lal Committee were accepted by the Government of India and a Hotel Classification Committee was set up in 1962 to classify hotels according to designated standards. The committee travelled extensively for more than nine months to 110 places all over India and classified 186 hotels with 7,085 rooms. The committee considered 299 hotels for classification. Only 186 made the grade. The committee was disappointed that only thirty four hotels in India had money changing facilities.

It may be interesting to know that originally several hoteliers were against the idea of classification. They were under the apprehension that it might bring in its wake rigid price control. However, they realised in due course that the classification was in their own interest to improve standards and to assure the foreign tourist of the type of service and facilities they may expect from a hotel in a given category.

The members of this committee had interesting experiences during their travels for classification. A member left a small bag in a hotel which he had inspected a few hours earlier. While travelling to the next destination, he remembered the bag left in the room and decided to drive back. When the committee members reappeared on the scene, they found the ultra-modern furniture in the rooms being taken out and put on bullock-carts, to be taken back to the furniture shop. Similarly, the committee members were impressed to see new radio sets in each room of a hotel in Calcutta at the time of inspection. Next day, when the members came back, they discovered that the radio sets had disappeared from the rooms.

The first classification of hotels generated considerable interest among hoteliers due to the visit of the committee. The owners of hotels and restaurants sought members' advice regarding improvements to be made. There were genuine improvements in practically all the hotels and restaurants which offered themselves for inspection. Kitchens were renovated, reception areas re-decorated and rooms given a fresh coat of paint. Apart from enforcing strict standards of classification, the committee took upon itself the task of educating hoteliers regarding the standards of comfort expected by new travellers and how these could be brought about. The first classification committee set the norms and recommended detailed periodic inspections of all approved establishments in the country to keep up the tempo. It was suggested that such check-ups or reclassifications should take place once every three years.

Assessment : The second Hotel Review and Survey Committee was set up in 1967. Regional representatives of the Travel Agents Association of India and the state governments were also included when the committee visited different regions.

The new committee travelled to all the states and centrally administered territories. It visited seventy one cities and inspected 221 hotels and ninety four restaurants. It interviewed several travel agents, government representatives and a few members of the public who, it thought, could make useful contribution towards its deliberations, particularly in the field of hotel rate structure and in surveying the hotel bed-capacity required during the next seven to eight years. Another interesting innovation was that the hotel industry volunteered to bear a substantial part of expenses of the committee by agreeing to a graduated levy payable by hotels or restaurants that applied for classification. It was estimated that the income from these fees would meet at least half the cost incurred by the government on the Classification Committee.

The committee's report divided into three parts dealt with:

- Classification of hotels;
- Projections of hotel capacity needed until 1974 and beyond; and
- The standardisation of hotel rates.

When the committee invited applications for new classifications, sixty hotels and forty seven restaurants already on the approved list of the Department of Tourism did not apply. On the other hand, sixty hotels and forty two restaurants which were not on the approved list of the department applied for the first time. Grading was done on unanimous basis and in accordance with the criteria evolved by the Hotel Classification Committee set up in 1962. Initially, the committee toyed with the idea that hotels and restaurants which had applied for classification and approval be inspected without any prior notice. However, they came to the conclusion that unannounced inspection was not expedient when the objective was classification based on designated criteria. It was, therefore, decided that the establishments concerned be informed in advance of the date of inspection so that their top management personnel were available to give answers to questions which could be raised. It also gave them time to improve standards to achieve higher grading.

The results were interesting. Forty three hotels and thirty five restaurants did not meet the requisite qualifications and were, therefore, not recommended for placement on the list of approved hotels and restaurants of the Department of Tourism. Of the twenty nine hotels which applied for five-star category gradation, only thirteen qualified. Of the forty three hotels which applied for four-star gradation, fifteen qualified for four-star, sixteen got three-stars, thirty-one got two-stars and the rest either qualified for one-star or did not qualify at all.

As pointed out earlier, the classification of hotels in India was essentially done to improve their standards and to introduce standardisation. In many countries of the world, there is no formal classification such as in the United States. In these countries, hotels are expected to provide a basic minimum and a customer cannot go wrong in one's choice on the basis of the price. According to J. David, Secretary General of International Hotel Association (IHA), there are, at present, thirty different national systems for classifying hotels. These can be divided into two main categories: the so-called European type where classification is based on factors relating to equipment, and the second type of classification, based on a points system prevalent in India. The Indian system is related to accumulation of points based on the facilities in a hotels. National variations exist in the value attributed to each factor and distinctions made between obligatory and optional elements.

The committee was not called upon to grade restaurants. As a result of its inspection, it found fifty nine out of the ninety four restaurants which applied for approval of the Department of Tourism suitable to be recommended to international travellers.

This classification of hotels led the hotel industry to further improve standards. The opening of Oberoi-Intercontinental in Delhi in 1965 was a landmark in the development of the hotel industry as it provided to the capital of India a hotel of internationally accepted standards and specifications. The popularity of the Oberoi-Intercontinental led other hotels in Delhi to improve their standards not only to meet the competition, but also to fall in line with the general specifications of international hotels. There were impressive improvements in the Ashok, New Delhi, after the opening of the Oberoi-Intercontinental. The Asiad in 1982 helped further and now India has some of the finest hotels in the world. In the new scheme of things entrepreneurs themselves decide the type of hotel they want to build — deluxe, five-star or budget—and they provide the facilities accordingly.

The other sections of the report makes an interesting reading for people interested in the hotel industry in India and its future. The committee was of the view that hotel rates should not be allowed to rise unchecked and to accomplish this, the hotel industry should be required to introduce internal discipline to keep prices at reasonable level. They were of the view that the Department of Tourism should continue applying the modified Hubbart Formula for supervising hotel rates.

Another recommendation of the committee was that a permanent central committee be set up by the Department of Tourism to encourage hotel establishments aspiring for a higher category to affect improvements without delay, and to enable new establishments to qualify for tax and fiscal benefits available to establishments in the approved category.

A permanent committee now exists in the Department of Tourism to inspect new establishments and they accord approval to existing establishments desiring to be approved. The approval of a hotel immediately entitles it to fiscal benefits as well as import entitlements against foreign exchange earnings. The permanent central committee inspects and classifies only five to three-star hotels. For classification and inspection of one and two-star hotels, committees have been set up at the state level with a representative of the central government co-opted.

With liberalisation of the Indian economy, the government no longer exercises the right to control hotel tariff. Hotels are free to determine the price that the market will bear. Hotels have also realised that they can charge a good price only if their product is deluxe.

The hotel industry in India has come of age. They are now in a position of build and operate quality hotels. Although governments' approval at the planning stage may be required to claim fiscal benefits, the government does not have any expertise to direct the entrepreneur which way to go. There are, at present, a number of highly qualified consultants to guide an entrepreneur in planning and developing a new hotel properly in the category he desires.

Nancy Cockerell is an authority on international hotels and consulting Editor of EIU's Travel Industry Monitor, London. Commenting on the Indian hotel industry, she wrote in 1992, "It is a paradox that a country which hardly recognises the value of tourism and which attracts only 1.3 million foreign visitors a year should have attained such high standards in terms of facilities and services in hotel industry. Indian hotels are one of its prime attractions and its best properties are the envy of most other tourism and business destinations around the world. No other country can boast of as many properties frequently quoted as the best in the world."

For more than three decades, the Government of India did not take any policy decision to help the hotel industry. The Department of Tourism, Government of India, which looked after the hotel industry, was always sympathetic to the needs of industry and in it own way tried to upgrade the hotel industry through classification and other measures. What the industry needed was low interest loans and tax incentives. It was only in 1968 that the Department of Tourism was allocated funds for low interest hotel loans and was also made the disbursing authority for such loans. The department soon realised that it could not cope with the disbursement and realisation of loans which amounted to crores of rupees every year. The responsibility was, subsequently, transferred to the Industrial Finance Corporation of India (IFCI) in 1974 which had the necessary expertise. IFCI sanctioned loans for amounts of rupees one crore and above, while the State Finance Corporations took care of loans of less than rupees one crore.

A few more facilities were offered in 1974 — tax holiday for five years under certain conditions to new hotels, priority treatment of loan applications from hotel industry like other priority industries, income-tax deductions on income of hotels built in backward areas, etc. The government allowed Indian hotels limited collaboration with well-known foreign hotel chains in respect of sales, marketing, publicity, etc. Indian hotels could also pay agreed fees in foreign exchange to foreign collaborators for rendering pre or post-opening technical services. That was the beginning of Indian hotels acquiring foreign franchises from chains like Holiday Inn, Intercontinental, Sheraton, etc. The new policy did make a difference and a number of new, modern international hotels were built in the late seventies and in the eighties.

Since 1990, government has further liberalised and the following concessions and incentives are available to Indian hotels.

Under section 80-L of the income-tax act, a hotel that started functioning after March 31, 1990, and before April 1, 1995, is eligible for the following deductions from Income-Tax:

- 30 per cent of the profit derived from the business of hotels, for a period of ten assessment years.

  It applies to companies.
- 25 per cent if the company is a cooperative society for 12 assessment years.
- 25 per cent in all other cases for ten years.
- Benefit from Foreign Exchange Earnings.

Under another section of the Income-Tax Act, the following deductions are allowed to hotel companies or tour-operators in respect of their foreign exchange earnings:

(1) 50 per cent of the profits derived from services provided to foreign tourists.

(2) The remaining amount, if it is credited to a reserve account, can be used for investment activity relating to the tourism industry.

Buildings used as hotels are eligible for depreciation at the rate of 20 per cent; for furniture and fittings the depreciation is 15 per cent, as against the general rate of 10 per cent.

The Department of Tourism offers a one per cent interest subsidy up to a loan amount of 75 lakhs for four and five-star hotels, and the subsidy is three per cent for one to three-star hotels. This is applicable on loans taken from the Industrial Finance Corporation, Tourism Finance Corporation or the state financial corporations.

There is an interest rebate of 20 per cent offered by the

Tourism Finance Corporation, IFCI, IDBI and ICICI for five-star hotels where more than 50 per cent of their turnover is earned in foreign exchange and in the case of the three or four-star category, where more than 25 per cent of their turnover is earned in foreign exchange.

Ten per cent of the direct foreign exchange earnings of approved hotels can be used for essential imports and overseas promotions and advertising. Essential imports also include motor vehicles.

Non-resident Indians are now investing in three to five-star hotels up to 100 per cent and can repatriate profits and investments.

Investments can be on two basis; repatriable and non-repatriable.

Non-repatriable investment can be made by NRIs in any public or private company without any obligation to associate resident Indians.

There are two schemes for investment on a repatriable basis.

Investments of 74 per cent can be made in the new issues of new or existing companies.

For permission to invest under this scheme, the NRI investor can apply directly to the Indian company.

Investments of 74 per cent can be made by NRIs only as new investment, including diversification of existing industrial units.

Rules for foreign collaboration have been further liberalised.

In the hotel industry, foreign collaboration is allowed with renowned international hotel chains, individuals or institutions having proven expertise in tourism-related projects.

Foreign investors can invest up to 51 per cent of the equity in foreign exchange. The principal and interest are repatriable. Foreign investors can have management control too.

The foreign collaborations can receive from the Indian partner lumpsum payments for the transfer of technology, planning, designing or equipping, etc.

The fee payable to a foreign party for sales, marketing and reservation will normally relate only to rooms.

Foreign managers and technicians can be appointed in key positions in such projects.

Among the major hotel chains already in India in one form or the other are: Intercontinental Hotels, Sheraton, Holiday Inn, Ramada Inn, Quality Inn, Le Meridien, Hyatt and Kempinski. Hilton is the latest entrant in Delhi.

Concessional custom duty is applicable on imports required for the initial setting up of a hotel or for substantial expansion of existing hotels.

Hotels are exempted from the purview of the MRTP Act.

Priority is given to allotment of telephones/telex communications/LPG cooking gas, etc., to approved hotels.

After the announcement of this policy, the hotel scene looks bright. Foreign investment proposals worth Rs 200 crore were approved till 1996, though it will take 2 to 5 years for new properties to take shape.

According to the Department of Tourism, Government of India, the number of available rooms approved and classified was 49,710 till January 1994. Among these, 15, 684 were in the category of deluxe or five-star category and 3,900 in four-star category. The total includes 611 rooms in the newly introduced category of Heritage Hotels. Heritage Hotels is the name given to havelis or minor palaces of feudal lords now converted into hotels with government help in the form of loans.

Besides, there are 509 approved hotel units with 30,345 rooms already under construction. Among these, five-star properties are 41 with an estimated number of 6,647 rooms, four-star with 4,602 rooms and three-star with 14,001 rooms.

Approved hotels are not the only accommodation that India offers. There are 615 hotels in India with 26,627 rooms which have not volunteered for government classification though they are members of Federation of Hotels and Restaurants Association of India (FHRAI). FHRAI too has its minimum standards for membership entitlement. These accommodations are often used by budget travellers.

In other words, the available hotel accommodation exceeds

75,000 rooms with a possibility of another 25,000 becoming available during the coming 2-3 years. This implies that in the coming years, hotel accommodation in India for visitors may not be in short supply, except at a few very popular tourist centres during busy seasons.

Chain of Hotels in India

The Ashok Chain is the largest hotel chain in India. It is run by India Tourism Development Corporation, a public sector undertaking. Originally, the India Tourism Development Corporation was set up to provide hotel accommodation at places where the private sector was shy of investing in hotel industry. Now, ITDC runs hotels all over India.

Its accommodation inventory ranges from five-star deluxe hotels like Ashok in New Delhi, to motel type accommodation like a Traveller, Lodge in Manali — a total or 34 hotels in 27 cities of India.

Ashok Group divides its accommodation units in three categories Elite, Classic and Comfort. The Elite hotels include five-star properties like Ashok and Samrat in New Delhi. The 16 classic hotels are three to four-star properties like Kanishka in New Delhi or Ashok in Jaipur and the remaining 12 Comfort hotels are two to three-star properties like Lodhi and Ranjit hotels in New Delhi.

The Government of India has taken a policy decision that they would like to sell the hotel properties owned by them at an appropriate time. The new thinking is that the hotel industry of India has now matured and the government has no business to be in this business. Despite massive government investments, ITDC's hotels seldom made worthwhile profit. Although there is policy to privatise hotel properties of ITDC, the political will is missing due to vested interests.

It is, therefore, only a matter of time when the government will sell most of its properties excepting, perhaps, Ashok, New Delhi, where they would like to put up government guests for their security.

The Oberoi is a familiar name all over the world. They run some of the finest hotels in India and abroad. The chain has the distinction of being the only one in the world with its nine properties featured in Rene Lector's the 300 best hotels in the world. The group was founded by M.S. Oberoi who was honoured by the American Society of Travel Agents (ASTA) in 1982 and admitted to the ASTA Hall of Fame for his contribution to the hotel industry in the world. In 1983, he was honoured by International Hotel Association with a Man of the World Award. At present the Oberoi chain has 26 hotels — 14 in India and 12 abroad including Saudi Arabia, Egypt, Indonesia, and Sri Lanka. Their new Oberoi Hotels in Madras, Bangalore and Agra are under construction.

The Oberois have started their second chain called Novotel Hotels. They have joined hands with the French Hotel Chain of Accor to develop 20 economy hotels under the brand name Novotel which will cater to mid-market travellers at a price range of US $ 40. So far, Oberois have been catering to only the upmarket visitors through their deluxe hotels. One Novotel Hotel in Agra has already opened and three more in Jaipur, Udaipur and Delhi are under construction.

Besides Novotel, the Oberoi Group has introduced a level of hotels specially geared to the needs of business travellers under the brand name "Trident Hotels". The first one, Trident Madras, opened in 1988 and Trident Ahmedabad opened in 1995. Similar Trident Hotels are also planned for Cochin and Jaipur.

Two Tridents have been opened in Egypt and Saudi Arabia.

The group now employs 12,000 people worldwide and manages 25 luxury hotels in six countries.

The Taj Group owned by the Tatas has 38 hotels in India and 15 overseas. Like the Oberois, the Taj Group has also started a second chain of hotels called Gateway Hotels to cater to the needs of mid-market travellers.

The Indian Hotels Company Ltd. which runs Taj Hotels in India was founded in 1903 when they opened their Taj Mahal Hotel in Bombay. At that time, it was the only hotel owned and operated by an Indian company. The present expansion of the Taj Group started in the mid-seventies and has been due largely to the vision and enterprise of one man, Ajit Kerker, who is currently the Chairman of the Taj Group.

The Welcomgroup is one of the fastest growing hotel chains

in India. They are a division of the Indian Tobacco Company, a major business corporation in the country. They diversified into hotel business in 1975 and built three luxury hotels in three years—Chola in Madras, Maurya in New Delhi, and Mughal in Agra. The three hotels have unique architecture and have set new standards of hoteliering in the country.

In the second phase of their business, they went into management, operations and marketing of hotels owned wholly by other entrepreneurs, or jointly with ITC. Today, they have 14 Welcomgroup Hotels in the country from New Delhi in the north to Port Blair in the Indian Ocean.

Seven Welcomgroup Hotels are operated on a franchise basis with the American Chain Sheraton. Its flagship hotel, Maurya Sheraton in New Delhi, has a consistent record of highest turnover of all hotel properties in the Indian capital. It has also been generating the maximum amount of foreign exchange earnings for some years. Much of it is due to its strength in food and beverage area. Its restaurant is called Bukhara, specialising in food from the North-Western Frontier—now part of Pakistan. Bukhara has already been opened in some of the Sheraton Hotels overseas.

All the four major hotel chains have their own successful travel agencies — Oberois own Mercury, Taj Cox and Kings, Welcomgroup owns Travel House and Ashok is linked to Ashok Travel and Tours.

The Hotel Corporation of India, a subsidiary of Air India, started with one hotel, Centaur, at Bombay airport. Presently, they have four hotels — two in Bombay and one each in Srinagar and New Delhi.

The Clarks Group owned by U.P. Hotels operates four hotels in Varanasi, Agra, Jaipur and Lucknow — all five-star properties.

Besides, there are two new groups — Eastern Hotels International has prestigious properties like Holiday Inn in Bombay, Majorda Beach Resort in Goa and Claridges Hotel in New Delhi.

Apart from Sheraton, a few other leading foreign hotels chains have registered their presence in India. There are two franchised Holiday Inns, though owned by different parties. Delhi has a Le Meridien, a Hyatt and a Hilton. The foreign chains present in India are Intercontinental, Kempinsky, Quality Inn and the Ramada International. Regent has signed for three properties in Agra, New Delhi and Bombay. A Parkroyal Hotel in New Delhi has recently opened under the banner of South Pacific Hotel Corporation (SPHC). The Taj Group has signed a contract with Club Med for developing three resorts on India's coast.

Trained manpower is an essential element in the smooth growth of hotel industry in any country. The Government of India took a very timely and wise decision in the late fifties opening institutes of Hotel Management and Catering Technology in the four metropolitan towns of India: Delhi, Bombay, Calcutta and Madras. Besides, a number of Food Craft Institutes offering short-term courses in Catering Technology were opened.

Initially, these institutes functioned under the control of Ministry of Food. In 1982, all these institutes were transferred to Ministry of Tourism as the manpower trained by these institutes was absorbed primarily by the hotel industry which was dealt with by the Ministry of Tourism. At the time of transfer, there were only ten Institutes of Hotel and Catering Technology and 14 Food Craft Institutes in India. After taking over the administrative control of these institutes, the Ministry of Tourism has added several more.

Today, there are 16 Institutes of Hotel Management and Catering Technology offering 3 years Diploma Course and another 16 Food Craft Institutes offering short-term Craft and Reception courses. There are a total of 32 institutes spread all over India. Together, they train over 500 young people annually.

The institutes have an apex body based in New Delhi—the Council of Hotel Management and Catering Technology—to provide direction to these institutes, to upgrade the curriculum and to conduct examinations on an all India basis.

These institutes have produced thousands of skilled managers and chefs — some of them at the helm of leading hotels in major cities of the world.

Besides the government, Oberois have their own Hotel School in Delhi where they train the executives needed for their hotels in India and abroad. The School is widely recognised internationally.

Welcomgroup was chosen as partner when Dr. T.M.A. Rai Foundation opened its first graduate school of Hotel Management at Manipal, Karnataka. This institution is managed by Welcomgroup and is run on the lines of Cornell School of Hotel Management in the United States.

The Taj Group has its own training programme for its managers. Generally, they pick the best from Government's Hotel Training Schools and give them extensive in-house training.

The government has also set up a separate institute for tourism training, called the Indian Institute of Travel and Tourism Management (HTM). Its headquarter is at Gwalior. The training is provided at post-graduate level. It also undertakes executive training courses for hotels and travel agencies.

Founded in London in 1946, the International Hotel Association (IHA) brings together about four thousand international standard hotels, one hundred and thirty one states and territories, sixty national hotel associations and about five hundred individual hoteliers. With headquarters in Paris, IHA work is directly linked to the everyday realities of hotel management.

The aim of IHA is to work at international level to unite the hotel associations of all countries, to offer them an opportunity to discuss problems of mutual interest, and to find solutions in keeping with the objectives of the hotel profession. Likewise, it defends the professional interests of hotels and restaurants and tries to enhance the standard and reputation of the industry.

IHA enjoys consultative status with the UN organisations like ILO, Council of Europe, and UNESCO, regarding international training programmes. It also works closely with WTO, and UFTAA.

IHA has compiled a booklet listing hotel schools and their syllabi and has set up an IHA training exchange network open to young workers in IHA hotels. It publishes an International Hotel Guide every year, listing commercial facts about member hotels.

A directory of travel agencies containing a list of travel agents all over the world who agree to respect IHA/UFTAA conventions is also brought out. Another publication is the International Hotel Review which gives information about tourism and reflects the point of view of the association on current issues.

The Federation with its headquarters at New Delhi is the national association of leading hotels and restaurants of India and serves as the watchdog of the organised sector of hotel and restaurant business. The idea of such an association originated in 1950 when four regional associations were set up at Delhi, Calcutta, Bombay and Madras. In 1954, the four associations federated into a national body called the Federation of Hotel and Restaurant Associations of India. Rai Bahadur M.S. Oberoi, the founder of Oberoi Group of Hotels, was elected its first president.

The Federation has about 1,000 members consisting of individual members (hotels and restaurants) and associate members (travel agents, hotel-ware manufacturers, etc.) who elect a new president every year.

The Federation, over the years, has made valuable contribution to the development of the hotel industry. Its persistent efforts with the government led to the introduction of the hotel development loan fund, tax reliefs and other benefits. Apart from liaisoning with the government in getting relief to the industry in day-to-day matters, the Federation undertakes surveys and studies on various aspects of the hotel industry in India. For new entrepreneurs, it has an information booklet, giving all details and guidance about starting a new hotel. Address M-75 (Market), Greater Kailash Part II, New Delhi-110048.

Endeavours and Weaknesses : The hotel industry has an interesting and colourful past. Through trials and errors, the business of Hotel-keeping has become one of the largest in the world. It is the most sophisticated industry catering to an increasing number of demanding travellers both business and leisure. It has matured to an extent that the brand name itself tells the visitor what facilities and comforts to expect from a hotel. A Sheraton in New York or New Delhi have similar ambience.

The hotel industry, today, is widely segmented in terms of types of accommodations available, from hotels and motels to camping sites and farm houses. Most of its marketing is done through computers which tell us who has been patronising the property more frequently and the need for special attentions to him. The manager need not remember the names of the guest who matters. The computer tells him what he likes and what he dislikes. And he makes sure that the guest is served accordingly.

Management of hotels ranges from individually owned and managed properties to hotels run by large hotel chains under a system of franchising or under management contracts. Though some individually run hotels are still surviving, most are opting to join one chain or the other. The chain gives them the advantages of scale — from purchasing hotel supplies at a special rate of the chain and to be part of its international reservation network which means more business.

International hotels are a Western concept planted on the soil of India. But, Indians picked up very fast and now some of their properties are included among the best in the world. Indian hotel chains like the Taj and Oberois have also crossed the oceans to build or manage properties in several countries of the world. They are competing with the best.

Hotel industry in India has a great future. The Government of India has offered several incentives and tax cuts for the new entrepreneurs. Foreign investments have been allowed and the foreign investors can have complete management control, if they prefer.

For training of hotel managers, the Government of India has set up 32 Hotel Training Institutes in different states of India. Some of the major Indian hotel chains like the Oberois too have their training schools.

The Federation of Hotels and Restaurants Association of India (FHRAI) is the national organisation representing the hotels industry of the country. At the international level, it is the International Hotel Association (IHA) based at Paris which is the watchdog of the interests of hotel industry in the world.

Large Corporate Hotel Chains in the World

Corporate Chain Headquarters	*Rooms*	*Hotels*
HFS Inc., Parsippany, NJ USA	509,500	5,430
Holiday Inn Worldwide, Atlanta GA USA	369,738	2,096
Best Western International Phoenix AZ USA	282,062	3,462

Contd...

Corporate Chain Headquarters	***Rooms***	***Hotels***
Accor Evry France	268,256	2,378
Choice Hotels International Silver Spring, MD USA	249,926	2,902
Marriott International Washington, DC USA	198,000	976
ITT Sheraton Corp., Boston, MA USA	129,201	414
Hilton Hotels Corp. Beverly Hills, CA USA	90,879	219
Promus Cos. Memphis, TN USA	88,117	669
Carlson/Radisson/SAS Minneapolis, MN USA	84,607	383
Hyatt Hotels/Hyatt International Chicago, IL USA	79,483	172
Inter-Continental Hotels, London, England	61,610	179
Hilton International, Watford Herts, England	52,063	161
Forte Hotels, London, England	49,183	270
Grupo Sol Melia Palma de Mallorca, Spain	46,825	185
Club Mediterranee SA, Paris, France	45,205	150
New World/Renaissance Hotels Hong Kong	45,104	140
Westin Hotels & Resorts, Seattle, WA USA	40,074	82
Societe due Louvre, Paris, France	32,926	511
La Quinta Inns, San Antonio, TX USA	30,000	240
Double Tree Hotels, Phoenic, AZ USA	28,501	105
Prince Hotels Inc., Tokyo, Japan	26,235	58
Red Roof Inns, Hilliard,OH USA	26,135	231
Tokyu Hotel Group, Tokyo, Japan	21,870	84
Circus Circus, Las Vegas, NV USA	17,739	11
Hotel & Compagnie, Les Ulis France	17,391	340
Wyndham Hotels & Resorts Dallas, TX USA	17,196	65
Nikko Hotels International, Tokyo, Japan	16,726	42
Scandic Hotels AB, Stockholm, Sweden	16,400	101
Walt Disney Co., Burbank, CA USA	16,163	13
Fujita Kanko Inc., Tokyo, Japan	15,941	70
Omni Hotel, Corpus Christi, TX USA	15,728	38
Hospitality International, Tucker, GA USA	15,366	269
Husa Hotels Group, Barcelona, Spain	15,354	182
Dusit Thani / Kempinski Bangkok, Thailand	15,150	64
Shangri-La Hotels & Resorts, Hong Kong	14,646	30
Red Lion Hotels & Inns Vancouver, WA USA	14,250	54

Contd...

Corporate Chain Headquarters	Rooms	Hotels
Queens Moat Houses Hotels Romford, Essex, England	14,092	122
Thistle & Mount Charlotte Hotels Leeds, England	13,556	100
Southern Pacific Hotels Corp. St. Leonards, Australia	13,187	77
Riu Hotels, Playa de Palma Mallorca, Spain	12,889	53
Park Plaza International Hotels Scottsdale, AZ USA	12,722	77
Four Seasons/Regent Toronto, Ontario, Canada	12,663	37
Budgetel Inns, Milwaukee, WI USA	12,613	120
Maritim Hotels, Bad Salzuflen, Germany	12,517	41
Occidental Hotels, Madrid, Spain	12,432	56
ANA Hotels, Tokyo, Japan	12,128	38
Canadian Pacific Hotels Toronto, Ontario, Canada	10,536	25
Barcelo Hotels, Palma de Mallorca, Spain	10,473	40
National 9 Inns, Salt Lake City, UT USA	10,420	181

Study of Specific Importance

In 1902, no one could fathom why Jamshedji Nasarwanju Tata was determined to build a hotel. Sceptics doubted the wisdom of his move. But Mr. Tata was not just a great philanthropist, he was also a pioneering industrialist and a visionary. A year later, on Bombay's seafront, the House of Tatas inaugurated the Taj Mahal Hotel.

It was not long before the Taj Bombay came to be one of the truly great hotels in the world, offering its guests the finest in Indian hospitality. Though the Taj of Bombay continued to be the epitome of grace and luxury, it was not until the '60s that the Indian Hotels Company Limited began to expand its chain.

Today, the Taj Group of Hotels has won international acclaim as being one of the finest hotel chains in India and also overseas.

This company which started expanding in the 1970s has become the fastest growing hotel chain in India. In two decades, it has increased its operations from one hotel in 1970 to 30 hotels in 1995 (within India) and 15 hotels worldwide. It has increased its room capacity from 270 to over 4,500 in India and over 3,735 rooms outside India.

Its hotels are architecturally impressive and offer the best of both worlds: the oriental and the Occidental. And that is more by design than by accident. Each of the Taj properties are centrally situated so as to be within easy reach of the commercial and entertainment areas of the city.

The hotels are beautifully designed and tastefully appointed with an eye for detail and comfort. Guest needs are carefully thought out — colour TV, telephone, piped music, attached bathrooms, 24-hour service, laundry service. There are always the added little extra touches to make a guest feel welcome, like fresh fruits and flowers and personal stationery. The food baskets are replenished every day.

For business travellers, the Taj Hotels offer brisk business service along with convention and banqueting facilities.

Among other amenities are its high profile restaurants featuring the finest international and Indian cuisines, high-spirited bars, health clubs, swimming pools, travel service counters, and recreational facilities in most of its hotels.

The Taj Group has targeted its hotels for the discerning tourist as well as for the exacting corporate executive in pursuit of leisure, pleasure and business-like efficiency and service.

The Indian Hotels Company Limited has recently promoted a new hotel company called Gateway Hotels and Gateway Resorts. This company will own and operate a spectrum of hotels from first class hotels to modest lodges. This new brand of hotels will serve as the alternative choice in the metropolitan cities and the primary chain in smaller towns and places of tourist interest.

While the Taj Group's top-of-the-line hotels in the major cities and tourist destinations will continue to provide luxury hotels and resorts, the Gateway chain will comprise a spectrum of hotels at a lower price range.

The first hotels to come under the Gateway banner are the Gateway Hotel on Banjara Hills in Hyderabad (120 rooms); the Gateway Riverview Lodge (38 rooms) at Chiplun, which is 250 kms from Bombay on the Bombay-Goa Highway, and the new 100-room Gateway Hotel in Bangalore. A few more have since been added.

The Taj Group's growth is not limited to India. The company gives technical knowhow and consultancy services to 12 properties spread across six countries in cities as far flung as New York and London to Sanaa in North Yemen. These are collectively known as "Taj International Hotels". The properties are:

	Name of Property	*No. of Rooms*
1.	St. James Court, London	519
2.	Hotel Lexington, New York	750
3.	The Canterbury Hotel, Washington D.C	100
4.	The Hampshire Hotel, Washington D.C	100
5.	Quality Hotel Downtown, Washington D.C	140
6.	Georgetown Marbury Hotel, Washington D.C	190
7.	Ramada Inn Central, Washington D.C	190
8.	Executive Hotel, Chicago	415
9.	Taj Sheba Hotel, Sanaa, Yemen Arab Republic	200
10.	Taj Samudra Hotel, Colombo, Sri Lanka	450
11.	Bi Ya Doo Island Resort, Bi yadhoo, Maldives	96
12.	Vilu Varu Island Resort, Vilungilveru, Maldives	60
13.	Hotel de L' Annapurna, Kathmandu	145
14.	Pamodzi Hotel, Lusaka, Zambia	200
15.	Al Falaj Hotel, Muscat	180
	Total	3735

Among other Taj projects under construction are a 300-room deluxe resort in Morocco, a 300-room hotel in Mauritius and three hotels in Tashkent, Samarkand and Bukhara.

The Taj Group and the Gateway chain in India comprise the following properties. We give below the list to give the readers an idea of different types of properties which a hotel chain operates:

	City Hotels	No. of Rooms
The Taj Mahal Hotel		
1.	The Taj Mahal Inter-continental, Bombay	650
2.	Hotel President, Bombay	300
3.	The Taj Mahal Hotel, New Delhi	350
4.	Taj Palace Intercontinental, New Delhi	504
5.	Taj Bengal, Calcutta	250
6.	Taj Coromandel Hotel, Madras	240
7.	Connemara Hotel, Madras	145
8.	Taj Residency, Bangalore	180
9.	West End Hotel, Bangalore	140
10.	Hotel Taj Ganges, Benaras (Varanasi)	120
11.	Hotel Chandela, Khajuraho	102
12.	Malabar Hotel, Cochin	100
13.	Taj View Hotel, Agra	105
14.	Taj Garden Retreats, Bangalore	60
Palace Hotels		
15.	The Rambagh Palace, Jaipur	110
16.	The Jai Mahal Palace Hotel, Jaipur	120
17.	The Raj Mahal Palace Hotel, Jaipur	12
18.	The Lake Palace, Udaipur	85
Resorts		
19.	The Aguada Hermitage, Goa	40
20.	The Fort Aguada Beach Resort, Goa	130
21.	The Taj Holiday Village, Goa	144
22.	The Fishermans Cove, Covelong, Madras	100
23.	Savoy Hotel, Ootacamund	60
Lodges		
24.	Sawai Madhopur Hunting Lodge, Ranthambore, Rajasthan	16
25.	Ramgarh Lodge, Ramgarh, Rajasthan	9

Contd..

City Hotels	No. of Rooms
Gateway Hotels and Gateway Resorts	
1. Gateway Hotel on Banjara Hills, Hyderabad	124
2. Gateway Riverview Lodge, Chiplun	38
3. Gateway Hotel, Bangalore	100
Total	4,270

Source: Report Taj Group.

The Taj group has established two large food processing units of Taj Flight Kitchens in Bombay and Delhi, each of which has the capacity to cater 10,000 meals a day, to meet the demands of airlines catering.

An affiliate company, the Taj Trade and Transport Company Limited runs guest facilitation services and shopping arcades in Taj properties. Another affiliate, Taj Services Limited, provides professional consultancy service in skills developed by the Taj Group, such as interior design, computer software, industrial engineering and systems, architecture, landscaping and other related areas pertaining to the hotel and hospitality industry.

Name of Hotel	Number of Rooms
Taj Luxury Hotels	
1. Taj Mahal Hotel, Mumbai	650
2. Taj Mahal Hotel, New Delhi	350
3. Taj Palace Hotel, New Delhi	250
4. Taj Bengal, Kolkata	250
5. Taj Coromandel, Chennai	240
6. Taj West End, Bangalore	140
7. Taj Krishna, Hyderabad	257
Taj Business Hotels	
8. Taj President, Mumbai	300
9. Taj Connemara, Chennai	150
10. Taj Residency, Bangalore	163

Contd...

	Name of Hotel	Number of Rooms
11.	Taj Residency, Hyderabad	118
12.	Taj Banjara, Hyderabad	140
13.	Taj Residency, Visakhapatnam	94
14.	Taj Residency, Ernakulam	108
15.	Taj Residency, Indore	78
16.	Taj Residency, Aurangabad	40
17.	Taj Residency, Nasik	68
18.	Taj Residency, Calicut	74
19.	Taj Residency, Lucknow	110
20.	Taj Residency Ummed, Ahmedabad	91
21.	Blue Diamond, Pune	109
Taj Leisure Hotels		
Taj Palace Hotels		
22.	Rambagh Palace, Jaipur	100
23.	Jai Mahal Palace, Jaipur	102
24.	Lake Palace. Udaipur	84
Taj Resort Hotels		
25.	The Aguada Hermitage, Goa	15 (Villas)
26.	Fort Aguada Beach Resort, Goa	130
27.	Taj Holiday Village, Goa	140
28.	Taj Exotica, Goa	140
29.	Fisherman's Cove, Chennai	28
Taj Garden Retreats		
30.	Taj Garden Retreat, Madurai	50
31.	Taj Garden Retreat, Coonoor	33
32.	Taj Garden Retreat, Kumarakom	22
33.	Taj Garden Retreat, Varkala	30
34.	Taj Garden Retreat, Thekkady	32
35.	Taj Garden Retreat, Chikamagalur	29

Contd...

	Name of Hotel	Number of Rooms
Taj Cultural Centre Hotels		
36.	Taj-View Hotel, Agra	100
37.	Taj Ganges, Banares	130
38.	Hotel Chandela, Khajuraho	94
39.	Taj Hari Mahal, Jodhpur	93
40.	Taj Malabar, Cochin	96
Other Hotels		
41.	The Ambassador Hotel, New Delhi	88
42.	Manjarun Hotel, Mangalore	101
43.	Savoy Hotel, Ooty	40
44.	Ramgarh Lodge, Jaipur	18
45.	Taj Mahal Palace, Jaipur	21
46.	The Gir Lodge, Sasan Gir	17
47.	The Sawai Madhopur Lodge, Sawai Madhopur	71
48.	Kuteeram, Bangalore	9 cottages
49.	City Inn, Baramati	34
Gateway Hotels & Gateway Resorts		
50.	Gateway Hotel on Residency Road, Bangalore	98
51.	Gateway Riverview Lodge, Chiplun	37
Taj International Hotels		
52.	Crown Plaza London, St. James, London	390
53.	Taj Samudra, Colombo	400
54.	Airport Garden Hotel, Colombo	120
55.	Taj Exotica, Bentota, Sri Lanka	162
56.	Taj Lagoon Resort, Maldives	64
57.	Taj Coral Reef Resort, Maldives	65
58.	Hotel de l'Annapurana, Kathmandu	160
59.	Admiral Plaza Hotel, Dubai	142
60.	Taj Sheba Hotel, Sanaa. Yemen	187
61.	Sohar Beach Hotel, Oman	40
62.	Taj Pamodzi Hotel, Lusaka, Zambia	200

4

Vital Dimensions

Travel agency sector is the distributor element in the travel and tourism marketing system. It can be considered to be a link between the producers of various travel services like tour operators, airline companies, transport operators and hoteliers on the one hand and their customers on the other. In other words, travel agents bring buyers and sellers together with a view to creating markets in places where these did not exist or to make existing markets more user friendly and efficient in order to expand the overall size of the travel market.

Today, the travel agent has become an important, integral, part of the travel and tourism industry world wide. Majority of people are using the services of travel agents for organising their travel both international as well as domestic. It is estimated that worldwide almost 70% of all international travel and 45% of all domestic travel are arranged by the travel agents. The figure however, may vary from country to country. The important role of the travel agent in the modern world is summarised in the principles of professional conduct and ethics of the American Society of Travel Agents. The role of travel agents in summarised as follows :

> "We live in a world in which travel has become increasingly important and complex in its variety of

> modes and choices. Travellers are faced with a myriad alternatives as to transportation, accommodation and other travel services. They must depend on travel agencies and others in the industry to guide them honestly and competently."

Product Sale

The main function of a travel agency is the product sale. Product sale is very complex subject specially when the product happens to be a tourist product. Because of the special nature of the tourist product and the multiplicity of manufacturers of the product, selling assumes greater importance. In addition, the distribution channels through which the tourist product finds its way to the consumers are multiple and varied. The tourist product, consists mainly of attractions, transport and accommodation. The producers of elements of the above products include air, sea, road transport companies and carriers, hotels and other forms of accommodation units, and the organisations which are responsible for putting together attractions both natural and man-made.

In most of the countries product sale is conducted through a distribution system controlled mostly by a network of retail travel agents, tour operators and wholesalers. The individual elements of a tourist product like international air tickets, domestic air or train tickets are also mostly sold through agents or representatives of airlines and railway companies, and purchased directly by consumers. The consumers have, therefore, a choice between direct booking and using the services of an agent. In addition, there are alternative channels available to the consumers through which they may buy their tourism products. These channels include clubs and societies, mail order, travel shops in supermarkets and departmental stores, tourist fairs and exhibitions and, more recently, electronic booking methods like computers.

Back to History

Any discussion on sale and organisation of travel must begin with the pioneer named Thomas Cook. The history of the business of the present Thomas Cook Group Limited can be traced back to over 150 years to its founder Thomas Cook, who not only was the first organised Travel Agent in the world, but who, it could be said, invented the travel business. A book salesman, a baptist preacher of Derbyshire was on his way to a temperance meeting in Leicester when he was inspired with "the idea of engaging a special train to carry the friends of temperance from Leicester to Loughborough in England and back to attend a quarterly delegate meeting." He thought that it was a sounder proposition to persuade a railway company, then in its infancy, to carry a train load of passengers at a very cheap fare than to run the train at 'standard' fares, but possibly only a quarter full. The man was Thomas Cook and his idea was put into operation with characteristic speed and efficiency. A few weeks later 570 travellers made the journey by the Midland Counties Railway at a specially reduced fare. This venture was soon followed by excursions to various other places, and in 1843, 3,000 school children were taken on a trip from Leicester to Derby in England.

Thomas Cook's real beginning as 'mass excursionist' was, however, the Liverpool-Caernaryon trip of 1845. The tourists travelled by rail to Liverpool, from where they took a steamer to Caernaryon. The advertisements for the trip caused a sensation and the response was so overwhelming that a second trip had to be arranged. Cook thought of every detail. He made a preliminary survey of accommodation and facilities and produced a handbook of the trip to Liverpool. The excursionist invasion of Scotland soon followed in 1846 and 1847. From 1848 to 1863 Cook conducted circular tours of Scotland, with 5,000 tourists a season. With the citadels of the landed aristocracy falling before him, he saw more enticing prospects opening before him: "I had become so thoroughly imbued with the tourist spirit that I began to contemplate Foreign Trips, including the continent of Europe, the United States and the Eastern land of the Bible."

Tour Around

By the mid-nineteenth century 'Holidays away from home' had become customary for a larger social group than ever before. Cook's initiative and organising genius provided the final impetus. In the winter of 1850-51, Cook was already negotiating for a tour of America, but his attention was diverted when he was offered the opportunity of conducting excursion trains to the Great Exhibition of 1851. Altogether, Cook conducted 1,65,000 people to and from the Crystal Palace. In 1856, Cook succeeded in organising his First grand circular tour of the continent. The tour was so successful that it had to be repeated six weeks later.

Thomas Cook's conquest of Europe began in 1862 when he made arrangements with Brighton and South Coast Railway for passenger traffic to the continent. Cook's Paris excursions are the first true 'package tours'; all the details of transport and accommodation were pre-arranged. In 1863 Cook visited Switzerland where his ideas were greeted with enthusiasm by hoteliers and railway proprietors. His next stop was Italy. Cook first made a personal survey of Turin, Milan, Florence and Genoa, to familiarise himself with their touristic attractions and facilities. In 1864 the first guided tour of Italy left England with applications far in excess of the available tickets. The 1860s also saw the introduction of Cook's 'railway and hotel coupons'. Cook personally examined the system by travelling through Italy to Vienna, down the Danube into Hungary and from there into Switzerland. By the 1890s, 1,200 hotels throughout the world accepted his coupons. Starting in 1868 Cook arranged regular circular tours of Switzerland and Northern Italy.

The first official London Office of Thomas Cook and Sons was established in 1865. John Mason Cook now joined his father as a permanent partner and took charge of the London office. From that year on, the history of Thomas Cook and Sons was one of continuous expansion. In the year 1880 John Mason Cook left for India and established offices in Bombay and Calcutta and formed the 'Eastern Princes' Department. In 1887 this department arranged the visits of Indian princes to Queen Victoria's Jubilee Celebrations.

By taking advantage of nineteenth century advances in transport technology, Thomas Cook and Sons had effected a revolution in tourism by the end of the century. No longer the preserve of the rich and the aristocrats, tourism was now an industry. Armed with Cook's hotel and rail coupons, the tourist could demand uniform prices and standards of service and accommodation. This new standardisation had distinct advantages. It meant comfort and convenience and less need for decision making on the part of the individual tourist. The tourist was less likely to experience discomfort or embarrassment.

The management of the Company passed on to John Mason Cook's three sons in the year 1898. At the time of John Mason Cook's death, the business included three main aspects of travel -selling tours, banking and shipping. Soon after the Second World War, the British government acquired the principal interest in the Company. In the year 1972, the British Government sold the company to Midland Bank Consortium.

Today, Thomas Cook Group is the parent company of a worldwide group of companies which are partially or wholly owned. The company also has a close trading relationship with Companie International des Wagon-Lits et Tourism, and the combined worldwide network of these companies, together with their authorised agents. The company also introduced traveller's cheques which were originally called 'circular notes'. Members of the Thomas Cook Group of companies now issue cheques as principals in different currencies and are associated with partner banks in various countries. It is also a large trader in the buying and selling of foreign currency bank notes. Thomas Cook Group Limited today provides a wide range of services to its customers in over 150 countries worldwide through their network of over 1,200 outlets. The company is considered to be one of the largest travel companies selling a wide range of travel services.

Much has changed since the year 1841, when Thomas Cook chartered a train to carry 570 travellers at a specially reduced fare from Leicester to Loughborough in England. Cook, who bought the railway tickets in bulk and resold them to members of his group, can be credited with being the first bona fide travel agent to work as a full-time professional. However, neither Thomas Cook & Sons, nor American Express Company or Cox and Kings were then a retail agent as the modern complex distribution chain had not yet evolved in any trade including travel.

Scope and Dimensions

The scope and the role of the travel agency was limited in the beginning since mass tourism as we know it today had not yet begun. It was, however, the introduction of the air travel which gave a boost to the travel agency business. The introduction of an economy class by various airline companies crossing the North Atlantic heralded the era of travel agency and was responsible for their growth. The introduction of an 'economy class' in effect was nothing more than a projection of Thomas Cook's original idea of adjusting prices to encourage full capacity use of every means of transport.

Rapid development of transport system, especially the jet travel, improved living standards combined with reduction in working hours is the root cause of today's upward surge in travel. Side by side with the rapid improvements in industry and technology, practically all aspects of life have become more and more complex particularly during the past half a century. This is certainly the case in the travel industry in which, only a century ago, the job consisted almost entirely of arranging a simple reservation for the travellers in some means of transport. Today the functions and duties of a person at the travel agency counter are vastly different and more varied. He is now called upon to perform a variety of duties rather than just issue tickets and reserve seats in a train, aeroplane or accommodation in the hotel. Travel today is no longer the privilege of the few, but is sought by millions. No longer does the travel agency exist for the sole purpose of selling tickets from one point to another. The travel industry developed along certain well-defined lines as the worldwide demand on its services increased. The urge to travel became very intense over the years resulting in widespread growth of travel agencies in the world. Most of the travellers wished to have their travel arrangements made in advance and to be relieved of the difficulties of coping with various pre-travel arrangements of which they had only a very limited knowledge.

Modern Approach

Over the years the range and activities of a retail travel agent have increased manifold. In the modern context, the role of a travel agent is rather different to that of most of other retailers selling merchandise. The travel agent does not purchase travel with a view to reselling the same to its customers. It is only when a customer has finally decided on the purchase of travel that the agent approaches the principal on behalf of his customer. The retail travel agent, unlike most other retailers, does not carry an inventory or stock of travel products in his premises.

The main role of retail travel agents is to provide to their customers a convenient location for the "purchase" of various elements of travel like transport, accommodation and several other ancillary services associated with holiday and travel. The travel agents act as booking agents for holidays and travel and disseminate information and give advice on such services. This role can be summed up as follows:

(i) to give advice to the potential tourist on the merits of alternative destinations, and

(ii) to make necessary arrangements for a chosen holiday which may involve booking of accommodation, transport or other relevant services associated with his travel.

A travel agent, in order to give an advice to his potential customers on the merits of a destination, must possess knowledge, expertise and up-to-date information about that destination. Besides, a travel agent has close contacts with providers of services, i.e., their principals from whom they purchase services for their customers. In other words, a retail travel agent is an intermediary providing a direct link between the consumer and the suppliers of tourist services, i.e.., airlines, transport companies, hotels, auto rental companies, etc. The retail agent is the one who acts on behalf of the principal, i.e., the original provider of tourist service such as an airline company, hotel company, shipping company, insurance company, railways or a tour operator. An agent sells the principal's services and is rewarded by a commission.

In Operation

The scope and range of travel agency operations would depend on the size of an agency. If the company is large in size, the range of activities will be more comprehensive. In this case the agency will have specialised departments, each having to perform different functions. To deal with the subject of a travel agency, the best method of approach is, perhaps, to consider its functions. These may be broadly classified as follows:

Provision for Information

One of the primary functions of a retail travel agent from the point of view of the tourist or the general public is to provide necessary information about travel. This information is provided at a convenient location where the intending tourist may ask certain questions and seek clarifications about his proposed travel. This is a very specialised job and the person behind the counter should be a specialist having excellent knowledge of various travel alternative plans. He should be in a position to give up-to-date and accurate information regarding various services and general information about travel, etc. The presentation to the potential customer must be forceful, and exciting variations must continually be devised to help sell tours. A good travel agent is something of a personal counsellor who knows all the details about the travel and also the needs and interests of the intending traveller. Communication plays a key role in dissemination of any type of information. This is equally true in the case of dissemination of travel information. The person behind the travel counter should be able to communicate with the customer in his language. The knowledge of foreign languages is an essential prerequisite for personnel working in a travel agency.

Guide Book

Tourist itinerary is a composition of a series of operations that are a result of the study of the market. A tourist journey is characterised by an itinerary using various means of transport to link one locality with another. Preparation of different types of itineraries is another important function of a travel agency. A travel agent gives advice to intending travellers on the type of programmes which they may choose for their holiday or business travel. The study and the realisation of the itineraries call for perfect organisation (technical and administrative) as also knowledge of the desires of the public for a holiday and the propensity to receive tourists by the receiving localities.

Liaison with Providers of Services : Before any form of travel can be sold over the counter to a customer, contracts have to be entered into with the providers of various services. These include transportation companies, hotel proprietors, the providers of surface transport like motor cars or coaches for transfer to and from hotels and for sightseeing, etc., and also for general servicing requirements. The work carried out under these headings is usually that of the owners or senior employees of agencies concerned. In the case of a large agency with worldwide branches, the liaison work involves a great deal of coordination with the principals.

Proper Planning

Once the contracts and arrangements have been entered into, there comes the task of planning and costing tours, both for inclusive programmes and to meet individual requirements. This job is intensely interesting and at the same time challenging. It calls for a great deal of initiative and drive, for travel to those places which are to be included in the itineraries. Paradoxically many of those who do this type of work visit comparatively few of the places included in the itineraries they prepare. This is essentially a job for a meticulous person and calls for considerable training and ability. Many agencies, with the cooperation of airlines and other transportation companies, take the opportunity of arranging educational tours for such staff to destinations with which they deal.

Many large agencies have experts who are authorities on particular countries and, in addition to a general programme, many will issue separate programmes dealing with specific territories. Separate programmes, dealing with holiday offers based on specific forms of transportation, e.g., air, rail, road or sea, may also be prepared. Programmes also have to be prepared to cover different seasons of the year.

Publicity is an important part of the programme. Having spent considerable time and money on preparing all that goes into the issue of a programme, publicity must feature considerably in the activities of a travel agency and more so if the agency happens to be a large one. The majority of large travel agencies have their own publicity departments under the management of an expert in the publicity field.

Ticketing : Selling tickets to clients using different modes of transport like air, rail and sea is yet another important function of a travel agency. This calls for a thorough knowledge of schedules of various modes of transport. Air carriers, railways and steamship companies have hundreds of schedules and the person behind the counter should be conversant with all these. Ticketing is, however, not an easy job as the range and diversity of international airfares is very complex and varied. There are several different types of fare combinations on the North Atlantic route alone. Changes in international as also in the local air schedules and additions of new flights from time to time makes the job of the travel agent one of constant challenge. An up-to-date knowledge about various schedules of air companies, steamship companies and railways is very essential.

Computerised reservation system has in recent years rather revolutionised the reservation system, both for air and rail seats, and also a room in a hotel. Many large travel agencies are using this system. This system comprises a computer network that can be used by the travel agent to reserve an air or rail accommodation as also accommodation in a hotel. Through a wide network, confirmation of reservations are available in a matter of seconds.

Settlement of Accounts : Linked with the function of ticketing and reservation of accommodation in a hotel is the settlement of accounts of the clients. Accountancy plays an important part and is one of the major duties to be performed by the travel agency. Dealing with the settlement of accounts in all parts of the world calls for a thorough knowledge of foreign currencies, their cross-values and, above all, the intricacies of exchange control regulations, which vary from country to country.

Provision of Foreign Currencies : Provision of foreign currencies to intending travellers is another specialised activity of a travel agency. Some of the larger travel agencies deal exclusively in the provision of foreign currencies, travellers' cheques, etc. This is an important facility to intending travellers as it saves them a lot of time and energy in avoiding visits to regular banking channels.

Insurance : Insurance, both for personal accident risks and of baggage, is yet another important activity of the travel agency. Some of the larger travel agents maintain sizeable shipping and forwarding departments, aimed at assisting the traveller, to transport personal effects and baggage to any part of the world, with a minimum of inconvenience.

The multifarious activities mentioned in the above paragraphs show that the travel agency's range of services in modern times has expanded a great deal. The field of expertise is quite large and is constantly growing with the fast changing travel needs of the people. The job description of a modern travel agency can be summed up as follows :

(i) Preparation of individual pre-planned itineraries, personally escorted tours and group tours and sale of pre- paid package tours.

(ii) Making arrangements for hotels, motels, resort accommodation, meals, car rentals, sightseeing, transfer of passengers and luggage between terminals and hotels, and special features such as music festivals and theatre tickets.

(iii) Handling of and giving advice on the many details involved in modern day travel, e.g., travel and baggage insurance, language study material, travellers' cheques, foreign currency exchange, documentary requirements (visas and passport) and health requirements (immunisation and inoculations).

(iv) Possession of professional knowledge and experience, as for instance, schedules of air and train connections, rates of hotels, their quality, whether rooms have baths, etc. All of this is information on which the traveller, but for the travel agent, will spend days or weeks of endless phone calls, letters and personal visits.

(v) Arrangement of reservations for special interest activities such as conventions, conferences, and business meetings and sports events, etc.

Important Travel Organisation

There are various activities which a travel agency has to perform in order that an intending traveller undertakes his proposed journey and enjoys a holiday of his choice. There are various steps involved from the time a traveller visits a travel agent to buy a ticket until he returns home after visiting a place of his choice.

Organised travel by a travel agency can be of two types, i.e. (i) single client, and (ii) group client. In order to effect the journey, the following main elements (in both types of travel) need to be considered:

(a) Study of the journey,

(b) Estimate of expenditure,

(c) Execution of the journey, and

(d) Presentation of accounts.

Individual or Ordinary Trips : The following steps are involved in organising individual or ordinary trips:

(i) The client turns to the travel agent to organise for him a particular journey (cultural, natural, business, religious, etc.).

(ii) The agency from this angle will examine as to what will be involved, e.g., scope of journey, when the journey is to take place, various services needed and the accessories required.

(iii) Based on the above evaluation and other elements in his possession, the travel agent will suggest an itinerary and will then communicate to the client the estimated maximum cost for the client's approval.

(iv) The travel agent will then compile the definite estimates, a total of a series of various costs added up, e.g., transport, accommodation, the services such as those of guides, operative costs such as (postage, telex, telefax, E-Mail, telephones, etc.).

(v) The travel agent then will present a document of the amount of money to be paid in duplicate to the customer. The client returns one of the debit copies signed on acceptance accompanied with a deposit (in anticipation). The deposit normally is about 25 per cent of the total cost.

(vi) Once the client's approval has been obtained, the travel agent's operation department then executes the journey.

(vii) The 'operation' department's task now is to book for the established dates the transport and various other services. After the booking confirmation has been received, the travel agent issues the vouchers.

(viii) The travel agent prepares the 'tourist itinerary' which will accompany the client through the entire journey. It will indicate the tickets to be used, the hotels and other services booked and will include vouchers, etc. Normally the itinerary is made in triplicate: one for the client, another for the agency and the third for the hotelier or those who will provide the required services paid by means of vouchers.

(ix) The last formality is the delivery to the client of the vouchers, confirmed tickets, the technical itinerary.

(x) When the group is particularly large, e.g., for sports, etc., the travel agent needs to take extra care by way of informing public authorities for purposes of security, etc.

Travel agents in a highly developed market cover all the above activities and range of services which depends upon the extent of the economic development of that country. The travel patterns of the population in advanced countries are different as compared to those in developing countries. The services of travel agents are increasingly utilised in developed countries. In some of the advanced countries like the USA, Canada, Germany and Japan a very large percentage of tourists are utilising the services of travel agents.

Tour Operator's Role

The dramatic growth of tourist traffic to the Mediterranean countries of Europe is a principal feature of the history of mass tourism in the last forty years. A major contributing factor in this growth of air travel holiday tourism has been the development of 'inclusive tour', a method of packaging a holiday. The idea of buying a package of travel, accommodation and perhaps some ancillary services such as entertainment etc., became established in Western Europe in the 1960s. Essentially an 'inclusive tour' is a package of transport and accommodation and perhaps some other service which is sold as a single holiday for an all inclusive price. This inclusive price is usually significantly lower than could be obtained by conventional methods of booking transport and accommodation separately from individual hotel and transport tariffs. The principal feature of the inclusive tour is that the tourist may buy, for a single price, a holiday which is much cheaper than would be possible for the holiday maker if he bought the components of his holiday separately and directly from individual hotels and from transport companies or from a retail travel agent.

The chief functionary or the principal in this system is the tour operator. It is the tour operator who buys aircraft seats and hotel beds and certain other facilities such as surface transport or entertainment and makes up the package. Historically, the tour operator has mostly emerged from retail travel agency. However, today a clear distinction must be made between tour operator and a travel agent. The latter, the retail travel agent, undertakes to sell the travel services of his principal, who will be airline companies and other transport undertakings, hotel groups, shipping lines and the providers of such ancillary services as traveller's cheques, etc. Unlike the travel agent who is the retailer of the tourism product, the tour operator is a manufacturer of a tourism product. He plans, organises and sells tours. The tour operator makes all the necessary arrangements - transport, accommodation, sight-seeing, insurance, entertainment and other matters and sells this package for an all-inclusive price. A package tour is designed to fit a particular group of travellers. These may be special interest tours, i.e., mountain tours and can be escorted. Escorted tour normally includes transportation, meals, sightseeing, accommodation, guide services, etc. It is the escort or the group leader who is responsible for maintaining the schedule of the tour and for looking after all the arrangements.

Group Inclusive Tour (GIT) : This is the most popular form of tour in this category where people travel in groups of 15 or more persons. These tours are available for any destination. The terms and conditions for group inclusive tours are laid down by IATA. The escort for such groups normally travels free as the airline provides him with free passage and accommodation. "Foreign Inclusive Tours' (FIT) on the other hand are unescorted package tours. These tours are comparatively more flexible. The traveller can buy a predetermined package with arrangements for sightseeing, hotels and certain meals, where necessary. He does not tour with a group. He can make his own arrangements and programmes according to his liking. The inclusive tour is one of the several devices which enable tourists to enjoy the lower prices.

How does the tour operator manage to sell the package to the traveller at such a low price? The low price of the package holiday or inclusive tour is made possible by reason of the lower unit costs obtainable both for the air travel and for the hotel accommodation. The tour operator enters into long-term contracts for aircraft seats and similar contracts with hotels for booking rooms. By mass-producing holidays in the form of package tours, the tour operators are able to procure substantial discounts from carriers, hoteliers, etc. and offer their package deals at much lower rates. The profits of the tour operators and the success of his operations, however, depend on achieving of very high load factors for the aircraft and very high occupancy rates for the hotel. In this way, unit costs can be maintained sufficiently low to enable the tour operator to offer his package at a price which is often less than the cheapest available fare alone. A breakthrough in the business of tour operation came when airlines recognised that tour operation can fill the empty seats and introduced special fares for use exclusively by tour operators for combining into an inclusive tour.

The tour operator has thus emerged as the true manufacturer of the inclusive tour product packaged, standardised and mass-produced. The tour operator may sell this product directly to the public or through the channels of the retail travel agencies. It can be marketed successfully in the tourist generating countries to a mass market just because it is standardised, packaged and quality controlled. The product is therefore susceptible to the similar marketing techniques that are applied to the marketing of consumer goods.

Some Guidelines

The agent's role in handling a client is very important. Once a client enters the agency it becomes necessary for an agent to properly anticipate his needs and requirements. The client also has come with a predetermined notion about a destination he is visiting. WATA, the World Association of Travel Agencies, has prepared comprehensive guidelines for handling a client. These guidelines are based on the WATA Master-Key, an annual publication of the World Association of Travel Agencies. Updated and published yearly, the WATA Master-Key is a selectively comprehensive source of travel information. Individual agency tariffs given in the publication, represent the selling tool for members, incoming and outgoing services. Along with the tariffs the Master-Key gives a country description sheet containing a wealth of useful background information of a destination. In addition, the Master-Key also gives detailed information about some hotels located in important cities and tourist centres together with prevalent confidential tariffs and other relevant information for travel agencies.

The WATA Master-Key is a valuable reference material for travel agents. Its presentation makes it easy for the users to extract the information they need. The guidelines as enumerated in the Master-Key are as follows:

Sale of Tour : It should first be determined whether the client who wants to book a tour prefers to:

a. Join an escorted tour, or

b. Choose a FIT, combining leisure and activity according to his individual tastes and interests.

FIT/Your Relations with Client : If your client wants a "tailor made" tour, let him make the suggestions, without imposing your own views, on the following points:

Itinerary

1. Determine the cities to be visited.
2. Number of days (overnights) in each place.
3. Mode of transportation between cities.
4. Establish a rough time schedule, taking into consideration the time at his disposal.

Transportation

1. Air transport should be used when time is limited and for long distances.
2. Surface transportation should be recommended for shorter distances.

3. For trains, determine whether advanced reservation is necessary. Indicate stations where trains are to be changed.
4. Bus should be recommended in some countries, as it usually allows additional sightseeing.
5. When arranging timetables, remember that your client is on vacation, and therefore avoid early departures.

Hotel Accommodation

Category of Hotels : Examine with your client which category of hotel he wants to stay at-Deluxe, First Class, Standard or Economy class. It is preferable that he is accommodated in a maximum rate room; however, if he must consider the cost, then rather suggest a lower grade hotel with best available room.

Type of Rooms : Examine whether your client wishes a special room on a special floor, with or without bath/ shower, sea view, outside or inside, etc. Draw his attention to the fact that in high season a room with a bath may be difficult to obtain in some places. In some cases a double room for single occupancy can be suggested, a single room being often small or not well situated. If your client insists on having a particular room, he may have to pay a supplement.

Meals : Ask your client whether he wants to have accommodation on bed and breakfast, semi-pension or full pension basis. If accommodation is on bed and breakfast basis, keep in mind that in certain resorts, semi or full pension is compulsory.

Check-in Time: Remind your client that check-in time at hotels is usually after 12 noon. Immediate occupancy on early morning arrivals can only be secured if the room is reserved for the previous night. If your client leaves late in the evening you may propose to him to pay for an additional night.

During periods of festivals, fairs or congresses, hotel space may not be available, rendering it necessary for your client to change the dates in those places; cabled hotel confirmation should, therefore, be suggested.

During periods, such as important festivals and events, a minimum stay of 5-7 days may be required. The same is applicable to some winter resorts, where a minimum stay of two weeks is required at Christmas and New Year.

Transfers

1. The need of transfers upon arrival or departure results from the fact that it is often difficult to find one's way at airport, piers or stations with which one is not familiar.
2. Transfers by agencies include interpreter meeting and assistance, accompanying clients (unless otherwise specified), porterage and transportation of 2 pieces of hand luggage per person between airport, station, bus or air terminal and hotels or vice versa, as well as tip to driver, but it does not include tip to hotel porter.
3. Type of vehicle varies according to cities, generally by private car or taxi/cab.
4. Airport transfers are naturally more expensive, but also the most convenient ones.
5. When opting for transfer from city air terminal, your client must know that there will be no assistance at the airport, that he will have to tip for baggage at the airport and pay for bus between the airport and the city terminal.
6. Bus Arrivals: Certain bus companies stop at the major hotels to drop or collect clients, the disadvantage of this being the clients' dependence on time schedules and waiting for his turn to be dropped off. In addition, it will be necessary for the client to contact the local agency if other services are not to be provided in that city.

Sightseeing/Excursions/Tours

1. The advantage of arranging sightseeing in advance is that your client does not have to waste his time, queuing up in the local agency. Also, a balance can be established in advance between leisure time and sightseeing, as well as for tours of the city and countryside.
2. Motor Coach Tours : Apart from the economic viewpoint, there is the advantage of meeting other travellers, but clients have to arrange their own transportation to meeting points, as pick-up is very seldom done on motor-coach tours.

3. Private Car Tours : Your client is picked up at the hotel, has the choice of time of departure and can stop wherever he likes, but this is the most expensive solution. In some places there are regular private car tours, or else sightseeing can be done on a seat-in-car basis.
4. Hire of Private Car with Chauffeur
   (a) City hire-must be recommended to deluxe clients, whose time is limited between trains, boats or planes, or who already know the city and want to see only special places or go shopping. Since very often the chauffeur cannot act as a guide, a private guide will be needed for sightseeing.

   (b) Touring hire-if a private car is used for travelling from one city to another, local guides in each place will be sufficient. Distance covered daily should not exceed 250 km. Client's attention has to be drawn to the fact that he will have to pay for empty run of car (return to point of departure). The full daily basic charge is due, even if the vehicle is picked up in the evening.
5. Motor Launch Tours/Boats Trips : The same applies here as for motor coach tours. Deluxe clients will be picked up at the hotel by private car and driven to embarkation pier.
6. Self-driven cars can also be provided when clients fill the necessary conditions and, if wanted, a local guide can be placed at their disposal.

Music Festival, Theatre and Concert Tickets

Clients must be told that advance reservation is necessary. Confirmation of requested tickets cannot be guaranteed and tickets are not refundable unless they can be resold.

Land Arrangements : On the basis of all details furnished by your clients, it will enable you to make an estimate of the land arrangements.

Transatlantic/Pacific Transportation : To the land arrangements, the cost of flight/boat tickets for Transatlantic/Pacific transportation has to be added.

Cost Price : Items a and b above give you the cost price.

Selling Price : In order to obtain the selling price you have to add your handling fees or mark-up, as well as a margin safeguarding any possible increase.

Suggested Itinerary

(a) A suggested itinerary should be drafted of what has been agreed with your client and submitted to him, together with the final price. The accompanying letter should clearly specify what is included in the price:

1. Price and type of land arrangements.
2. Price and class of air/sea/rail tickets, indicating that they are subject to change without notice.
3. The agency's conditions regarding handling charge , cancellation fees, possible deposit request, etc.

(b) It should also point out what is NOT included, such as cost of passport, visa, gratuities, tips to hotel porters, beverages, laundry, taxes (government, landing, embarkation), etc.

(c) Acceptance of suggested itinerary should be requested to enable you to proceed with reservation, and a deposit should be asked.

Your Relation with Service Suppliers : Reservation Procedures

(a) Once you are in possession of the client's agreement you can start reservations with carriers and hotels.

(b) In case your client requests only hotel reservations in a few places, it is advisable to make the reservations directly with the hotels.

(c) However, if transfer, sightseeing or other services are also requested, then it is preferable to go through the local agent, who is in a better position to replace a hotel by a similar one, in case of full occupancy.

Transfers : Due to frequent changes in time schedules and/ or due to changes your client may require, it is NOT advisable to send transfer requests earlier than one month prior to final documentation. An exception can be made if a special service is required and rate confirmation is needed.

Transfers should be requested by vouchers, indicating the following items:

(a) Full name of client(s) and number of passengers (for a child or an aged person give their age also).

(b) Date of transfer.

(c) Full description (indicate type of car, name of airport, city air terminal or station, exact flight or train number and arrival/ departure time).

(d) Name of hotel the client is staying at.

(e) Town and date of issue.

(f) If you do not have the rate of a service, request the rate of confirmation on the voucher copies.

Transportation : Whenever possible, obtain all tickets for rail, bus, boat, cruise, sleeping cars, etc., that may be required locally from agencies of foreign railroads, bus companies, steamship lines, etc.

Hotel Accommodation

1. Depending on the time you have, hotel reservations can be made by reservation requests, by telex or cable (give paid reply), through hotel representatives, or through a WATA office. If you reserve through a hotel representative or WATA office, their conditions should be respected.
2. Once you have a hotel confirmation, issue a voucher for re- confirmation, indicating the following items:

   (a) Full name of client(s) and number of persons (for a child or an aged person give their age also).

   (b) Type of room.

   (c) Arrival and departure date, time of arrival and flight/ train number.

   (d) Meal conditions - clearly indicate whether rooms only, bed and breakfast (Continental or American/English), half or full pension.

   (e) Always mention on hotel vouchers: "All taxes and service charges included".

(f) Method of payment-indicate who will pay the bill. If the client settles the bill directly with the hotel, even when a deposit has been sent, hotels do not always pay a commission.

(g) Always ask for a re-confirmation of the rate on the voucher copies.

3. If the best room is required, it should be determined as DELUXE, and a 10 per cent supplement foreseen.
4. If a suite is required, it can be estimated a 2½ times the normal tariff.
5. Whenever necessary, an extra night is to be foreseen for early arrival or late departure. Indicate on voucher early a.m. arrival the following day or request additional night or day use, advising the exact departure time.
6. In case of split stays at the same hotel, a separate voucher should be issued for each day.

Sightseeing/Excursions/Tours

The same applies as for transfers - regular sightseeing tours should not be requested earlier than one month prior to the final documentation, except when a special service is required (e.g., sightseeing starting at airport) or for excursions/tours of two or more days' duration.

1. Sightseeing/Excursions/Tours should be requested for WATA affiliates by vouchers, indicating the following items:

(a) Full name of client(s) and number of persons (for a child or an aged person give their age also).

(b) Date of sight-seeing/excursions/tours.

(c) Reference number of tour (if given), tour designation and title.

(d) By private car or by regular scheduled motor coach.

(e) For regular tours, give time and place of departure for private car tours, indicate "pick-up at hotel".

(f) Name of hotel client is staying at.

(g) Town and date of issue.

(h) In case a complete description does not appear in the agent's tariff, ask for additional information and rate confirmation.

2. If your client wants to start a sightseeing tour from airport or station, add transfer-rate to sightseeing rate.

Chauffeur Driven Car Hire

1. If private car hire with chauffeur is required, it has to be reserved in advance on the basis of rates quoted in the Master-Key. If rates are not given, apply to the agency for rates and details.
2. For requests, issue voucher, indicating the following details:
   (a) Full name of client(s) and number of passengers.
   (b) Type of car (year of construction if available).
   (c) For city hire : Date and time of beginning of hire, length of hire or time of termination.
   (d) For touring hire: Date of beginning and termination of hire, starting time of hire and termination point, as well as stopovers.
   (e) Special requests, such as automatic cars, air conditioning, luggage, rack, etc.
   (f) Name of hotel client is staying at.
3. City and Touring hire must be issued on separate vouchers, as tariffs and minimum daily averages are not the same. Also, if more than one day city hire is required issue one voucher for each day.
4. Touring rate is established on the basis of a reliable map. Ten per cent of total mileage should be added for detours. If there are overnight stops, an additional 20 miles should be foreseen for possible use of car during the stay in city.
5. For empty runs, it should be noted that the law does not authorise chauffeurs to drive more than 310 miles/500 km per day, therefore, the total distance should be divided by this authorised maximum to reckon the number of chauffeur's overnights to be added to the touring rate.

6. For chauffeur's accommodation, the rate appearing in the tariff has to be multiplied by the number of days the car has been used (special rates if outside the country).

Self-Driven Cars : If given, use rates appearing in the WATA Master-Key, otherwise, apply to the agency or consult Hertz, Avis, etc., for details and rates, whenever so indicated.

WATA Master-Key is a valuable document for a travel agent. The guidelines given in 'key' make the job of a travel agent a lot easier. As a comprehensive source of travel information it facilitates the work of a travel agent. The destination profiles provide a wealth of background information not only for a travel agent but also for a traveller. The 'key' is updated every year making it a valuable reference material.

IATA Accredition : Travel agents are the marketplace intermediaries responsible for selling the services of airlines worldwide. Considering the role and importance of air transport which is at the heart of travel and tourism selling, its services becomes the key motivation for engaging in travel agency business. Therefore, the importance of IATA approval for a travel agency is essential to enable it to sell the services of airlines.

For setting up a travel agency business there are no legal requirements. In some countries, however, governments exercise some kind of a licensing control over agencies. Most principals license the sale of their services through the issue of an agency contract, or agency agreement. In the absence of such a contract or an agreement, a travel agency will not get any commission from selling the services on behalf of the principal. The income of a travel agent is derived only from a commission which he receives from the principal after selling their services.

A licence is required by a travel agency for a commission to be payable on the sale of services of air carriers who are members of the International Air Transport Association. Domestic air services are, however, exempted from this. Most airlines want to sell their services worldwide but cannot do so on their own as it is not economically viable for them to set up extensive network of sales offices in every city of the world. It is the travel agents who are the marketplace intermediaries who make the sale of the services of the airlines possible worldwide through their own network.

As IATA travel makes up a substantial proportion of a total sale of a travel agency turnover, it is important for the travel agent who wishes to offer his clients the full range of travel services to obtain the necessary IATA approval or appointment.

IATA-Controlled Approval : The travel agency approval of IATA is controlled by its Agency Administration Board. This Board is made up of a number of IATA members operating from a particular country. Before approval is granted by IATA, a travel agency has to fulfil certain conditions. The most important condition is the demonstration by an agency of its financial soundness or financial standing. It has to prove that it has sufficient finances to settle the accounts of various airlines whose business it is handling. Another condition which an agency has to fulfil is to ensure the suitability and security of its premises. The premises of a travel agency are to be centrally located preferably in the centre of the town in a commercial district having proper security. The security aspect is very important as the agency has to keep the ticket stock of various airlines and this is quite expensive.

Proficiency of the staff of a travel agency is another important aspect which is considered by IATA before giving an approval. The staff has to be professionally trained in the handling of airlines business. IATA in association with UFTAA conducts the International Travel Agents Training Programme to meet the growing demand for a professionally trained manpower for the travel industry. The IATA-UFTAA training programme operates under the authority of the Passenger Agency Training Board. IATA's Agency Training Services (ATS) located in Geneva (Switzerland) is responsible for the general administration of the programme.

In the field, the training programme is administered by a Local Coordinator who is responsible for the promotion of the training courses, the distribution of the training materials and the organisation of the examinations. The Local Coordinator is provided by the local IATA Agency Services, the National Airlines or the National Travel Agents Association in a particular country.

The IATA-UFTAA training courses have been designed primarily for travel professionals who work in IATA accredited travel agencies and whose main task is to sell international air transportation on behalf of IATA member airlines. The agents' staff can demonstrate proficiency by completing an IATA/ UFTAA (passenger) training course.

The applicant's ability to generate new business is another requirement to be taken into consideration by IATA before considering an application for approval. This is to ensure that an agent is capable of generating new business in the market and has sufficient contacts to do so. To sum up, any travel agency, in order to get IATA approval for selling the services of IATA airlines worldwide, has to ensure the following: (i) Financial standing, (ii) Suitability of the premises, (iii) Security for control of ticket stock, (iv) Proficiency of the staff, (v) Ability to generate new business

After considering the above aspects and if the IATAs Agency Administration Board is satisfied, necessary IATA approval is accorded to an agency. Once approved, a Passenger Sales Agreement is issued and a numeric ticket validation code is provided which will be stamped on all tickets issued by that IATA-approved agent. IATA approval enables the agent to do business on behalf of all IATA members. It enables the agent to sell the services of all IATA member airlines throughout the world. The entire process of getting IATA approval can be quite time-consuming and lengthy and in the meantime agents applying for IATA approval are expected to generate business without getting any commissions.

Additional Approvals : In addition to the IATA approval which is basic for a travel agency, there are certain other approvals/ recognitions required for running a travel agency. These approvals, however, will depend on the extent of activities and range of services which a particular agency would like to offer to its clients. For instance, in order to make commissionable sales on the services of railways, domestic airlines services and other principals such as car hire companies, shipping and cruise services, necessary approval is to be obtained. These approvals will enable travel agents to sell services on behalf of these principals with remuneration. In case a travel agency is an IATA-approved agent, or a member of the National Travel Agents Association, obtaining approvals for most of other principals becomes largely a formality.

Travel and Trade Associations

Formation of associations by independent firms in a particular trade or a group of industries is primarily done with a view to protecting the interests of its members. Trade Organisations are voluntary bodies formed by individual firms belonging to a particular trade not only to protect but also to advance the common interests of their members. The main objective of forming an association by independent firms is to get strong representations which act as channels of communication with the government and other organised groups to further the interests of their members. In almost all disciplines, members sharing similar interests or complementing each other's interests in some way or other have formed organisations/associations.

The ever-increasing importance of the tourism sector and the increase in the growth in its volume over the years have resulted in the formation of associations in this sector. Secondly, the ever-increasing international character of the modern day tourism and the growing influence of international agencies in various fields have also influenced the growth of international cooperations in the field of tourism. All these developments in turn have brought together members of the travel associations at national, regional and international levels collectively to further their trade interests. Different producers and sellers of various tourist services like tour operators, travel agents, hotel companies, airline companies, ground operators, etc., have formed associations of their members.

The scope of discussion in this chapter is limited to the associations of travel agents and tour operators. These associations today have assumed great importance and provide a platform to their members where ideas are exchanged and topics of mutual interest discussed and solutions arrived at. They provide services like information, assistance and advice in the conduct of their business to their members. The various associations in the field of tourism can take different forms. Broadly, the following five forms can be identified:

(i) Those based on the education and training needs of the industry. These may include professional bodies like Hotel and Catering Management Association, Travel and Tourism Management Association which are primarily concerned with the training and educational standards of personnel working in hotel and travel agencies.

(ii) Those which are concerned with the sectoral interests of their members. They include the National Associations of Travel Agents and Tour Operators. Each country has such associations. For instance, the American Society of Travel Agents (ASTA), the Australian Federation of Travel Agents (AFTA), the Association of British Travel Agents (ABTA), the Japan Association of Travel Agents (JATA), the Indian Association of Travel Agents (IATA), the Swiss Travel Agents Association, the German Travel Agencies' Association, etc.

(iii) Those which are responsible for developing, promoting and facilitating tourism among a particular region. These regional organisations draw their membership from public or private sector organisations dealing with tourism and sharing a common interest in the promotion and development or marketing of a specific tourism geographical area or a region. This area may represent a region, a state, a country or a resort. The membership is opened to groups or organisations, both in public and private sectors, rather than individuals, such as Pacific Area Travel Association (PATA), etc.

(iv) Those which are concerned with the promotion and development of tourism globally. These organisations deal with all the aspects of tourism. The rapid expansion in tourism activity globally was responsible for creating a need for world bodies to deal with tourism issues at the government level. The World Tourism Organisation (WTO) is one such global tourism organisation representing public sector tourism from most countries of the world.

(v) Those which are responsible for promoting and furthering interests of specific trade groups in the travel industry, like travel agents, and tour operators at the global level. Unlike the sectoral trade association of travel agents and tour operators, these have international impact. They play an important role in representing the common interests of travel agents and tour operators worldwide in crucial international issues like negotiation of travel agency commission rates with International Air Transport Association (IATA). Universal Federation of Travel Agents Association (UFTAA) and the World Association of Travel Agencies (WATA) are such associations. Both UFTAA and WATA play an important role in representing the interests of travel agents worldwide. The following pages will discuss in detail the roles and functions of these two international organisations of travel agents.

Universal Federation of Travel Agents Association (UFTAA): Universal Federation of Travel Agents Association (UFTAA), an important organisation of travel agents on a worldwide basis, was founded in Rome in November, 1966 by the merger of the International Federation of Travel Agencies (IFTA) and the Universal Organisation of Travel Agents' Associations (UOTAA). The General Secretariat of UFTAA is located in Monaco.

The membership of the Federation consists of the National, Travel Agents' Associations from most of the countries in the world. Today it represents over 33,000 travel agencies globally. National Travel Agents Associations are the full members of UFTAA. The membership of the Federation is split into nine regions each covering a group of countries.

List of Countries of which the National Association is a Member of UFTAA

Algeria	Guatemala	Norway
Argentina	Hungary	Pakistan
Australia	Hong Kong	Paraguay
Austria	India	Peru
Barbados	Indonesia	Philippines
Belgium	Iraq	Poland
Bolivia	Ireland	Portugal
Brazil	Israel	Puerto Rico
Bulgaria	Italy	Senegal
Canada	Ivory Coast	Singapore
Chile	Japan	South Africa
Colombia	Jordan	South Korea
Costa Rica	Kenya	Spain

Cuba	Kuwait	Sri Lanka
Cyprus	Lebanon	Sweden
Czech Republic	Malaysia	Sudan
Dominican	Malawi	Syria
Denmark	Malta	Thailand
Egypt	Mexico	Trinidad & Tobago
Ecuador	Mauritius	Tunisia
El Salvador	Monaco	Turkey
Finland	Morocco	Uruguay
France	Nepal	Venezuela
Germany	Netherlands	Zaire
Ghana	New Zealand	Zambia
Greece	Nigeria	Zimbabwe

The Aims of the Federation : The following are the main aims of the federation :

(i) To act as the negotiating body with the various branches of tourism and travel industry on behalf of its members and also in the interest of the public;

(ii) To ensure for all travel agents through their national associations the maximum degree of cohesion and understanding, prestige and public recognition, advancement of the member's interest and protection from legislation and legal points of view; and

(iii) To offer to its member all the necessary professional and technical advice and assistance in matters concerning their trade.

UFTAA provides several advantages to its members which include the right to reproduce the symbol on the stationery, information service on all matters of legal or professional nature, free of charge assistance by its Legal Department for the recovery of outstanding debts, arbitration services for litigations between a member agency and a hotel company in different countries, etc.

The Annual General Assembly of UFTAA is the policy-making body. The Assembly decides on the general policy of the Federation and makes recommendations on any matter within its competence. The Board of Directors, consisting of Directors elected from candidates proposed by National Member Associations handle the routine business of the Federation. The Executive Committee is responsible for handling day-to-day activities and also urgent matters. The UFTAA world congress which normally takes place annually is the advisory body of the Federation. The world congress is open to UFTAA registered agents and enterprises, UFTAA individual members, suppliers of services and regional, national and international public authorities.

UFTAA claims to have a series of achievements since its inception in the year 1966. Prominent among its achievements is its collaboration with the International Rail Union resulting in obtaining increased commission on several railway networks, creation of professional training courses and introduction of Rail inclusive Tours. With regard to air transport, the cooperation between the Federation and IATA over a number of years has resulted in the raising of commission, introduction of an overriding commission, 50 per cent reduction for the spouses of travel agents and creation of international correspondence courses for the training of agency sales staff. In the sphere of hotel industry, the federation, following negotiations with the International Hotel Association has created an international convention, setting down regulations for booking, and cancellation fees. A court of arbitration to settle disputes between hotels and travel agents located in different countries has also been created.

World Association of Travel Agencies (WATA) : WATA, the World Association of Travel Agencies, is another important worldwide association representing travel agencies. Founded in the year 1949, WATA is a non-profit organisation created by independent travel agents for the benefit of all travel agencies around the world. The Association has over 200 members from 175 cities in 80 countries. The headquarters of WATA are located in Geneva, Switzerland. The basic idea of WATA is to bring together local travel agencies into an international network, so that every member is offered all the facilities and advantages of being associated with an international body in addition to enjoying local prominence. WATA is registered as an association under Swiss Civil Law, and is essentially a non-profit making organisation. Under its statutes, WATA and its members are required to assist one another.

The General Assembly of WATA held every year provides a forum for discussion of the Association's business and an opportunity to talk with fellow members. It enables members to have an exposure to new business and ideas applied successfully elsewhere. One day, before the General Assembly, the meetings of the Regional Assemblies are held which provide a chance to its members to discuss regional travel problems as well as the implementation on the regional level of the decisions taken by WATA governing bodies. The regions also have the possibility to submit to the General Assembly ideas and suggestions.

Advantages of a WATA Membership : The advantages of WATA membership include :

Guaranteed Payment of IHA Invoices : WATA headquarters guarantees payment of all invoices for services rendered by the International Hotel Association (IHA) hotel members to WATA members, up to a certain amount. In return, the IHA has requested its members to accept vouchers for individual clients issued by WATA members to be billed after the client's departure.

Internal Guarantee : Subject to certain conditions, unsettled services rendered by one WATA member agency to another, are paid by WATA headquarters.

WATA Standard Exchange Voucher : An agency's own exchange voucher bearing the WATA logo and the reference to the IHA/WATA agreement or the standard WATA exchange voucher printed by the headquarters with the name of agency, are widely accepted by hotels worldwide. In the majority of the cases, hotels accepting these vouchers will agree to bill the services after the departure of the clients without prepayment or deposit.

Membership List and Introduction Card : A small booklet listing all WATA members and their addresses is available for agencies to give to clients who go on extended trips, in case they need assistance and service en route. For specially important clients, a special introduction card is available for the members.

WATA Master-Key : Updated and published yearly, the WATA Master-Key is a comprehensive source of travel information. Individual WATA agency tariffs represent an invaluable selling tool for members' incoming and outgoing services. Master-Key carries the tariffs of WATA members offering incoming services. A standard presentation makes it easy for users to extract the information they need. Along with the tariffs is a country description sheet provided by the respective National Tourist Offices containing a wealth of background information.

WATA Circular Letters for Latest Developments : This internal newsletter keeps members abreast of new developments in WATA. It also gives members an opportunity to describe special activities of their own.

WATA's Overriding Commission : A supplementary commission of 5 per cent is allowed between members, on prices published in WATA Master-Key for transfers, sightseeing, excursions, tours and chauffeur-driven car hire.

WATA Membership Categories

Full Members : Membership in WATA is open to any travel agency, preferably privately-owned, which can prove a sound financial structure, adheres to the highest professional ethics expected in the industry and enjoys prominent standing in the local community.

All WATA members have the same rights, privileges and obligations within the association. Individual members are grouped into three sub-categories depending on the scope of their activities, as follows:

(1) Agencies offering both outgoing and incoming services.

(2) Agencies offering outgoing activities only.

(3) Agencies offering incoming service only.

Associate Members : A travel agency may apply to become an associate member. This category offers the possibility to become a WATA associate member for a trial period of 2 years. The associate members have the same rights and obligations as the full members but the fees are generally reduced.

Allied Members : A category open to hotels, airlines, shipping lines and car hire companies. The aim of this category is to develop the business relations between the members and their partners. Allied members may attend the WATA General Assembly, they will be listed in the WATA publications, receive all WATA publications and circulate letters and have the right to display on all their printed matter, the WATA logo created for this category. They have no voting right nor can they be elected to the WATA governing bodies. Both UFTAA and WATA are playing a valuable role in representing the interests of travel agents worldwide. In addition to the above two international travel associations representing travel agents, there are some important national travel agents organisations like the American Society of Travel Agents (ASTA) which has influence beyond the confines of USA. The American Society of Travel Agents draws its membership not only from travel agents and principals within the country but also from principals throughout the world who have interest in promoting overseas tourism from United States to their country.

The American Society of Travel Agents (ASTA) : American Society of Travel Agents (ASTA) is the leading professional society of travel agents in the USA. The world's largest professional travel trade association, ASTA was established in New York in the year 1931. Originally named the American Steamship and Tourist Agent's Association, the present name was adopted in the year 1944. The Society was established to foster programmes for the advancement of the travel agency industry, promote ethical practices and provide a public forum for travel agents. It has now over 25,000 members and is the only organisation representing all segments of the travel industry. The membership consists of travel agents, carriers, hotels, etc.

Purpose : The purpose of ASTA is the promotion and advancement of the interests of the travel agency industry and the safeguarding of the travelling public against fraud, misrepresentation and other unethical practices. The Society maintains legal representation and also a Government Affairs office in Washington, D.C. to provide direct contact with the Federal Government and the regulatory agencies in the travel and transportation field, and to protect the legitimate interests of travel agents.

Services : ASTA's services to travel agents also benefit the general public. Such activities include sponsorship of frequent conferences on travel matters, involving airlines, steamship companies, agents, municipal and government officials, and other interested parties; discussions with airlines on fare structures and travel destinations; research studies into traveller preferences; close cooperation with various city, state and government agencies across the country in travel-oriented matters, assistance to all agencies across the country in travel-oriented matters; assistance to all levels of government consumerism departments in upgrading standards of service to travellers.

The American Society of Travel Agents is primarily the trade association of the travel agency industry. There are more than 25,000 members in the Society covering all segments of the travel industry. Out of the total membership of 25,000 over 14,000 are travel agents in the United States of America and Canada. In addition to travel agents, there are allied members representing airlines, railways, hotels, government tourist offices, etc. The Society has a membership in over 140 countries all over the world. In order to qualify for the membership of the Society, an applicant must be in the business of travel under its present ownership or control for a minimum period of three years.

Membership : There are two basic classifications of membership-Active and Allied. Active members are year-round travel agents or tour operators. Allied members include airlines and steamship companies, railroad, bus lines, car rental firms, hotels, resorts, government tourist offices and other organisations regularly engaged in the travel industry or associated industries.

ASTA has over 2,500 travel agency members outside the USA and Canada. All are engaged in travel agency operations on a year-round basis and have been in business for at least three consecutive years. The international roster has its own elected governors and actively participates in all phases of Society meetings. International members come from Algeria, Bolivia, Sri Lanka, Denmark, Ethiopia, Fiji Island, Ghana, India, Iran, Japan, the Netherlands, Portugal, South Africa and Sweden.

ASTA World Travel Congress : The year's foremost meeting place is the ASTA World Travel Congress. The Congress is the single most important meeting held annually in the travel industry and the programme includes workshops, seminars, business meetings, film presentations, and social events. Members from throughout the world travel industry participate, give talks, lead discussion groups and conduct sessions. The ASTA World Travel Congress has been the platform for launching many important and beneficial education programmes for agents. The Congress grants Travel Hall of Fame awards, an honour given to those whose careers have made long standing impacts on the development and expansion of the travel industry and tourism. The awards are given every year to outstanding members. ASTA consists of the following departments: (a) policy implementation, (b) administration, (c) Industry relations, (d) Membership relationsm, (e) Communication

The members of the society derive various advantages which include education and training. ASTA has a comprehensive list of travel courses and seminars which are attended by its members. The society also offers professional training courses to senior travel agency personnel. Various research papers and newsletters are brought out from the Society's headquarters for use of its members.

ASTA Chapters : The society has 28 chapters in the United States of America and Canada and another 28 chapters overseas. Each chapter has elected officers and appointed committees. There is a National Board of Directors which establishes policies of the Society. Every two years a new President and Chairman of the Board are elected by Active Members. Day-to-day activities of the Society are looked after by a professional staff which works under the guidance of an Executive Vice-President who, in fact, is the Chief Operating Officer of the society and makes recommendations on policy matters to the Board and Executive Board. The Vice-President directs the headquarters staff in providing a broad programme of services and facilities to ASTA's membership and carrying on the day-to-day business of the Society. ASTA world headquarters are located in New York City, USA.

Indian Scenario

As long back as in the year 1954, the Government of India was aware of the important role which the travel agents were to play in the development of tourism. It was recognised by the Government that tourists who visit a foreign country often prefer to secure the services of travel agents who assist them in order to make best use of time and money at their disposal. The government felt that many a time unauthorised persons offer themselves as agents and in return fail to render satisfactory services, and even exploit the ignorance of the tourists for their personal benefit. With a view to curb this the government evolved a system of granting recognition to travel agents. The rules for recognition were as follows:

(i) No firm shall be granted recognition unless it has been engaged actively in handling tourist traffic for at least one year before the date of the application.

(ii) Firms granted recognition shall be entitled to such right and privileges as may be granted by the government from time to time and shall abide by several terms and conditions of recognition.

(iii) Firms granted recognition shall undertake to maintain an office under the charge of full time members of their staff who should, apart from issuing rail tickets, be in a position to give up to date and accurate information regarding transport and accommodation facilities, currency and customs regulations and general information about travel, etc.

(iv) The recognition may be extended for the whole of the country or be limited to a particular region.

(v) Firms granted recognition shall undertake to employ only guides approved by the Ministry of Tourism.

(vi) All recognised firms shall furnish yearly statement of their activities and such other information in regard to the volume of tourist traffic actually handled and other relevant matters.

(vii) The decision of the government in the matter of recognition shall be final and it reserves the right to cancel or withdraw it at any time.

Subsequently, following clauses were also added:

(i) The recognition to be granted by Ministry of Tourism shall not automatically entitle the firm to be appointed agents for the sale of rail tickets by the Ministry of Railways (Railway Board). The agencies thus recognised shall apply separately to the Railway Board.

(ii) Firms seeking recognition as travel agents should have a minimum paid-up capital of rupees one hundred thousand.

(iii) Applications for grant of recognition by the Ministry of Tourism will be considered only if the firm:

(a) is approved by the IATA;

(b) has licence to book foreign passages issued by the Reserve Bank of India;

(c) has the approval of the Ministry of External Affairs to handle travel documents and to deal with passport offices;

(d) is registered under the Local Shops and Establishment Act.

The recognition is now granted by the Ministry of Tourism in the Ministry of Tourism and Culture. The application for grant of recognition is to be made in the prescribed form and is to be addressed to the Director General, Ministry of Tourism who is the authority empowered to grant such recognition.

Travel Agents Association of India (TAAI) : The travel agents decided to form an association on all-India basis as long back as in the year 1952, when an All India Travel Agents Association was established. The main objective of the association is to safeguard and protect the interests of its members by way of having a constant dialogue with the concerned government agencies. The annual convention of the association is attended by a large number of representatives from travel trade both government as well as non-government. Important matters related with the promotion of product are discussed in these conventions. The Travel Agents Association of India has its registered office in Mumbai and regional offices in Kolkata, Delhi and Chennai. The association publishes a monthly magazine *Travel News* for of its members.

The vital role played by the travel agents in the growth and development of tourism in the country and its promotion is recognised by all segments of the travel industry. The government works in close collaboration with them not only in India but abroad as well, encouraging them to plan and organize package tours for various destinations in India. In suitable cases, the Ministry of Tourism recommends the foreign exchange to travel agents to enable them to open their branch offices abroad. The ministry has also instituted a special tourism award which is given every year to the agency earning the maximum amount of foreign exchange.

5

Tourism and Hospitality

What is its Meaning ? : As in other fields, this simple term 'tourism' has different meanings. In Britain, the word 'tourism' covers all travel for whatever purpose, whereas in the USA it refers to leisure travel only. In India, the British use of term is adopted. The tourism covers what is generally referred to as the visitor industry, the hospitality industry, the travel industry or the convention and tourism industry. The world tourism organization definition of a tourist is some one who moves away from home on a temporary or short-term basis for at least 24-hours, whether travelling in his or her own country (domestic tourism) or going to another country (international tourism).

To be useful, survey the travel needs, to measure the distance moved, the length of stay and the purpose of the trip. Most people in the industry or those who study it find a definition which limits a 'tourist' to a person who spends at least 24-hours away from home, too restrictive. One may argue that day trippers or excursionists should be included. In Britain, these have been defined as people spending at least three hours away from home and involving a round journey of at least 20-miles which they do not regularly make, thus moving outside the area of their normal daily journeys. However, any distance used is open to discussion. As travel has become easier, the boundaries of commuting areas have increased. For some cities this may be up to 100-miles, although for most people ten miles might be a more appropriate figure. Excluded from this definition of a tourist are students, and workers migrating temporality. The term Visitors' could cover both the over-night stayer and the day trappers.

Definition of who is counted as tourist is important when assessments are made of the impact of tourism. It is necessary to define a tourist in order to count their number and to use surveys of expenditure to estimate the revenue generated by the tourist industry. In particular, the size and nature of destination area may also determine the volume of tourists.

Tourism as an Industry

The boundaries of tourism industry are not very clear cut. Many of the firms associated with tourism supply both tourists and residents, and there is no way to recording division of trade. An industry is often defined on the basis of a product, but how is this defined for tourism? Some authors use the term tourism system instead of tourist' industry. These authors use the notion of component which would include the tourist, the transporter, the attraction, the ancillary facilities, and the planners and promoters of a place. In case of a tourist product we may define it as what attracts the tourist to a place, which include historic buildings, urban landscapes, museums and art galleries, theatres, sport and events. These may be called as primary elements. There are other facilities also which are important for the experience of the tourist, but are unlikely to be the cause of the visitor coming to the city. These include hotels, shops, and other services and are described as the secondary elements. Some visitors travel to a place to purchase one product only, while others are attracted by the possibility of consuming several products during their stay. Many of them are unique to a place, and these include historic buildings, museums, and special events. They can only be consumed by traveling to place where they are found. Just because these attractions are unique does not mean that tourist will come. Individual have special interests for which they will travel a long distance. Most people will travel for something that they perceive as really impressive. The hierarchy of there attractions could be presented as follows:

Tourism and its Elements

1.. Local appeal
2. Regional appeal
3. National recognition with specialized appeal.
4. National recognition with wide appeal.
5. International recognition limited for special appeal, such as, Pyramids, Taj Mahal.
6. International recognition: Many elements of appeal and at tracking people from all over the world, e.g., Paris, London, etc.

The higher up the hierarchy a product as classified, the more it is able to attract visitors from a distance. The appeal of places are not fixed for all time. New product could be developed, existing product may be promoted. There may be a life-cycle for some products.

The second main component of tourism system is the consumer who supplies the demand, in this case the tourist. The development of a tourism industry in a place will depend on being able to appeal to the potential tourists and this in turn requires an understanding of their wants and requirements.

Planning for Regional Tourism : Many areas in this region are loosing or have absence of economic activities. They require new ones which will generate income for the area and create jobs. New activities are required which will stimulate physical regeneration. Tourism is on the increase and needs thorough examination to assess whether it could play a role in the economic and physical regeneration of the areas. On the basis that there would be increasing affluence, easier travel and greater leisure time, it is assumed that the tourism industry is bound to grow. It brings income to the areas. Acting as an economic base it is assumed to be able to give support to the regional economy. Tourism should never be perceived as a panacea for regional development problems but as a part of the solution.

It would be wrong to see tourism promotion simply as one

component of regional development policy. Investment for tourism involves the development of facilities, activities, physical environments and infrastructure that will have benefits for the local community. It also involves marketing the region and selling an image, which will assist in the attraction of industrial and commercial activities. Advertising the region engaged in tourism activities will raise the profile and visibility of the region and will also assist in economic promotion. Many activities being expanded, such as culture, and sport will persuade potential residents that the region is a good place in which to live, that it has the right life-style opportunities.

With the renewal of villages and the new image, it will be easier to bring resident back to the interior regions. The money which tourists spend on facilities may make tourism activities more economically viable, which will be of benefit to the local community. *Finally,* the development of these facilities, the physical regeneration of areas and the arrival of visitors may increase the region's pride. The local residents will take much greater case of the environment.

The tourist industry must be substantially increased in size so as it may play a larger role in the regional economy. It means attracting hundreds of thousands of extra tourist to bring in extra income that will create jobs. To bring in more tourists the tourism resources must be expanded. Tourism resources comprise — primary elements and secondary elements. Primary elements are those which attract people, and consists of historic buildings and landscapes, museums and art galleries, concerts, specter sports, conferences exhibitions, entertainment and special events. A person may be attracted by one element and use only that element. He/ she could come to a region for one component and then use other elements as well. Tourists come because of mix of attractions. Secondary elements enhance these attractions or assist in the process of attracting tourists, and include shopping, catering, accommodations and transport and tourism agencies. Any expansion of tourism will involve the development of all there components. In addition to these elements, a region may act as a 'gateway' to other areas.

The prime visitor markets for tourism are: 1. Business travellers, 2. Conference and exhibition delegates, 3. Short-break holiday makers, 4. Day trippers, 5. Visitors to friend and relatives, holiday makers using the region as a gateway to the neighbouring region, 6. Long holiday makers on a tour, stopping off for a short visit.

Strategy for Regional Tourism : The strategy of regional tourism development has been universally adopted. Some critics mostly elected representatives, do not think that tourism is a 'proper' industry and still look to other industries to restore the fortunes of the region. The region need to expand the service sector and thereby create jobs. Tourism is one of the service sector which is growing rapidly. Another criticism of the strategy arise because tourism is often perceived as providing low-paid, low-skilled and seasonal jobs. We will find that many of the activities of the industry such as conferences, do not experience great seasonal variations, and the hotel industry has a different seasonal profile from that of resorts. No doubt, many of the jobs are low skilled, this could be in favour of regional tourism when it is located near the villages with its labour resources of the unskilled. Another strong argument against expanding the tourist industry is that it involves spending money on visitors when the priority should be to spend it on residents. Studies have found that the community benefits from tourism and public sector investment is worthwhile.

This ambiguous attitude toward tourism has meant that the funding has been denied or limited. An attempt to cut public expenditure have impeded on the funding of tourism administration and project, and this has affected the regions differently.

Other critics perceive tourism as having adverse consequences for the region. Bringing more visitors to a region might add to existing congestion. More tourists will add to the wear and tear on facilities and increase the cost of management. Further, local resident, sometimes does not welcome the influx of visitors, and facilities favoured by the tourist may not be those denied or, needed by the community. Thus, specialty shopping has been described as 'commercial gentrification'.

The incorporation of tourism in to regional economic development strategies is fairly widespread. A lengthy comprehensive regional tourism plan could be prepared. The role of tourism can be gauged from statement in economic development strategies and in structure plans. Tourism promotion unit could be within the economic development department provided the later does not concentrate on traditional policies such as those of constructing industrial estates. With or without tourism strategy document, such tourism development is a product of pragmatic opportunities.

Pleasure Travel Market : The growth of tourism has been enabled by increasing influence, easier travel, and greater leisure. The basic task of a region is to persuade tourists to come to it. A study of the pleasure market classified trips into eight types:

1. Visit to friend and relatives
2. Touring
3. Close to home trip (mainly out-doors)
4. Out-door activities in village/rural areas
5. A resort trip
6. A city trip
7. Theme park, exhibition or special event
8. Cruise.

Exhibitions and Conferences : Conferences and exhibition activities are one of the staple of tourism. These are the growth industries in which visitor spends an above-average amount, and which operate for most of the year. These can be considered as two separate kind of events but there are increasing links between them. Many conferences include an exhibition.

Conferences are convened for a number of different purposes, such as:

1. Policy making
2. The exchange of ideas and information
3. Training
4. Selling
5. Social purposes, (a) meeting old friends, (b) making deals not connected directly with the purpose of conferences, and (c) meeting people for the first time.
6. Recreational purposes—short holiday during or after the conference.

Conferences are organized by or on behalf of a wide range of bodies which can generally be classified as either corporate or association. Companies and other organizations to achieve their objectives arrange corporate meetings. The association conference may involve educational, professional, political, religions and social organizations. Apart from achieving the objectives of the association, they are also a means of generating income which is often easier and less painful than raising subscription. Conferences vary from an inter-governmental summit, the convention of a political party, a company strategy meeting, a religions synod, a symposium of scientists, to the annual conference of a trade common or professional or social association.

Some conferences take place on a regular basis, while others are one-off and may evolve a unique set of circumstances. Meetings may last from one day to a week or more. Conferences occur though last the year although there is a lull in some period of the year. Conferences vary in size from 10-people to over 2000. The term convention is usually reserved for the large meeting. A significant portions of all conferences is organized by companies, the corporate market, either for policy making training or selling. The larger the organization and wider the area from which it draws it membership, and longer the conference, the more likely it is that delegates will have to stop overnight, a factor of great importance when measuring the impact of conferences.

Accommodation Requirements : The basic accommodation requirement for a meeting is large room or hall of sufficient size to take the expected attendance. Extra facilities are required in the form of special lighting, microphones, and loudspeakers, projection equipment, the possibility of simultaneous translation, and catering, including banquets. Conference venues include:

1. Large halls, arenas, civic centers, concert halls, and theatres.
2. Purpose-built conference/convention/congress centers.
3. Hotels, having large rooms, other built banquets which can be used for conferences.
4. University and other educational establishments having large lecture rooms.

Exhibition is described as an organized pubic display of manufactured goods and works of arts. These serve as a very useful purpose for sellers and buyers. Exhibition can be organized by a trade association, by a company associated with the exhibition site, or by a company which specializes in organizing exhibitions. These are held in large halls, many exhibition centers may have out-door space. A special type of exhibition center could be an agricultural fair ground, which is mainly out-door display space. Exhibition centers require catering facilities and office spaces, and may provide rooms for meetings. Some exhibitions may take place in hotels. Convention business is also on the increase and may prove fruitful to the area.

The Attractions : The region as a part of its economic strategy needs to develop attractions of a large and high quality. There is a hierarchy of attractions and only those attractions, which rank high that will be able to pull in visitors from a distance. Vision wants something that is unique and interesting, is popular, is entertaining and includes attraction and sight-seeing.

When visiting a region many people ask the following questions:

1. What is there to see?
2. What are the attractions?

These attraction generally include museums and art galleries historic building, theatres, and concert, sport, and the sight, the general landscape of buildings. In addition to these, new types of attraction may be developed such as:

1. Industrial tourism factory tour/visit
2. Theme park
3. Zoos
4. Wildlife attraction
5. Heritage center
6. Wax work, planetarium and various forms of entertainment
7. Fun fairs.

Events of Special Importance : The cultural and sporting activities of the region have not been regarded as part of the tourist industry. Initially, theatres, concert halls and sports grounds were all built to meet the need of the resident population. Now, these are perceived to bring prestige to a region and raise its profile in the outside world. As the region is desperate to attract inward investment, having a high profile in the arts and sport is a good starting point. These can be perceived as having tourism potential. If the events are of a sufficiently high quality then people will be prepared to travel some distance to attend. There is clearly some validity in this idea since many places around the world have traded on arts tourism for many years.

The term 'art industry' and 'cultural industry' are sometime used to include the performing arts, museums and art galleries, cultural heritage, special events such as art festival and the producing art. Here let us concentrate on performing art, and in particular to the role of theatres, and concert halls. Mostly, drama, concert, ballet, opera and other art have been concentrating in cities. Patrons living in interior areas have to travel to big cities to experience live performances and in the process become tourists.

Sports : Sport activities may be perceived to project a high status image of the area via media coverage which may help attract economic development, persuade people to live in the city and attract visitors. It increases civic pride, community spirit and collective self-image. The profits from hosting a mega- event could pay for high-quality facilities which could be of permanent value to the region. To keep teams in the region and to attract them from elsewhere, local governments be prepared to offer inducement, including building and retiring ownership of a stadium which can be let to the team, sometimes on an uneconomic basis. Sport programmes can have their greatest economic impact on the region when they are linked with other tourist attractions and they are family leisure activities. As regards to impact of sport on general economic development, this is the only factor, which will affect the growth performance to the region. It may have both positive and negative effects, positive as the prospect of large numbers of people may encourage investment in other activities, (e.g. catering) and negative because crowd and congestion may discourage investment. Much may depend on the characteristics of spectators. The maximum impact of a stadium is likely to be felt when it is close to other tourist attractions and hotel.

It includes the events, which occur infrequently. A football match or a concert could be described as an event. Typical special event are ones that occur only on an annual basis in the same locality. Another type of special event is the one-of celebration, (e.g. bi-centenaries). Special event may have almost any theme and take any form. A special event could be as simple as Annual Street parade. Many special events use related to existing attractions. An art gallery may have a special exhibition, perhaps of pictures on loan from elsewhere, the terms mega-event or hall mark even describe large events of world importance and high profile which have a major impact on the image of the host region. This definition is mainly psychological, as it is difficult to specify a quantitative one that would be widely applicable. Special events can therefore be any thing from the annual village carnival to the national games.

Often special events involve a considerable amount of spectacle, which acts as a visitor draw. Most special events are only of short duration, lasting either a few days or a few weeks, but some last several months and even up to a year.

Many special events have a long history but new ones are constantly created. Special events could be used as a means of attracting tourists, and raising the profiles and changing the image of places. The large special events, whether it be a festival, a sport competition or a political convention, gains tremendous television coverage which can be more effective publicity than any other method. Some regions for special events are given below:

1. To attract people into the area.
2. To attract people outside the main season.
3. To attract media attention and raise the profile of the area.
4. To add animation and life to existing attraction.
5. To encourage repeat visit.
6. To assist regeneration.

An attempt may be made to measure the level of knowledge of the event in other part of the region. An assessment can be made of the long-term effects, including the amount of inward investment and the growth of tourism. Because of the wide diversity of special events it is not possible to cover all of them and attention will be concentrated on art festival, sport events, world fairs and garden festival.

Art Festivals : A festival may be defined as a theme public celebration, which extends leisure and cultural opportunities beyond every day experiences and choices. Art festivals may cover several arts or focus on a single art such as classic music, jazz, literature, drama, film, etc. Arts festivals attract mainly the middle class and only the largest or most specialized attract a majority of attention from outside the locality. Many cities have attempted to introduce art festivals. To attract attention and to be able to draw people from distance they have to increasingly focus on a particular art form, such as film or jazz. A recent innovation has been the introduction of year long art events which move from one area to another. In this region an area (place) could be given the little of 'Garhwal Culture', Kumaon Culture' or Himalayan Culture' and it could be projected across the whole region. Similarly, arts years for an area could be decided and each year could be a specific theme. Each area may bid for the tittle. Festivals have multiple objectives of extending the arts experience of the residents, of raising the profile of the region and attracting visitors.

The success of these art festivals in terms of drawing audience from outside the local area will depend on having a clear theme and achieving high quality. The more attractive the sitting, the easier it is to draw an audience. The negative impact of art festivals is congestion during the event and the under-utilization of facilities during the rest of the year.

Games : Games, national, regional or Olympics are the greatest mega-event. Each time events are held, it gets bigger. The competitive national element plus the various spectacles associated with the event ensure interest well beyond the relatively few that follow sports. The transformation of the economics of the games persuaded many regions of the benefits of hosting them. The profit made could be used to pay for the facilities that are required and which will be left behind after the event. Given the regional prestige, host region hope that government will pour money into the facilities and general infrastructure of the area. Ring roads and railways could be build, new airport constructed, and derelict water-front area cleared and re-developed for as game villages. For the host region, winning the games offers the prospects of worldwide publicity as well as investment in permanent facilities and infrastructure, which could enable it to attract further general investment, future events and more tourists. During the bidding process public money could be provided to build some facilities and infrastructure. Private finance be covered, both for the bid and for facilities. The greatest importance is the element of unity. Politicians of different parties, leaders of private sector and voluntary groups may come together and agree on the proposals as well as on the direction in which the region should be moving. A tourist industry could be developed and the region could be marketed with arts and manufactures, with pavilions being provided for different regions.

Historical Celebrations : It should be made common place for regions and area to celebrate the anniversary of some land mark achievement in its history. Many region/countries have bi-centennial celebration. Areas may celebrate the anniversary of their foundation or some events of national and international significance. The motives should be pure celebration, promotion and visibility, attraction of tourists. The celebration may take various forms including festival, fine work and other outdoor spectacles, new buildings and infrastructure, including museum, and art venues, and fairs. The event may last for a few weeks or a whole year. In the event of regional celebration the events may take place in the capital or in an area with a historical connection. Historical celebrations have not been as positive as the organizers expected.

Garden Festivals : The aim of the garden festival is to celebrate the reclamation of derelict land, to bring short-term benefit to a locality in the form of tourists, to bring longer-term benefits in the form of image enhancement, and to provide sites for new land uses including the provision of jobs, to replace those lost in the site then the industries close down. There could be *two* model: *one* laying emphasis on the after-used, and *second,* less on the involvement of the horticultural sector and the provision for park land. The government should pay for the costs of reclamation, while the festival would pay for itself.

The economic impact studies of sport events—costs and revenues to the organizers and the impact of the event on the area, indicates that the cost of the games involve direct expenditures on sport facilities, indirect expenditures on infrastructure from transport to hotels for the operating costs of the games themselves and the subsequent expenditures of all visitors, including competitors, team appeals and the media. The larger the injection of funds into the area, from whatever source, the greater the impact of the event on the area.

There are long-term tangible and intangible benefits such as improved infrastructure, the ability to host further sport events, improved image, and the attraction of economic development, and civic pride.

Fairs and Expos : There are various and inter-linked objectives for holding a fair, such as, encouraging trade, increasing the visibility of an area, and region, developing tourism, attracting economic development and thus promoting employment, stimulating land re-development and infrastructure improvement, the celebration of past event, and the entertainment of the masses, as well as the often unstated one of obtaining extra funds from higher levels of government. The prime motive holding a fair is to boost the area, but as well as selling the area there is also the selling of ideas. The host area should prepare a special site for the event where many buildings and structures hoped for architectural distinction be erected. These will remain a permanent legacy to the area, as will be general infrastructure put in place. The fair itself usually contains exhibitions of both. Subsequently, some costs would be recovered though the sale of land. In case the festival makes a small loss, the local council for the area Development Corporation could meet it. Garden festival could use a tourism event to support a specific piece of rural regeneration. There are short-term benefits in the form of extra income to the region and resultant employment. These benefits can be increased by an associated promotion of local attractions so that the tourists are encouraged to stay longer in the area. After use of the site need to be carefully considered to get the long-term environmental and economic benefits. The region may get high profile and enhance image resulting in more tourists and general economic gains. Most of these gains are short-term but long-term strategy of event and development is required. Garden festivals have a limited role in urban regeneration and the long-term development of tourism. Garden festivals may act as a catalyst, persuading local authorities to increase funding for tourism promotion and development.

Elements of Secondary Importance : Secondary elements are not the main reasons to visit an area, however, they influence the quality of the experience of the tourists. The development of the tourist industry should give due consideration to these elements, access the exiting situation and plan for improvement. These elements include: 1. Hotels, 2. Shopping facilities, 3. Restaurants, 4. Clubs, 5. Pubs, 6. Other forms of entertainment, 7. Transport, and 8. Car parking.

Visitor could travel a long distance because of good hotel, interesting shops and varied range of activities for the evening and night. On the other hand the visitor might be deterred from visiting an area if there is a shortage of hotel rooms and it is known that it is very expensive place. Easy availability of these elements, and good quality and not too expensive may provide an additional reason for visiting the area. The provision of these secondary elements is essential if we want to make the area a successful tourist center.

The secondary elements are the principle forms of expenditure and have the most economic compact on the region. The approximate percentage of expenditure made by the tourist on these elements is given below:

1.	Accommodation	34.9%
2.	Food and Beverage	24.1%
3.	Travel	14.0%
4.	Shopping	18.9%
5.	Entertainment	5.5%
6.	Other	2.6%

The nature of their activities helps in determining the type of employment created, they tend to employ a significant proportion of low-skilled and low-paid jobs.

Hotels : Any region, area, city or town, which inspire to be an important tourist center will require a substantial stock of hotel rooms. Although we presume that not all tourists will stay in hotels, some of them may be day visitors, others may stay with friend and relatives and some may choose to stay in bed-and-breakfast or unserviced accommodation. More important an area is as a tourist center, the higher the proportion that will require some type of hotel accommodation. It is the visitor who stays in a hotel who has the greatest economic impact. It is estimated that about 60 per cent of expenditure may be accounted for by the cost of accommodation and meals bought in hotel restaurants, it is, therefore, pertinent to examine the factors behind the growth of hotels in the area, the type of hotels required, where should they be located, and the employment impressions.

For most hotel users, staying in a hotel in a means to an end, not an end itself. Hotels can be classified by sizes, tariff, ownership, and location. The quality and price of services provided may be indicated by star system. Other terms used include luxury, first class, upscale and budget. Much business travel is at the upper end of the market, while the leisure traveler is often looking for the cheaper budget-priced hotel. The nature of the market in the area is reflected in the type of the hotel. The region should attempt to offer accommodation of varying quality and price.

The demand for hotel accommodation varies over the week and over the year. Business travel generally concentrates into weekend, leaving the week with low demand. Leisure market is concentrated towards the weekend. A region should fill its hotels during the week with business travellers and the weekend with the short-break leisure market. These markets are rarely balanced. It is often necessary for hotels to offer cut-price rates at the weekend to attract visitors.

The business and conference markets decrease the summer holidays, while the short-break market peaks in spring-early summer and autumn periods. At any time of the year there may be peaks and through. A large conference or exhibition can fully use all the capacity, while in between events there may be a low occupancy.

Hotels can be built by either a hotel company or an independent developer and plan leased to a hotel chain. The investor will have to decide whether there is sufficient demand and of what type need to be planned as part of multi-use structure. It will be better to build hotel by a developer rather than a hotel company. The demand for hotel services is a derived demand. The demand for hotel services can be broken-down by market type into business, tourist, conferences, and other. The exact composition will vary greatly from one hotel to another and particularly with location hotels, situated in well developed areas, depend much more on business travel and less on the leisure market, whereas for resorts, it would be reverse. The business market consists of executives travelling to visit other establishment to transact business, salesman visiting clients, as well as many other activities such as activities working at theatres and official government business. The size of business market will depend on the nature of activities undertaken in the area and the role of the area in the region. Well-developed areas with high proportion of manual jobs are likely to require less stock than in important financial center. The conference and leisure market will also vary in size from an area to another. Although most areas are attempting to develop these markets, there may be differing degrees of success. As regards to conferences, a supply of hotel rooms is an essential ingredient in attracting the business. Without the trade, hotels will not be built, but without the hotels, the trade will not be attracted.

A growing market in the region is the traveler/ a tourist where the demand is likely to be either on the edge of an area or between the areas. Hotel may derive business from non-staying clients through providing meals in restaurant and space for receptions.

The basic economics of hotels reveal the following:

Income		**Costs**	
Rooms	60.5%	Employees	28.1%
Food	23.5%	Cost of goods	12.1%
Beverages	8.9%	Operating cost	30.7%
Others	7.1%	Tax	5.5%
		Interest/profit depreciation	23.6%

The prime income in hotel business comes from the letting of rooms and the selling of food and beverages to guests. Profit on rooms are higher than those on meals and other services. On the cost side a significant proportion goes on interest and depreciation.

The greater the capital cost of the facility, the higher their overhead will be, and hence there will be a need for high occupancy rates. For this reason the break-even occupancy rate is usually lower for budget-price hotel than for luxury ones. Land and capital costs may be high in prosperous area and this deters the construction of hotels. Employees costs in these area is also higher: given these factors the cost of hotel accommodation varies in different areas of the region.

The physical requirements for a hotel building are affected by the rising expectations of customers and high safety standard. Most customers may expect an en-suite bathroom even in low-price accommodation. At the luxury end of the market patron expects a very high standard of design both inside and outside the building.

Another factor affecting supply is the hotel development. As demand grows for accommodation, occupancy rates and profit increase. This will increase developers and hotel chains to invest in new properties, thus increasing the stock of hotel rooms. However, because the economy is cyclical as this extra capacity comes on stream, there is an economic downturn, and demand for hotel accommodation falls. With more capacity and lower throughout occupancy rates, profits falls. During the recession period some of the older, less profitable hotels may close. Low occupancy and low profit discourage any further building of hotels. It may take several years of recovery before occupancy rates and profits reach former levels and even further time before increased demand encourages further building.

The supply of hotel accommodation is also greatly affected by the rise in importance of the large company. Most of the small hotels are independently owned and often-family run large firms develop because of certain advantages. They are able to use marketing techniques effective in order to reach potential customers, and can make use of central reservation systems. They can agree special terms with major clients. They know of major firm that needs conference facilities and offer them a wide range of location. They offer the same formula around the world so that customer know what to expect and comes back to them. Their size can extract good terms from suppliers. All these factors give them an advantage over the independent firm. Having established themselves, they seek to have a presence in all the major markets. Areas that are revitalizing inner areas and may even be given grants as an incentive to invest may count them.

The location of hotels is also an important factor. Guests will want hotel close to the place they wish to visit and so cut down intermediate transport as much as possible. Developers look for sites, which are proven generators of patronage. The traditional location for the hotel was the city center, near railway station, or on the fringe of the retail and business zones away from the highest land values. In city center hotel may be included the most expensive and luxurious. Cheaper hotels may be located along the main radial routes. Old buildings can be converted and extended. Hotels could also be constructed on the edge of the built up area, either near the main road which connect with other parts of the area or near airports. The budget-priced hotels/ motels may be located on highways.

The size of the hotel stock, as measured by the number of bedrooms together with the range in the price of accommodation, is an important indicator of the area as a tourist destination. It is a critical factor in determining whether the area can function as a conference and exhibition center. Its size will also reflect the importance of business and leisure tourism.

Many areas may attempt to encourage the building of hotels so as to assist the development of the tourist industry. The areas should be designated for hotels. Grants may be given to encourage the building of hotels. Exemption of the payment of property taxes for a number of years to stimulate employment may also be granted to encourage hotel construction near the specific areas. Hotel development may also be encouraged on the areas where land prices are lower and where budget-priced hotels could operate profitably.

Hotels have a distinctive employment structure. A catering and cleaning staff complement a small management staff. Many of the later are unskilled and low paid. While some may be part-time, many have full-time jobs. About 50-per cent of all workers may be part-time. In well-developed areas, hotel work is available throughout the year, as the industry is not subject to seasonal variations. Some decry these types of jobs. For many city residents they are suitable jobs. Hotels generally employ about one person per bed room.

Shopping : An analysis of the behaviour of tourists indicates that a significant amount of time and money is spend on shopping. Surveys of tourists, which ask the purpose of the trip rarely, find shopping mentioned, but when asked what they did, visitors list shopping as one of the most important activities. For many people shopping is a pleasure experience and something they like to do when they have time. People like to spend their leisure time in shopping and so they should wish to do so on holidays. There is also a desire to see if different goods will be found in another place. A survey of festival market places indicate that about 60-per cent of the patrons come with no specific purchase to mind. A pleasant environment may make shopping more enjoyable. Many people like to take gifts back for friends and relatives when they return. A day out or a short break or a long holiday or even a business trip, there is always an element of shopping. Most of the retail processes are found within, adjacent to near the principal tourist attractions. These may vary from the simple gift/souvenir shop to outlet selling a wide rang of speciality goods. When there are many shops of this type they become part of attraction of the place. Right kind of retail facilities can enhance the attractiveness of an area to tourists.

Very large and specialized retail center may be able to attract tourists. Development of comparable facility will attract tourists. 'Speciality' retailing attracts tourists. This includes the goods, which are not found every where. They are not mass produced, and in some cases are genuine craft goods. They could be described as luxuries in the sense that they are not goods, which are essential for living. It includes goods such as art and crafts, including pottery, unusual and designer cloths, books, perfumes and annual household articles. Developers should attempt to bring the various elements together to create speciality shopping areas.

The concept of 'festival market place' could also be introduced. It combines speciality shopping, eating and drinking, and entertainment. It may remain open all evening and at the week-ends and may attract office workers, sub-urbanities, and tourists in large numbers. Close attention must be given to the quality of the shops, the tenant mix, their environment, and security. The festival market could be successful in an area where there are a large numbei of office workers.

The Restaurants : All visitors to an area will require food and drink. This is to meet an essential need or to be pleasurable experience in itself. Therefore, the area should provide the right kind of catering facilities. A successful tourist place should have a wide array of restaurants in or near the area.

In recent years there has been a great growth in the demand for restaurant. Restaurant is an establishment, which serves food and drink, which can be consumed on the premises. People travel further away from their homes whether for work, to shop or for leisure activities, and while away they need food and drink.

Many people eat out as a leisure activity. There is a growing importance of eating out. The market for restaurants is in various ways such as business market, individual, and as a leisure activity. Therefore, eating out may be classified into *two:* body food and soul food. Body food is consumed to keep the body going. It may be simple, taken quickly and relatively cheap. Soul food does satisfy basic needs, it is sought after as an enjoyable experience. The food will be more sophisticated, the cost greater, the surroundings more important, and time taken much longer. It is also a social event, rarely undertaken alone, and often undertaken as part of an important personal relationship, or as a special family or group occasion. As standard of living arise, individuals want to experience life to the full. Eating in good restaurants is perceived to be one of the experiences of life.

We may classify restaurants by the type of cuisine. There is an enormous range of foods available from the ethnic, such as Chinese, Indian and Italian, to the traditional sea food, the gourmet, to the menu of the fast food chain such as burgers or chicken. This new range of cuisine is perhaps why dining out has become a leisure activity.

Restaurant can also be classified by price. Snacks can be provided not only in fast food restaurants or in cafes, but also in more up market surroundings. Full meal can be provided at a range of prices, at different levels of quality and indifferent settings. At the cheaper levels the food is tending to be mass produced or proceeded to a tight formula, a trend that reaches its climate in the fast food restaurants.

The demand for restaurant facilities varies throughout the day or week or from season to season depending upon the location. Restaurants are busy around lunch-time and also in the evening. In the day time the customers perhaps business people are more likely to be shopper, local workers and some will be in the position of searching for good restaurant with the type of meal they want and at price they can afford. Seasonal factors may reflect several influences, such as business fluctuations, tourist flows, and special event such as New Year, Deepawali, Dussehra, etc., when many people eat out. The demand for restaurant meal is bound to increase.

At the international level, large corporations increasingly dominate the restaurant business. These corporation gain economies of scale in purchasing and marketing. Restaurants are also found within hotels, departmental stores and other places. There are many independent businesses also.

The three important factors for success of a restaurant are: location, location and location. Two important ideas in understanding restaurant are location and visibility. The location of an outlet is to be chosen on the basis of customer counts, other multiple retailers, car parking, entertainment, etc. Once the sales potential is established, search for a site is the right rent is 5.7 per cent of the sales projected. The concept of visibility describes the fact that restaurants and fast food outlets often cluster, not because they all choose the same accessible locations.

Customers are attracted to clusters of establishments where they feel confident that they will find an outlet to their liking. Customer's can head for the cluster without the need to divide which store they are going to patronize. Body food establishment and fast food ones, sought accessibility. They are located in the city center, in malls and office park, near where people worked, shopped and attended leisure activities and also along the main arterial roads. 'Soul food' establishments are found in the city center, usually on the fringe of the retail and business quarters, accessible for business people and convention less. These restaurant attract people from all over the city. With the growth in the number of restaurants, the employment could grow rapidly. Many of these jobs are low paid, part-time and on casual basis.

Entertainment : Many tourist staying over-night in an area will want some form of entertainment. This could be in the form of visit to a theatre or concert hall for music, opera, ballet or drama, or possibly a visit to a club for music and dancing. Arts and culture are also a source of entertainment. More tourism resource such as 'adult entertainment' quarters could be developed.

Transport : Tourists be attracted from a wide range of distances, from the surrounding region to the inter-continental, and different forms of transport will be required. There is a need for good transport systems. Differences in quality and cost could influence tourist flows. Air, rail and road is important. A station which is modal in the network and which is central to the city is important. For those arriving by car, a lack of congestion and ample car parking is an important factor. Every effort should be made to improve transport and advertise its availability.

Tourism and Hotels : Correlation

The world of travel and tourism has been revolutionized. Tourism is today's fast growing business and expected to be the world's largest industry in the 2001-millenium. The world have become a global community for travellers, opening up places, unimaginable decade earlier—the secrets of Himalayas, the wonders of Antarctica, the rain forests of the Amazon, the beauty of the Tahiti, the Great Wall of China, the dramatic Victoria Falls, the origin of Nile, and the wilds of Scottish Islands. Tourism has become a global business whose expanding market now leaves no place untouched. Tourism and travel now affect every continent, country, and city. Every one's economy is impacted either by their people travelling elsewhere (import spending in other places) or travel service exports (expenditure by nonresidents in that place). The Himalayan region has to decide how much travel service it want to capture.

In discussing tourism in the Himalayan region, following factors need to be considered:

Importance in Economy : Due to location, climate, limited resources, size and cultural heritage, this region have no real choice but to engage in tourism to grow, develop and improve its living standards. The areas in the region differ in their dependence on/or interest in, attracting tourists. Areas engage in tourism with mixed emotions, and at times, ambivalence. There are instances, where places are concerned that tourism is destroying its culture, as farm land becomes resort and new jobs unravel family values. These areas may not formally welcome tourists. Some people and businesses benefit, others may not. The regional economy may be better off from tourism, however, the costs and losses—quality of life, convenience, cultural or social values—are not worth the benefits. Should the region place too much emphasis on tourism and hospitality industries? Are these full of risks? These are the questions need to be debated.

The region must decide the three broad alternatives:

1. Pursue tourism even more aggressively in well-developed areas because its physical and historical beauty provides it with a competitive advantage in this industry.
2. Hold tourism in its present level and invest in building other industries more aggressively, and
3. Build tourism and other industries in a balanced way.

The decision is quite tough because of conflicting interest of different voting blocks. Not all regions and people are enthusiastic about tourist generated jobs. This region may think of expanding tourism when its thriving business decline. Tourism's primary benefit is jobs through hotel, restaurants, retail establishment and transportation.

Segmentation of the Tourist Market of the Region, and Monitoring for Shifting Trends, Life-Style, Needs and Preferences. The region must decide on not only how many tourists it wants and how to balance tourism with other industries or strategies but also what kind of tourists it wants. The choice will be constrained by the area's climate, natural topography and resources, history, culture and facilities. Like any other business, tourist marketers must know the actual and potential customers, their needs and wants, determine which markets to serve and decide on appropriate products services and programmes to serve these markets.

Not every tourist is interested in a particular destination. The region will waste its money trying to attract everyone who travels. The region, instead of a short gun approach, should take a rifle approach and sharply define its target market. The region should identify its natural target markets in two ways.

One is to collect information about its current tourists:

1. Where do they come from?
2. Why do they come to this place?
3. What are their demographic characteristics?
4. How satisfied they are?
5. How many are repeat tourists?
6. How much do they spend?

Examine all these questions and determine which tourists are easiest to attract and which are worth attracting.

The approach is to audit *the* region's attraction and conjecture about the types of tourists who would have an natural interest in them. The aim in this approach is to identify new sources of tourists. Do not assume that the current tourists reflect all the potentially interested groups. Different tourists are attracted by different place features. The local/ area/ district/ municipal authorities must ask questions keyed to segmentation visually, such as, attractions sought, market areas or locations, customers.

After identifying its natural target market, the region has to see research where these tourists are found. Which areas out side contain a large number of citizen who have the means and motivation to enjoy the particular place.? Badrinath area attracts mainly religious tourists. The best source for these tourists are Gujrat, Maharastra, Uttar Pradesh, Madhya Pradesh and even foreign markets. This analysis can uncover too many or too few natural target market. If you have identified many, next step is to calculate the potential profit from attracting each segment. The potential profit of a target tourist segment is the difference between the amount that the tourist segment would spend and the cost of attracting and serving this segment. The attraction cost will depend on the master plan. The serving cost depend on the infrastructure requirements. Now rank the potential segments in order of their profitability and concentrate on attracting those segments highest on the list.

For example, Haridwar, Rishikesh Badri-Kedar region of Utttaranchal/Uttarakhand's primary market is religious tourists for sentimental, historical, and religious reasons are drawn to this area. The area should create a deep infrastructure of educational, social, and political groups that are likely to visit this region. Summer work-study vacations for young students, groups for to study artifacts and religions questions, etc., could be arranged. Some religious minded people visit this area as many as ten or fifteen times during their life time. They receive deep experience rather than a superficial one. Depending on their special interest, they meet leaders, study with scholars, with village residents. So doing, they bond with the region and through word of mouth encourage others to visit their 'Deva Bhumi'. The region can begun marketing to a broader audience by launching a campaign with these tourist generating market, that feature a combined visit. The task is to build these new markets and not allow erosion of its successful primary market.

If the analysis identifies too few natural tourist segments in the area, the local government must undertake investment marketing. A natural market is attracted by existing features of the place where as an investment market is attracted by new features that might be added to the region. Investment marketing consists of allocating money toward infrastructure improvements, such as hotels, transportation, etc., and attraction that can potentially attract new types of tourist. The pay-off from investment marketing comes only some years later but this lag is necessary if the region can not identify a sufficient number of natural tourist segments.

The region should better off attract fewer but higher income tourists who stay longer and spend more. Back packers and campers should spend more to enjoy its natural, unspoiled beauty. They should tour not only its mountains, water and ancient building but also its literary treasure and attract high income culture-seeking tourists to visit this area where the speech and wit of old can be experienced today. Hotel and restaurant facilities should be improved as an act of investment marketing.

Whatever tourist segment the region aims at, it needs to be

very specific. A ski resort like Auli could attract only skiers; swimming and natural reef would attracts snorkels and divers; arts, and crafts would attract the art crowd; gambling would attracts gaming tourists. Tourist must be segmented by additional characteristics such as the Valley of Flowers, Winter Park; snow slopes, lakes, winter resort, river boating, rafting, mountain trails, etc. to elude the tourists. The area should expand from single season to year-around business. For example, from winter skiing to summer recreational, educational and cultural attractions.

Market and attractions of these areas are subjected to change over time. A small area attraction may grow to natural and international attraction and later on the entire region explode in competition for tourists competition, results is hot and cold tourist attractions, ups and downs, or ins and outs. A region's attractiveness can be minimized by violence, political instability, natural catastrophe, adverse environmental factors, and overcrowding. There are examples, of Greece and Thailand, highly depended on tourism, where infrastructure investment has lagged tourist development. The results are tourist fall off due to high pollution, inadequate sanitation and major traffic congestion. Greece's natural treasure, the formerly white marble Parthenon in Athens, stand as a pollution-stained symbol of environmental neglect. Similarly, Thailand's beautiful beach resort and temples have been severely damaged by pollution and poor sanitation.

Regions that fail to maintain the necessary infrastructure run significant risks. The region should be ready to respond to changing demographics and life-styles. The growing percentage of retired people and vacations may expand the tourist business. Hotel and airlines should accommodate these trends with low-cost excursion packages. Business travel should include mixed business and leisure. To capture the trend towards shorter vacations, with in driving distance of home, will help in the growth of new local and regional tourist attractions. The whole region should determine its best tourism target. Older citizen and retires drive the regional economy. They have high income, high consumption, and low service demand levels. They take their pension, social security checks securities to the region. Thus, older citizens are much more than a tourist marketing, their visits lead to permanent residency.

The region should market to families, college students, and foreign visitors. Attracting the fixed income elderly, the region could gain the distinction of having the oldest population. Accommodating changing life-styles and need is a dynamic challenge for the tourism in the light of demographic trends.

Strategies and Investments for the Region and Businesses to be Competitive in the Tourist Industry?

Tourist competition is going to be fierce amidst a growing and constantly changing tourist market. Besides new areas, competition expands when declining area up-grade and make new investment in regional development. A major trend in regional revival is heritage development, i.e., the task of preserving the history of the region, their buildings, their people and customers, the machinery and other artifacts that portray history. Counter examples exists of regions/area rediscovering their past, capitalizing on the birth place of famous person; and event, a battle or other hidden gems. A region should rely on various monitors for identification. The area may bear nickname of its economic heritage. With shorter holidays, and family vacation, many areas have new opportunities to access to the tourist market.

The environmental movement has compelled the tourist industry to adopt earth-friendly approaches, and the region should seek to develop 'green' images. Developers and architects should accommodate changing tastes in designs hotels — low rise, more green space, nature architecture, and energy efficient. We find the tourist places in this region are more sensitive to zoning, density land use, and the problems of over-building. Now government tourist agencies, airlines, hotel chains and tourist organizations are all talking about green issues, and how best to accommodate growth while respecting environmental values.

Event based tourism will be a vital component of tourist attraction programmes. Small and rural areas should begin with village festival/ melas or to establish their identify. All local newspapers should publish listing of events, festival, and celebration occurring with in 2-3 kilometer. Regional and local/ area tourism offices should do the same. Travel agencies, restaurants, hotels, airport, train and bus stations should all have even-based calendars for posting.

Every area/region should have a listing of forth-coming events and programmes of scheduled events to attract tourists regionally and nationally.

Tourism Investment : Tourism investment ranges from relatively low-cost market entry for festivals or event to multi-million rupee infrastructure, costs of stadiums, transits systems, airport and convention center. To create a strong destination pull, attractions, facilities and services should be in a convenient and accessible location. In a planned economy the government controls, plans and directs tourists development. Tourism is necessary for an area/region to earn currencies for trade and development and serves regional purposes. Tourist development and expansion in this region is totally dependent on public investment. This is inadequate because of lack of private investment and market mechanism to respond to changing consumer need and wants. The region should promote investment through joint ventures, foreign ownership and time sharing for individual investors. The state investment in infrastructure should work with private investment in tourist amenities such as hotels, restaurants, golf courses, shopping areas, etc. Regional tourism could be build on public-private partnerships, joint development in planning, financing and implementation. Public authority should clear, develop, and write down land costs and make infrastructure investment. The region should provide or subsidize tax incentives for private investment in hotels, convention centers, transit, and parkings. Non-profit Development Corporation from airlines to hotels should carry out restoration. The tourist industry should provide tax revenues, from fuels, leases, bed taxes and sales taxes to support long-term bond for capital construction of tourist-related infrastructure and other public improvements. Such steps will make it possible for this region to increase its tourist attraction.

The region could also require much more finance and investment for tourism promotion. The area/region must expand public services, public safety, traffic and crowd, emergency health, sanitation and street cleaning. It should promote tourism internally to it's own citizens, and businesses—retailers, travel agencies, restaurant, financial institutions, public and private tourist, lodging, police and public servants. It should invest in recruiting, training, licensing, and monitoring tourist—related business and employees cab drivers should have professional training and service, which should include language exams, safety programmes, and location skills.

How can the Area/Region Gaining Access to or Establish a Niche in the Tourist Business, and the Risks and Opportunities to such a Venture?

The region should respond to the travel-basics of 'cost', 'convenience' and 'timeliness' in order to attract tourists. Every tourists to this region would weigh the costs against the benefits of the destination — and investment of time, effort, and resource against a reasonable return in education, experience, fun, revolution and prospective memories. Convenience includes time involved in travel airport to lodging, language barriers, cleanliness and sanitary concerns, access to interests, (i.e., valleys, attractions, amenities), and special needs (elderly, disabled, children, dietary, medical care, communication, auto rental, etc. Timeliness embraces those factors that introduce risk to travel; wars, terrorism, civil disturbances and political instability, currency fluctuations and convertibility, airlines and transit safety, and sanitary conditions.

It is a general rule, that all the areas of the region and tourist business should be competitive in costs, minimize risks, and maximize conveniences and amenities. Tourist packages should range from total planning of hour-by-hour details to multiple options and choices. To accommodate multiple tourist needs, packages should range from destination to destination, no frills only to site- and event-based full-frills luxury. Travellers also make comparisons about the relative advantages and disadvantages of competing destination, e.g., geography (local, regional, national, international), special interests (hiking, snorkeling, trekking, recreation), and amenities (music, art, entertainment, etc.) 'Should I ski in Auli or in the Gulmarg? 'Should I take a chance on central Himalayas or north-eastern Himalayas? The tourist would like to make trade-offs between cost and convenience, quality and reliability, service and beauty, and soon.

The region should market its specific attractions. The region should provide easy access to its attraction by bus, boats, carriages, and planes. It should distribute brochures, audio-tapes, and video-tapes to travel agent and individual prospects. All major hotels should provide in home video packages to assist visitors in planning local tours, booking events, including skiing various sites. Bus companies should prepare half-day, full-day and evening tours to highlight the area's attractions. Concentrating attractions, services and facilities on an area will definitely create excitement, adventure, and crowds. A major strategy for regional tourist attraction is concept integration, i.e., try all diverse elements into one center theme. Associating honeymoon with snow hills, and water-falls, the tourist season could be extended. It would appeal to newly married. Hotels could offer honeymooners a choice of heart-shaped both tubs, Jacuzzis, Canopy beds and waterbeds. The entire romantic aura of champagne waiting in the room, mirror on the ceilings, and quiet and discreet quarters, will encourage the honeymoon market. The large number of honeymooners could find a complete package of dramatic beauty and business community, resulting in a satisfying tourist experience.

The region needs to monitor closely, the relative popularity of its various attractions by determining the number and type of tourists attracted to each location. It should seek to deepen its attractions quality which will transcend the specific attraction and become a platform for building a place's appeal, features, and sites alone will not attract visitors. The region should seek to deepen the travel experience by holding greater values and making the experience more significant and rewarding. Such appeals should be couched in history, culture, and people. The region should be made foreign friendly by creating tours that emphasize nationality interest designing vouchers in a variety of languages, and providing hassle-free currency exchanges. Tour packages should try to deepen cultural bond and ties between the region and the visitors and thus provide value-added dimension and friendship.

Competition extends to restaurants, facilities, sports, cultural amenities, and entertainment. The region/area should have best hotels, best culinary fairs, museums and theatres, athletic teams, best wine and drinks, best chefs, and best natives, cultural or ethical flair. Regional campaign should be carried out in special publication. In addition to specific sites and attractions, critical amenities are also of vital importance to tourism and hospitality business.

The whole region-at first glance seems to bad set as a tourist attraction. It suffered from a poor image and a non-existence industrial base. It requires to recognize the problems and allocate one time grant to explore tourist markets. The audit of potential attractions may be promising, which require a crucial decision. The region needs to be reinvented as a short-break holiday market and be promoted as a weekend packages. The message should reach the main stream tourists. The locals will take pride in the new attention. A general confidence could be derived with the cooperation of all. The result could be a sharp pick-up in holiday packages.

Role of the Media : Tourist competition involves image-making. The regional image will be heavily influenced by pictorial creation of the area, often in movies, and on television and some times by music, and other cases of by popular entertainers, and celebrities. Decades later, this regional image still persists. The region exploits the pilgrim as a successful image of the Himalayas. The region should take advantages of its news events, sport and entertainment stars, movies, and whatever else it could do to stimulate tourist interest and convey a regional image. Television also affects relative regional/area attractiveness.

Changing of an image of an area is quite difficult. In selecting a mix of communication messages and channels will help in determining the regional identify. State's media investment in attracting tourist is bound to grow rapidly in the future. It should produce multi-language travel guides, video-tapes, radio segments, and selected segments for hikers, trackers golfers, fishers, bicyclists and adventure enthusiasts.

Partnership could be formed with travel, recreation and communication business on joint marketing efforts. Advertise in national magazines and travel publications and thus help in vertical marketing with business travel promotions to link the growing business leisure segment of the travelling public. Target its own travel agencies and agent. The region should also target tourism to its own resident, regionalizing attractions with brochures, maps and calendars of event targeted for sub-regions.

The region should constantly discover hidden assets that have vast tourism potentials, for example, Auli skiing discovered in Uttranchal/Uttarakhand, needs to be advertised as a tourist product to a particular target. Effective regional image requires congruence between advertising and the region. Glossy photographs of sunrise, sunset, valleys, streams, wildlife, fountains, springs, houses, and events need to have some relationship to what tourist actually experience, otherwise there is a great risk of the region loosing tourist-goodwill and generating bad word-of-mouth. Travel agents should be extremely responsive to region/area. Feedback from customers and tourist could provide the best or worst privation of a place depending on their experience.

How to Organise and Manage ? : Making an area/region tourist friendly is the task of the central tourist authority, i.e., the Ministry of Tourism. Tourism promotion is the responsibility of the government and promotion hospitality business is entrusted to be travel-tourist business. In smaller area tourist-travel activities could be assigned to local chamber of commerce and private organizations.

Business of Hospitality

The five groups that define the meetings market are:

1. Trade shows
2. Conventions
3. Assemblies
4. Conferences, and
5. Consumers shows.

The key revenue factors are the size of the group, its length of stay and its service demands. The meetings market is growing very fast and there is a need for meeting space requirement. The hospitality business requires attractive exhibition facilities combined with ample meeting space. Convention includes exhibits and displays, and combining exhibitions with meetings. When hotel's occupancy falls below profitability, pressure mounts to expand exhibition and meeting space as a method to increase hotel occupancy rates. Convention and trade show business involves dealing with dedicated specialists such as trade association directors, site selection committees, and convention specialists who make site selection recommendations based on price, facilities, and various amenities. Space at reasonable rate, discounted hotels, restaurants, theatres, airlines, auto rentals, and other amenities are all part of competitive packaging. Facilities should be upgraded to meet aesthetic and convenience needs—restaurants, shops, rest rooms, cleanliness, security, proximity to shopping areas and recreations, etc.

The Himalayan region is not an interesting site for conventioneers. It has outstanding dry weather, and beautiful natural scenery that includes some of the greatest mountain ranges, snow and skiing in the world. The region is not in a position to attract large conventions and trade shows. The space compares unfavorably. Hospitality locations know their target market and respective niches. It travels a growing universe of new and expanding player whose markets may be local villages, cities, statewide, regional, national and international. When time is tough, organizations out-back on travel for professional development, trade shows, and even sales contact. Some travel is being replaced by video conferences, teleconferences, and other media methods.

While no exact test exists to measure how friendly a place is, the 10-questions as given in Table below provides a rough approximation, with 10-points for each favourable answer, a passing score is 60. Anything less probably spells trouble.

Table Friendly Test for an Area

Quiz.1	Are the central access points to your community/ area (road, rail, plane) equipped with visitor information centers or do they provide instruction to easily accessible information?
Quiz.2	Should an airport be the primary access point, does it provide a full range of visitor information services, (e.g. accommodations, tourists booths, visuals on sites, listing of events and what to do, specialized information for elderly, foreigners, families, etc.)?

Quiz.3 Do visitor facilitators—cabs, buses, airline personnel, security, air operators, reservations personnel—receive any formal training, and does a system exist to monitor quality of visitor facilitator services?

Quiz.4 Do hotel/motel offer in house television access channels for visitors with information or events, attraction, restaurants, and things to do?

Quiz .5 Is a single organization/ agency responsible for visitor business, and are public funds provided for it activities?

Quiz. 6 Does that organization/agency have a marketing profile of visitor, and is this profile used on marketing activities?

Quiz.7 Does the place's hospitality industry accommodates foreign visitors needs (language, directors, special interest, do's and don'ts, etc.)?

Quiz.8 Does a range of accommodations exists to meet actual or expected visitor needs (by price, range, size, facilities, access to sites, etc.)?

Quiz.9 Is access to sites, attractions and amenities (events, recreational location) easily available at reasonable costs frequency?

Quiz. 10 Does the place welcome visitors and accommodate their needs (commercial hours, credit cards, language, sign-age, traffics parking, public services, etc.)?

6

Ticketing and Travelling

Tourism in its present form, which makes millions of people move from their homes in search of a holiday, began by a mere coincidence. It was 1841. Thomas Cook, a very intelligent and active member of a Temperance Society of England, organised a trip by a train for five hundred and seventy members of his Society, to a distance of twenty-two miles. He was the first agent to buy tickets in bulk to sell them back to other people. The experiment was successful and everybody was happy. The cost of the return trip was only one shilling each. Mr. Cook had done this job on a no-profit basis. But, it gave him new ideas. Could he turn it into a business, he wondered.

In 1845, Thomas Cook set up a full-time excursion agency to organise excursions. The Railway Company gave him a five per cent commission on sale of tickets which was not adequate to meet all his overheads. So, he decided to diversify. He started operating package tours which included transport, hotel accommodation, sightseeing, guide-services and meals at the other end of the journey.

Thomas Cook must have been a genius, because he introduced some new businesses which are still in vogue. For instance, he invented the system of travellers' cheques and hotel vouchers which eliminated payment in cash. Tourists prepaid the cost of their trip and in return got the hotel vouchers, which took care of all the services provided by the hotel, including meals. Hotels, in turn, gave him the commission for bringing in the business. Similarly, the travellers took Cook's travellers cheques—at that time called circular notes—which were honoured at many establishments and could also be encashed at Thomas Cook offices or banks in the local currency. These were gradually upgraded and have stood the test of time—these have now become the inseparable part of travel and holiday.

Now, travellers' cheques worth billions of dollars are bought and sold everyday all over the world. Travellers' cheques are a unique phenomenon—only a nominal charge is made for the service but the banks can use the money collected by them and earn interest or make short-term investments. After all, travellers' cheques are not used immediately. Travellers' cheques are also insured against loss. The traveller, therefore, does not have to worry about the safe-keeping of his money.

Almost at the same time, other travel companies like American Express, were set up in the USA. American Express is now a household name because of its banking and travel activities in almost every country of the world. In credit cards, American Express was the pioneer and still a market leader.

While Thomas Cook was the first travel agent and tour operator in the world, several others followed him. They opened their offices in major cities of Europe and America. In India also, we had a few travel agencies in the late nineteenth century, including the offices of the Thomas Cook.

In 1878, Thomas Cook brought the first group of rich British tourists to India by the P & O Steamship Company. The group landed in Mumbai, travelled to Agra by train to see the Taj Mahal and also visited the valley of Kashmir.

In his old age, Thomas Cook became blind and the business passed on to his only son, John. John Cook expanded the business further, and when he died in 1898, Cooks had diversified into selling package tours, banking and shipping. Today, Thomas Cook has a thousand offices in one hundred and forty-five countries of the world. They move about ten million people annually. This is how tourism operates in the world.

Across the Atlantic from London, the American Express Company (AMEXO) is perhaps the world's largest travel company with an international banking network, selling American Express Travellers' cheques and related banking facilities like the American Express credit cards to tourists and businessmen.

This company pioneered the credit card system. The American Express card is perhaps the world's most cherished and popular card. A credit card entitles the holder to buy anything (up to a given limit) against the card, without having to pay cash. The shops and establishments accepting a credit card, are immediately paid cash by the credit card company's local office, after deducting a three per cent commission. The company then raises a bill against the credit card holder. The bill has to be paid in ninety days. If the money is not paid within ninety days, interest is charged. Credit cards are issued after due scrutiny of the credit-worthiness of an applicant. People with low credit ratings are not issued such cards. Since the Indian rupee is not a convertible currency as yet, our banks do not issue international credit cards. But some international banking companies now issue credit cards valid all over the world, including foreign currency payments. Most Indian hotels, leading restaurants and many shops dealing with foreign tourists, accept international credit cards like American Express, Visa, Bank of America, Diners' Club, etc. The travellers can pay for their air-tickets, hotel accommodation, meals and shopping with these credit cards and need not bring any cash. You can appreciate how convenient it is to carry an international credit card and international travellers' cheques. No worry, no fear of falling short of cash or of losing it. The lost card is immediately replaced by any office of the issuing agency.

So long as travel was limited to steamships or the railways, the companies did not need travel agents to sell their tickets. They could sell their rail tickets at the stations and steamship tickets at their offices or at the pier.

But the advent of aeroplanes changed the travel scene. In the thirties, PAN AM—which subsequently became America's number one international carrier (it closed its shop in 1991)—was so small that they could not afford to rent an office to sell their tickets. They approached Cooks to let them open a counter in their travel offices and, in return, agreed to give them ten per cent commission on the sale of their tickets, instead of the usual five per cent given to other agents. This is how most airlines discovered travel agents as their marketing arms. Now, some seventy per cent of international and sixty per cent of domestic airlines tickets are sold and issued by travel agents all over the world. Internet has, however, reduced the travel agent's share.

World War II disrupted holiday travel and it was only after the war ended in 1945, that travel and tourism for fun and pleasure restarted. The advent of commercial planes set a new trend because the cost of air travel which was very high in the initial stages, tumbled down with the introduction of larger aircrafts. The three hundred and seventy-five-seater Boeing-747 in the seventies brought about a price revolution in travel. Holiday travel by air became cheaper than by sea. The shipping companies started folding up. The railways were replaced, to a great extent, in the USA and Canada by personal cars, and to a lesser extent in Europe. Air travel came within the reach of an average middle class and salaried classes. To fill up the seats in their wide-bodied planes, the airlines needed sales outlets. While in the early fifties there were three thousand travel agency offices worldwide, the number exceeded sixty thousand by 1998. About twenty-five thousand of these travel agency offices are in the USA alone. Scheduled airlines flew more than two billion passengers—twenty-five hundred million to be exact—in the year 2000. One can imagine the scale of travel. Non-scheduled or chartered airlines fly another five hundred million people annually.

Different Types

Among travel agents, there are the *Wholesalers* and *Retailers.* The wholesalers develop package tours to many a destination and sell them either directly to travellers, or through retail travel agents—small travel agencies operating in each country. Retailers get a ten per cent commission from wholesalers for every package tour sold. The retailers need not make any arrangement for their customers themselves—that is the responsibility of the wholesalers who are in touch with hotels and travel agencies overseas, if it is an overseas package, or within the country if it is a domestic package, for making what in travel agents' terminology is called 'ground arrangements'. The tour operators who receive guests and handle arrangements in the host country are called 'Inbound tour operators'. They service the inbound travellers from foreign countries. Those who promote tours to foreign destinations are called 'Outbound tour operators', while those who operate tours only within their own country, are called 'Domestic tour operators'. Several of them combine both types of businesses. Tour operation is a complicated business—wheels within wheels, each doing its job to make travel trouble-free for the tourists.

There is a thin line between the different kinds of travel agencies—big travel agencies often combine all the functions including retail selling. They have several branches in a country. Sometimes they act as wholesalers and permit other travel agencies also to retail their tour packages. Wholesaling is a popular business in countries like the USA where one company may move as many as half a million people in a year. In India, it is not so common as yet. Often, wholesalers have their retail outlets as well. With the taking over of large Indian companies like Sita World Travel by Kuonis, a multinational travel company, wholesaling will be a big business in future.

Basically, there are two types of travel agencies: the general travel agency and the specialised travel agency. The general travel agency is a small organisation (two to ten employees) that deals with almost all types of travel and offers nearly every type of travel-related service. The specialised travel agency is a fairly large operation and may specialise in one form of travel, or travel service to a group or a community. In India, most travel agencies belong to the category of general travel agencies.

The specialised travel agencies—not very common in India—may specialise in corporate and commercial accounts, exclusively dealing with business travel, organising air tickets, arranging hotel accommodation, car rentals, etc., for corporate executives. The other areas of specialisation are ship or cruise travel, outbound travel, specially in packaging and marketing overseas holidays, organising and promoting conferences and conventions, and creating and catering to an incentive travel market, etc. Some travel agencies confine their business to developing and marketing domestic tours only. This is an excellent business in developed countries and is now becoming profitable in India too.

Important Commissions

Surprisingly, most travel agencies do not charge anything from their clients for their professional services. They survive on commission given by their principals, i.e., airlines, hotels, motels, railways, car rental companies, bus and insurance companies, etc. Where they do not get commissions, they may make a service charge. For instance, the Indian Railways do not give commissions to travel agents. So, a travel agency will add its service charge if a client wants them to buy rail-ticket. However, Indian Railways makes an exception. They permit ten per cent commission to travel agents selling *Ind-Rail Passes* to foreign visitors against foreign currency. They also offer the same commission on sale of Palace on Wheels' tickets.

Commissions to travel agents vary from country to country, depending on the competitive situation. For instance, commissions go up to fifteen per cent and more in the USA where the international airlines are free to offer any commission to make a sale. There is virtually no ceiling on payment of commission due to the policy of deregulation followed by the US Government. But now the airlines are getting wiser and some of them have put a ceiling or 'Caps' as they call it. It has made travel agencies less profitable. The scene is changing due to tight economic situation of airlines.

In India, we follow the IATA norms—seven per cent commission on international tickets. Till recently, Indian Airlines followed their own rules. They had the monopoly and paid a low four per cent commission. With the entry of private airlines, Indian Airlines now pays five per cent commission—the same as the private airlines. Now, the Government has added its ten per cent tax on the total value of the domestic air ticket, which a travel agent is required to collect. No commission is paid to him by the Government for this service. Tax goes to the Government coffers.

Membership of IATA

Although one may find all travel shops calling themselves travel agencies, a dependable travel agency is one displaying the logo of IATA (International Air Transport Association) appointed agent—their symbol is reproduced below.

An IATA appointed travel agency is reliable, because such a company has been approved by this international organisation, after due scrutiny of their professional competence and financial reliability. Such agencies have given financial guarantees to the airlines against default. The agencies which are not IATA members, may not be trustworthy because they buy tickets from other approved IATA agents, or the general sales agents of airlines and resell these to their clients, sharing a part of the commission with their clients. Their margin is so small that they cannot give good service. Until a travel agency is approved by IATA, it cannot get commissions directly from an international airline. IATA approval does not automatically make an agency eligible for commission from Indian Airlines or private domestic airlines. The IATA approval helps. Airlines, however, have their own rules, regulations and yardsticks for approval.

Indian Travel Agents Association : Most IATA approved travel agents in India, are also members of a national organisation called Travel Agents Association of India (TAAI). Its membership is further proof of their reliability. The TAAI logo displayed in such travel agencies is like an ISI mark, indicating professionalism and reliability. TAAI makes a close scrutiny before accepting new members and expects all its members to follow a code of conduct.

The TAAI, has its headquarters in Mumbai and the organisation has seven chapters or branches in major cities of India. The objectives of TAAI are to protect the genuine, and legitimate interests of the professional travel agency members. TAAI membership includes not only travel agencies but also domestic and international airlines, hotels, motels, resorts, etc. At the annual conference of TAAI, called the Indian Travel Congress, they discuss their common problems. TAAI was established in 1950 by a group of eight travel agents led by late Nari. J. Katgara. Membership exceeds two hundred.

Indian Travel Agents Federation : Travel Agents Federation of India (TAFI), is yet another organisation of India, claiming to represent travel agents. Headquartered in Mumbai, it started as TAAI had very stringent rules for membership. It is now fairly large and both the organisation—TAAI and TAFI—try to work together to protect the interests of travel agents and tour operators.

Tour Operators Association of India : Delhi-based IATO (Indian Association of Tour Operators) is the representative organisation of tour operators handling inbound tourism. It is a young and active organisation and has among its members, all those involved in tourism industry, including hotels, transporters, state tourism department and airlines. It holds annual conventions to deliberate over its problems.

Universal Federation of Travel Agents Associations (UFTAA) : At the world level, there is the Universal Federation of Travel Agents Associations (UFTAA). Travel Agents Associations of more than one hundred and twenty-one countries, including India's Travel Agents Association of India (TAAI), are members of UFTAA. Travel agency membership exceeds forty-eight thousand. The world body represents the interests and viewpoints of travel agents all over the world, vis-a-vis organisations like IATA and IHRA (International Hotels and Restaurant Association). UFTAA also provides training opportunities to travel agents who are members of this organisation.

There are about one thousand five hundred IATA-appointed agencies in India. A few of them have a dozen or more offices all over the country and provide employment to a large number of educated young people. A travel agent tries to give full service to his clients—prepares their itineraries, issues tickets after necessary reservations, arranges passports and visas for international travellers, books hotels at the place or places to be visited by his clients, sells travel insurance and if requested, arranges cars on arrival at the destination. In fact, there is hardly anything which a travel agent cannot do for his client at the other end of the journey, provided the client is in the hands of an experienced travel agency.

ASTA (American Society of Travel Agents) is another major

international travel organisation of travel agents. Due to the global nature of travel business, ASTA's agenda is more international now. It permits travel agents from all countries of the world to become its members. While the American members are active members, others are called allied members. Its annual conventions—called World Travel Congress—are attended by seven thousand to eight thousand travel agents every year. It is held one year in the USA and in the alternative year in a foreign country. The participation is so large that a country like India does not have enough hotel rooms in one city, to be able to invite ASTA conference. So far, ASTA has not met in India.

Beginning of Agency

For opening a new travel agency, the first important step is to select a proper location. The selection of the location can make the difference between success and failure.

Careful attention must be given to the evaluation of different areas with high potential for growth and profits. While selecting the location, the agency owner must choose an area which is appealing and accessible to the types of clientele he wishes to attract. It must be an expanding area or a new suburb with possibilities of growth. It must be convenient to businessmen enroute to or returning from work.

The owner must also look at the competition—preferably, there should be less competition in the type of business he wishes to attract.

As for budget, the rule of thumb is that rent and utilities should not exceed ten per cent of the projected budget.

A travel agency office must be well-designed, neat and attractive. Outdoor signs and window displays are essential features of a good travel agency. Telex, fax and photocopying machines have become an essential part of office equipment. Computer terminals from airlines will have to be rented once business starts growing. More successful travel agencies have back-room computerisation too—for accounting, billing and to follow-up on outstanding payments.

A new agency is not immediately approved by IATA. It has to

function successfully for one year, giving business to airlines. During the first year, the agency does not get the commission, but as soon as it is approved, the commission earned in the past year is paid back.

The Endorsement

Since travel agency business is highly competitive, the management of the agency must have a comprehensive marketing plan to facilitate sale of its services.

Under the broad term 'marketing', promotion means all the activities undertaken to promote a business and its products and services. It includes the projection of a proper image of the agency and creation of demands for the services of the travel agency. It can be done by personal contacts, through a sales force and advertising.

A travel agent sells his services. Sometimes, there may be some malfunctioning somewhere in the long chain of travel, not necessarily due to the fault of the agent. It may be the fault of an airline which did not operate a service on time, or of the hotel which did not honour a reservation due to overbooking. But, the travel agent gets the blame from his clients. It is a business full of tensions. There is an interesting story of a travel agent who died and was face to face with St. Peter. He was trembling and expecting to be confined to hell because he never had time to pray in his lifetime. St. Peter asked,

"What was your profession on earth?"

"A travel agent, sir."

St. Peter gave a benevolent smile and ordered, "Let him go to heaven. The poor fellow had enough of hell on earth at the hands of his clients."

Importance in International Tourism

Travel agencies play a key role in promoting international tourism. In India, only twenty-five per cent of incoming business is handled by established travel agencies—mostly groups. Other visitors make independent arrangements. But they should have a larger share and should be helped by the Government to handle more inbound business. The travel agents of India have a good reputation overseas and are known for their efficiency, reliability and hospitality.

The National Committee on Tourism set up by the Government of India, underlined the importance of travel agencies in marketing Indian tourism overseas. The Committee said:

Considering that the travel trade industry is an important link in the total tourism chain, we recommend that the industry should be extended suitable incentives to help improve its performance. We believe that the activities of the travel trade are in the nature of export services, earning foreign exchange as they do. As such, the industry needs to be given selected fiscal and monetary incentives which are already available to the export industry.

Some concessions were extended to travel agents earning foreign exchange in the budget presented by Dr. Manmohan Singh, for the year 1992 - 93. More concessions have been added by the Finance Minister in 1997 and subsequently in 2000.

The Committee suggested that travel agents should get the same concessions for earning foreign exchange as the hotel industry. The plants and machinery of the travel agents are cars, coaches, camping, sports and skiing equipment...low customs duty on such equipment should be levied as for project imports. According to an American Express Travel Agency Survey in India, corporate business for travel agents in India is increasing at the rate of ten per cent annually (American Express Survey, 1996).

No wonder, therefore, the rate of IATA approved travel agencies folding up in India is one of the lowest, in fact, negligible.

Changing Scenario

The travel agency scene in the world, specially in the developed countries, is fast changing. Deregulation of civil aviation in the USA, followed by several other countries, brought in a plethora of reduced airfares and tempting commission structures. Lower airfares resulted in expanded business and higher commissions for travel agents. Business has never been so good. In the USA, membership of IATA is no longer necessary to claim commission from IATA or other scheduled carriers. America has set up its own Air Transport

Association (ATA) which works closely with IATA. Agent members of ATC—a division of ATA of America— are as good as IATA agents and IATA has endorsed them.

Many Governments including those of the USA, UK, Japan and Singapore, have enacted legislation regulating the working of travel agencies to protect the consumers. The regulations insist that new travel agencies will have trained staff, minimum capitalisation and consumer protection insurance, etc. There have been instances of large travel agencies declaring bankruptcies, while hundreds of their clients were travelling in many countries—leaving them high and dry as airlines refused to honour their tickets. In India, there is no legislation regulating travel agencies or protecting travellers. The newly set-up of Consumers Forums can, however, take note of complaints against travel agents.

Attracted by new opportunities in expanding travel business, the number of IATA-approved travel agencies has doubled in ten years, from thirty thousand in 1980 to over sixty thousand in 2000, according to an IATA report.

Statistics pertaining to the travel agency business in the USA are mind-boggling. In 1995, travel agencies in the USA wrote a record US$45 billion in airlines ticketing—commission payments amounted to US$4 billion. In India, statistics pertaining to legal payment in the form of commissions are seldom available— airlines are secretive about it as part of it is often paid under the table. The Indian Airlines which has no reason to be secretive about commission is also reluctant to part with this information in an attempt to expand their area of direct sales at the cost of travel agents.

Overall, approved Indian travel agents sell more than sixty per cent of domestic and seventy-five per cent of international tickets. The rest of the selling is done either directly by the Airlines or through their General Sales Agents (GSAs), which have mushroomed everywhere. GSAs are normally appointed by an airline at a place where there are no IATA agents. A GSA sells tickets of only one airline which he represents and operates his office as the Airlines' own office, entitling him to a higher commission. Over the years, GSAs in India have become an outlet for price-cutting by airlines to beat the competition. They have become experts in cross-border selling—selling across the area of their jurisdiction. Air India, the national carrier, has its GSA in New Delhi where there are more than a score of IATA agents, not setting a very good example for foreign carriers. IATA agents are often hostile to the institution of GSAs because they know that this is a way of taking away their legitimate business from them, by their own principals—the international airlines.

Suppliers and Travel Agents : An idea of the suppliers dependence on travel agents can be had from the following table.

USA: Estimated percentage of business booked by travel agents-wholesalers

Airlines	60 per cent (Domestic)
	70 per cent (International)
Hotels	25 per cent (Domestic)
	75 per cent (International)
Bus	10 per cent
Rail	30 per cent
Rental Car	50 per cent
Packaged Tours	90 per cent

Source: Travel Industry World Year Book.

In India, the suppliers' dependence on travel agents is a little less.

New Wave

Deregulation of airlines in the USA in the eighties, enabled airlines to offer any fare to travel agents or consumers. It has led to two new developments in the travel agency distribution system. One is the emergence of *Consolidators*—business organisations which buy airlines and cruise tickets in bulk at special rates from the principals and offer these at discounted prices to travel agents. The other is *Consortium* or *Co-ops.*

A Consortium is composed of affiliated travel agencies whose purpose is to enhance the volume sales' profits of independently-owned travel agencies. This is done by means of group advertising, production of promotional material, educational opportunities, consulting resources, suppliers' discounts and other aids. This development has occurred to meet the challenge of mega-travel agencies which have a greater bargaining power with the suppliers. A recent example of this development is an arrangement arrived at between North-Western Airlines, Thomas Cook, a mega-travel agency, and Ford Motors whereby Ford personnel are expected to travel by North-Western through Thomas Cook only. North-Western in turn gives a better price to Ford travellers and a higher commission to Thomas Cook. The consortium concept seeks to achieve the same bargaining position for small travel agencies.

These concepts have also seeped down to other countries during the first decade of the new millennium.

In India, Thomas Cook has introduced their bid or buy.com site which offers last minute bargain sales of international tickets as well as holidays—both domestic and international. Many products are on sale.

India Outbound

Outbound travellers from India touched four million mark during 2000—up from only 1.9 million in 1991. Till the mid eighties, Indians—particularly the leisure travellers—were discouraged to go abroad and foreign exchange was not released in their favour, if they declared their purpose as leisure. Foreign exchange was only released to travellers declaring their mission as business promotion, official or occasionally medical treatment abroad. The bureaucrats and politicians used the release of foreign exchange as patronage. At one time, Indian travellers could take only US$20 with them if they were on any mission other than business or official. How did they manage with this paltry sum in countries where even the taxi fare from airport to city costs more? Well, either they were sponsored by their friends or relatives abroad or they cheated—collecting US dollars from an intermediate point where they had parked their dollar accounts secretly, or buying it in black market paying more rupees. It was a peculiar philosophy of the Government to save foreign exchange. They encouraged their citizens to cheat. Overseas, Indian travellers were not respected as they acted like beggars. The scene changed a little when in the late seventies, the Government of India allowed US$300 for leisure travellers, later raised to US$500 in three years and some travel agents in India started marketing tours with this amount on shoe-string budgets. It became possible as air ticket could be bought in Indian rupees and for sightseeing purposes, buses and trains were used abroad which were relatively less expensive.

However, India decided to liberalise its economy in early 1990s. The country achieved an average growth rate of 4.5 per cent annually during this decade, with an accelerated growth in the later part of the decade. Allied to a strong economic growth, demand for international travel increased Until 1996, basic travel quota allowed by the Government—(BTQ) remained at US$500. It was increased to US$2000 per year per person in June 2000 and later, further enhanced to US$3000 a year. Now, it is US$5000 a year per person. For business travellers and for those attending conferences or those going for medical treatment, the foreign exchange quota was enhanced to US$25,000—up from US$15,000. The system was further simplified as the release of foreign exchange was administered by designated commercial banks, as a matter of routine and the people did not have to get prior clearance from the Reserve Bank of India or the Government, for foreign exchange quota to travel overseas. It acted as a major stimulus for overseas travel.

Economic Globalisation

The liberalisation of economy has resulted in greater exposure to the international business community and increased travel among the middle classes, who could afford to travel. There were other factors too—popularity of colour TV in India—with almost every other household having one or two colour TVs at their homes in urban areas. Indian films were shot in far-off foreign destinations like New Zealand, Switzerland and other European countries thereby twelve creating interest in these foreign destinations. The market is now big enough to attract twelve foreign government Tourist Boards to open representative offices in India, to lure Indian citizens to their respective destinations including Great Britain and Australia. The departures from India in the year 2000 were 3,996600—small for the size of a country like India but growing at a fast rate—specially in the leisure segment. The outbound travellers were 3.5 million in 1995 and 3.8 million in 1998. And, about 4 million in 2000.

PATA Report : The increase in outbound travellers, especially the leisure travellers from India, made Pacific Asia Travel Association (PATA) sit up and take note. They asked Travel Research International, a research organisation based in UK, to conduct a survey of India's outbound market for its members. This hundred-page study is a comprehensive survey of the current spread of outbound travel from India and its future potential. The first of its kind, it is an attempt on the part of an international organisation to do such a research on its own. The report, a priced publication, was published in January 2001 and examines India's present status as an international outbound market, its potential for the future and reasons that deter its faster growth. So far, the focus of the Ministry of Tourism, Government of India, has always been on inbound tourism which earned for the country foreign exchange and India annually spends some US$75 million dollars to lure foreign travellers to this country—not very successfully. In less than a decade, outbound market has left the inbound far behind with the number of foreign inbound travellers pegged at less than 2.6 million in 2000 and outbound touching four million. India's balance of trade in tourism is now in the red. Indian travellers abroad are respected as their average spending is more than that of citizens of affluent countries. According to official statistics of Singapore, the average Indian spending in that country exceeds that of the US visitors.

Foreign Destinations

PATA Report estimates that out of the four million outbound travellers, thirty-five per cent were leisure travellers which includes a sizeable chunk who fall in the category of Visiting Friends and Relatives (VFR). And among the VFRs, the USA and UK have the largest share. Other popular destinations are nearer home—Singapore, Thailand, UAE, Nepal and Hong Kong, in that order. One reason for Indians opting for foreign destinations nearer home is perhaps the high price tag of air tickets for domestic air travel. The Government of India, for reasons of its own, keeps the price of air tickets for travel in India high to an extent that it is now cheaper for Indian citizens to travel to Singapore or Bangkok from Delhi, than from Delhi to Cochin or Chennai. Naturally, they prefer foreign destinations. Tickets to these destinations are cheaper because of intense competition among foreign carriers.

What is the Purpose of the Trip ? : Pure outbound leisure tourism in India is still in its infancy but it has grown out of all recognition compared with ten years ago and continuing to increase at a rate of fifteen to twenty per cent annually. According to an International Passenger Survey done on behalf of the Government of India in 1996 - 97, thirty per cent of the outbound tourists were travelling for business-related purposes, twenty per cent were visiting friends and relatives, thirteen per cent were joining their families, thirteen per cent went for employment and only thirteen per cent declared their purpose as pure leisure. India being a vast country, purpose also varies from region to region depending on the nature of the people. Most leisure travellers came from metro cities but the share of smaller towns was not insignificant. The impact of liberalisation of the economy is spread all over the country.

PATA report estimates that at present some twenty-five million Indians are affluent enough to be able to afford overseas holidays. With only four million Indians travelling abroad, the potential is six times more and it is rising with levels of incomes going up in the country.

Within the broad spectrum of outbound travel, the composition of the outbound market has changed radically in recent years. Business travel has changed from being a market composed primarily of businessmen and entrepreneurs pursuing business opportunities within the region, to encompass incentive and conference travel, as well as long-haul trips for increasing number of Indian companies with offices overseas on the one hand and multinational companies based in India on the other. Indian as well as multinational companies sponsor incentive travel holidays for their good workers or salesmen, or hold seminars and training programmes for their staff abroad. Travel Corporation of India (TCI), one of the largest travel outfits in India, reported sending eight thousand Indians in one year, representing white goods manufacturers—automobile and pharmaceutical sectors. Air India reported that such groups could vary from two hundred to UK, to five hundred to Singapore. American Express has estimated that business travel out of India is worth more than US$1 billion a year.

Travel Agency as an Industry

Only eight years ago, travel agency industry worldwide was in a state of euphoria as profits were soaring, business was up, commissions were high and airlines wooed the travel agents as their main source for higher sales. The number of travel agency outlets all over the world was increasing at a fast rate. Almost at the same time, an internet *Guru,* Dr. Nicholas Nagarpente, predicted at the annual convention of PATA in Auckland, that three years from now people will be able to make direct bookings of all their travel plans by moving one finger on the mouse of their personal computers. Since then, the business of internet has increased at a fast pace leaving everyone amazed. Travel is an information-based industry, already exposed to computers for twenty years and the impact of internet on this business is most marked. A downhill trend in travel agency business worldwide is already evident. Many travel agents have taken advantage of the challenge posed by internet and started their own websites, reaching a much larger audience.

ASTA conducted a research study of the member travel agents and discovered that sixty-seven per cent of their members were now charging fees for their services as commission income was not adequate, thus making up the loss due to capping of travel agency commissions. Again, the travel business worldwide has grown from an average of three to five per cent annually. According to the Travel Industry of America (TIA) survey, the business conducted on the Net in 1997 was US$900 million while the total travel business in the country was estimated to be US$500 billion. By 2002, TIA estimated the business on the Net will soar to US$9 billion but the overall travel business in the USA may well be nearer to 800 billion US$. The business on the Net will thus be only 1.2 per cent of the total travel business, leaving the rest to travel agency players—enough for everyone to have his share of the cake.

Parameters of Internet

In today's marketplace, it is necessary to talk about internet as a channel of distribution. It makes direct selling from suppliers to the consumers easy and hassle-free. The internet is an evolving communications tool with greater potential than any of its predecessors. Information technology is beneficial to every major principles like airlines, hotel chains who can market their products worldwide on their websites; the tour operators can market their destinations. National Tourist Organisations can have their websites to expose tourist attractions of their countries; individual travel agents can showcase their products—fair chance to all the players.

But it is only the travel agent who can add value and pleasure to the product. We were, therefore, not surprised to read a research paper which revealed that for every person ecstatic about booking on the Net, there were many more who were frustrated by the vast data and bewildering information which their head could not digest. Another IATA research further tells us that of the five passengers who book globally, four come through travel agents—not very different than what was happening thirty years ago. Again, only one in five explores the surf for information—but only one in ten actually books.

E-commerce is coming of age; in fact, it is doubling every three months. Creating this growth are supplier' websites and internet booking services such as Microsoft Expedia, Sabre's Travelocity, Internet Travel Network, Preview Travel, American Express and Travel Web, etc. These are full service mega sites doing business in millions. Most airlines too have mega sites but they only give their schedules and prices. They do not give comparative prices. This difficulty is overcome by sites like, www.travelocity.com, which gives comparative prices as well as airline schedules. There are several other websites offering similar services. Although the impact of internet on travel agency business is going to affect it adversely in the long run, the travel agent will not be out of business. European budget hotels are some of the best beneficiaries of the internet revolution— receiving bookings from all over the world from travellers wanting economical accommodation.

According to Cyrus Gazdar, former President of the Travel Agents Association of India and a leading expert on new technology, by 2005 the revenue of travel agents from travel agency commissions will come down by fifty per cent.

Indian Profile

India is one country where IATA discipline still holds. Though the price war has left no standard tariffs—all airlines are offering major discounts to sell their seats including those with excellent reputation as dependable carriers. Another innovation in the Indian market is the emergence of consolidators, appointed by airlines to offer cut-throat prices. Consolidators are bulk-buyers of airlines seat who then retail it to individuals as well as travel agents, keeping a small margin for themselves. Another new institution to reappear in India will be travel agent Co-ops or Consortia as in USA. It may be in the offing as the industry reshapes.

The number of IATA-affiliated travel agencies in India has not declined, in fact it has increased from one thousand two hundred two years ago to about one thousand five hundred at present. Travel business in India is increasing at a good rate—five per cent annually. Outbound business is even better, the shortage of airlines seats make travel agents kind of indispensable.

Adi Katgara, Director TCI, expressed his anguish at airlines policy to introduce consolidators, throwing away their seats to beat each other in preference to regular IATA travel agents who worked for them for small commissions. Now, they end up paying higher commissions unprecedented in the history of Indian travel industry. Another development in Indian travel industry is the merger or amalgamation of large Indian travel outfits with much larger multinationals. The trend was started by Airfreight Ltd. with Carlson, followed by Sita Travels joining the Kuonis. This is an indication of the shape of things to come and we can predict more mergers, but it is good for the travel industry of India. Both our inbound and outbound tourism will grow.

Model Case History

TCI of India : The Travel Corporation of India with its headquarters in Mumbai, is India's largest travel agency in terms of financial turnover, offices in India and abroad, and the staff employed.

July 1961 was a watershed year for the travel trade in India. It marked the merger of three leading Indian travel agencies, Jeena & Co., Lee & Muirhead (India) Pvt. Ltd. and N. Jamnadas & Co., to form the Travel Corporation (India) Ltd.

Since then, TCI has pioneered new areas in tourism and helped thousands of tourists to discover India and other parts of the world. Along the way, they have earned on behalf of the Indian exchequer, millions of dollars in foreign exchange, collected many prestigious tourism awards and secured a global reputation as successful travel agents. It has won the Government of India's National Tourism Award around fourteen times.

Complete Travel Shop : TCIs services range from international and domestic ticketing to travel documentation and hotel reservations. Their exclusive "Speedotel" service assures instant room reservations at over seventy hotels all over India. TCI has its own fleet of the latest air-conditioned and non-air-conditioned deluxe coaches and limousines. TCI are agents for India's extensive rail network, *Ind-Rail* passes. They are also special representatives of Eurail, Japan Rail, Amtrak, Greyhound and Cosmos in India.

TCI has an annual turnover of Rs 2500 million. It has over a thousand professionals in its twenty-seven offices in India and twelve sales offices in London, Paris, Frankfurt, Milan, Madrid, Barcelona, New York, Seoul, Sydney, Tokyo and Toronto and Beunos Aires.

TCI has achieved international recognition and is a member of almost all major international travel trade associations. It represents more than a thousand international tour operators.

TCI has achieved distinction through its innovative efforts. It was often first with new travel ideas, like exploring and developing new areas for tourism like Sikkim, Bhutan, Lakshadweep Islands, Andaman Islands and Ladakh, promoting India as a conference destination and pioneering cruises in the Indian Ocean; introducing air charters and developing incentive and special interest tours to India. TCI was the first to offer scuba-diving facilities in India at its Andaman Beach Resort, achieving the position of an undisputed leader in its field. Due to their large volume of business with hotels and airlines, TCI is in a position to get better rates for their clients.

Inbound Business

In promoting inbound business, TCI has been very innovative. For instance, they were one of the first agencies to introduce special interest tours. A fantastic variety of special interest tours is offered. Among these are:

Anthropology	Yoga
Archaeology	Angling
Architecture	Biking
Astrology	Desert Safari
Buddhism	Golf
Cuisines	Hang Gliding
Fairs and Festivals	Heli-skiing
Horticulture	Rock Climbing
India by Rail	Scuba Diving
Museums	Skiing
Ornithology	Trekking and Mountaineering
Palaces	Water Sports
Photography	White-water-rafting
Gems and Jewellery	Wild-life
Shopping	

Travel Incentives

Another area of their specialisation is incentive travel to India. Incentive travel tours are luxurious travel programmes offered by major international companies as rewards to their best workers. TCI designs their programme in India with great care and imagination, adding special touches like the flowers and sandalwood welcome, elephant and camel rides, mock Indian weddings, folk and classical dances, palmistry, magic shows, juggling and other folk entertainment. Lavish banquets and theme parties are organised in chandelier-lit ballrooms of Maharajas' palaces and royal gardens. Sometimes, desert camps are organised for guests. Hospitality for each group is different. Bazaars and fashion shows are also organised. Special souvenirs, video films and photo albums pertaining to their visit are gifted to clients.

Conferences on Global Level

International conferences are also an area where TCI has done a good job. They have set up a special conference management cell to undertake the handling of international and national conferences with precision. Their services include selection of conference venues, hotel and airline reservations, local transportation, sightseeing, pre-and post-conference tours and all the supporting services required for the smooth operation of an international or national conference.

Air Charters and Cruise Ships : TCI has pioneered the development of tourist air charters to India. With the liberalisation of the Government of India's regulations on charter movement, TCI is now handling tourist charters from UK, Germany and Scandinavia.

Similarly, TCI handles ground arrangements for many luxury liners calling on Indian ports, looking after their tour and travel arrangements while these ships berth in Mumbai, Chennai Goa or Cochin ports.

Exploring New Areas

Discovering new areas for tourism has been a tradition with TCI. They were the first agency to discover the potential of both Andaman as well as the Lakshadweep Islands. TCI built the Andaman Beach Resort, the first deluxe resort in Port Blair in 1978, opening up the area for international tourism. It was the first to introduce cruises in the Indian Ocean in 1974. They have ambitious plans to develop more cruises to South-East Asia, Africa, Mauritius and the Seychelles.

Ladakh was yet another area which TCI promoted and brought on the international tourist map.

India Outbound : TCI is a major promoter of overseas holidays, tailored for Indians and is one of the largest outbound tour operators of the country.

TCI's "Fun tours" are carefully planned and include accommodation at first class hotels, offering Indian vegetarian and non-vegetarian meals, transportation by deluxe coaches and sightseeing with knowledgeable local guides. Every tour is accompanied by a trained and experienced TCI tour escort.

Destinations include Europe, UK, USA, South-East Asia, South-East Africa, Mauritius, Maldives, Nepal, Turkey, Greece, Egypt, Dubai and Australia. Every year thousands of Indians make use of their services for overseas holidays.

Tourism Inside the Country

TCI is also active in domestic tourism, though it is not their strongest area.

Specially designed for the Indian holiday market, the TCI's "24 Carat Indian Holidays" are flexible and economical packages to popular holiday destinations like Goa, Shimla, Kulu-Manali, Darjeeling, Bangalore, Mysore, Ooty, Kodaikanal, Kerala, Andaman Islands, Lakshadweep Islands, Mahabalipuram and Delhi-Agra-Jaipur.

During the four decades of its existence, TCI has grown from strength to strength mainly due to its creative marketing approach to tourism. In promoting international tourism to India, TCI has several firsts to its credit. It was the first Indian travel agency to open offices overseas. It responded to the needs of the market and wherever it found potential, it opened an office. For instance, it opened its office in Tokyo immediately after the Japanese started travelling overseas in the mid-sixties.

Now, it has opened an office in Beuros Aires to tap the tourist potential from South America.

TCI is also one of the first to introduce automation in its operations and put up its website: www.tcindia.com to market tourism services worldwide.

The success of any modern travel agency depends upon its ability to respond to the needs of customers—TCI seems to follow that golden rule.

To summarise most leisure travel business today revolves around travel agents and tour operators. They promote and sell all kinds of travel and travel-related services to the public.

The travel agency business is not very old. The first travel agency was set up by Thomas Cook in the year 1845, as he discovered accidentally that packaging of travel services could be a profitable business. He also introduced travellers' cheques and hotel vouchers, eliminating the need of cash in travel. Today, there are over sixty thousand travel agencies appointed by IATA and perhaps the same number which do not have the official approval. In India, there are only one thousand five hundred IATA-appointed travel agencies, but several of them have more than one office.

Travel agencies are of two kinds: one, the general services travel agency which undertakes all kinds of travel and travel-related business and two, specialised travel agencies specialising in business travel, conventions and conferences, incentive travel, outbound or inbound travel. Travel agencies can be further sub-divided into wholesalers and retailers, but several of them combine both functions.

Among the services provided by travel agencies are airlines, rail and cruise reservations, booking of hotels and rent-a-car vehicles at the other end of the journey, developing and marketing overseas and domestic package holidays, organising conferences/ conventions, entertainments/sports, developing incentive tours, insurance, etc. Their main source of profits is from the commissions earned from their principals like airlines, hotels, steamship companies, car rental companies and railways.

To open a new travel agency, it is important to select a location, which is easily accessible to the type of customers whom it wishes to attract. To make it profitable, the owner has to get IATA and other licences in the first year of its operation. Only then is an agency entitled to get commissions from international airlines.

New technologies like the computerised Central Reservation System (CRS) has made the task of travel agencies easier and more profitable. With a touch of a few buttons, they can hand over the entire itinerary to a client duly printed. But a newer technology-communications through internet opens new horizons. It may help travel agents further but it also threatens their very existence. Any person owning a personal computer can access any travel information through internet, make reservations and is already in a position to pay by fibre cash. There are at present five million internet connections in India but within the next few years there may be several million. Payment through internet may take time to reach India but Lufthansa Guman Airlines has announced that a potential traveller could do any travel transaction with the help of their 'Smart Card' through internet on all their flights as well as the flights of seven hundred other airlines through their Reservation System. Other airlines are not far behind.

Due to recent liberalisation of the Indian economy, and relaxation of foreign exchange restrictions, Indians are travelling overseas in large numbers. The outbound business today is more than inbound—four million against 2.6 million inbound. The balance of trade in tourism is no longer in India's favour. It helps Indian trade, industry, exports and expands educational horizons. Several foreign government have opened their tourist offices in India to lure Indians to travel to their lands—a healthy competition. We should welcome that.

PATA has done a survey on India's outbound tourism. According to its estimates, twenty-five million Indians are today in a position to afford foreign travel. Only four million are travelling, leaving a vast potential untapped.

7

Package Deals

A travel agency plays a vital role in the entire process of developing and promoting tourism. It plans and organises tours for various areas or tourist spots of a country. This country can be different from its own country in which, it is based. Combinations of various travel agencies are not uncommon nowadays. That is because all the travel agencies cannot provide all-inclusive packages to their clients in all the parts of the world. Thus, these agencies sign tie-up agreements with those of the other nations so that the latter are able to cater to the needs of their clients as and when they arrive in those countries. Travel agencies plan package tours and sell these to tourists. Package tours are very economical and convenient for tourists as they help them locate tourist spots, hotels and modes of conveyance with ease and at the opportune moments. Thus, a travel agency has to:

(a) attract customers so that they could use its tourism services;

(b) prepare their plans for specific tours; and

(c) coordinate with their affiliates in other parts of the region or world so that these tours could be completed by the clients with flying colours.

We shall study the vital aspects related to the origin, structure and operations of travel agencies in this chapter.

Tour and Travel

Man has been on the move since tunes immemorial. But professional travel activities were not in his mind while he was exploring this planet. Scientists have discovered bodies of primitive men in or around the Arctic and Antarctica regions., These findings prove that man had tried to explore the most hostile terrain of the world despite the fact that he had limited resources. Only things he had got with him were primitive tools, water, food (which was available en route) and above all, will power. Today, he needs not only the will power, but also the financial resources, adequate travel gear and legal permissions to travel to lands that are unknown to him. He is bound by procedures and the limitations of time. The system of travel has become complicated and he must conform to certain norms, which are followed universally.

Travel's Historic Development : During the Paleolithic Age (30000 BC to 10000 BC), the travel activity had only one motive survival. Slowly, man started developing primitive tools and made shelters for himself. He had to travel to new hunting grounds to arrange food. During the Neolithic the (10000 BC), man settled in permanent settlements. Agricultural communities were formed and humans started depending upon farms or fields for survival. In this Age, sailing vessels were developed in Egypt (in 4000 BC). In 3500 BC, the Sumerians developed the wheel (in Mesopotamia). They also used the concept of money (mohurs) to indulge in trade and business activities. In ancient Babylonia (the present region of Iraq), rulers made roads and provided rest houses along their sides so that travellers could stay in them for short time periods.

India and China were also the popular destinations of ancient travellers. Spices of India were the coveted items of the Europeans. When Ashoka sent his religious emissaries to Sri Lanka, Thailand, China and Cambodia, the people of those nations suddenly found themselves to be in love with his land. Thus, Fa Hien and Huen T'sang visited India on religious tours. Marco Polo, Vasco da Gama, Ibn Batuta, Al Beruni and many other travellers came to India and explored her length and breadth. Even before their visits, traders were arriving on the eastern and western coasts of India from far-off places. The historic Silk Route was treated by thousands of people. China and India were engaged in trading and barter activities. This had necessitated the need to travel. The roads were primitive and facilities on the roadside were anything but satisfactory. Incidents of dacoity and arson were common. The Indian travellers had quite often faced the wrath of Pindaris, a specialised gang of looters. This gang was decimated by the British later.

In Rome, luxury bathrooms (in city centres) and places of pleasure (prostitution) were flourishing. Rome was cruel towards slaves. Hence, the rulers would make the prisoners accused of treason face the lions or professional warriors. These prisoners were termed Gladiators, whose only destination used to be death (after their gruesome fights with multiple numbers of State warriors). People used to flock to the grand theatre at Rome to watch the gory ends of those prisoners. Thus, they used to travel from far-off places to have witness the game of death that went on in the middle of the stadium.

The famous silk route had a total length of 12,000 km. It started from the Mediterranian Sea and ended at Pacific Ocean. It linked China, India, Persia, Egypt, Mesopotamia, Greece and Rome. Trade was the chief activity carried out by the travellers along this route. Resting places, palaces, temples, caravan sarais and towns were built along this route. This route still exists, though it is not used for trade and travel nowadays.

The Romans were curious travellers. They used to visit Pyramids of Egypt and temples in the Mediterranean region. They also used to travel during the course of Olympic Games. Medicinal baths, seaside resorts and health spas were developed during the primacy period of the Roman empire. Entertainment, pleasure and health were their objectives while they travelled to far-off places. The Roman empire fell between 400 AD and 500 AD. The activities of travel were subdued in Asia Minor, the erstwhile Roman empire and Europe. During the dark ages, only stout and adventurous people used to undertake long trips to far-off places. Further, the fall of Rome led to reduction in the activities related to trade and commerce. This phenomenon led to a decline in the number of travellers. The concept of luxury travel come into being after the decline of this empire.

Christianity spread in Europe and America. Constantan, the ruler of Rome and his mother, Helen, were responsible for the spread of this religion in Europe. Helen travelled to Jerusalem and tried to locate the Cross of Jesus Christ that was used to execute Him. Buddhism spread in Thailand, China, Cambodia, Korea, Sri Lanka and Japan. Travellers undertaking religious tours used to travel on horsebacks and by foot. There were no roads to travel on. There was also no security of life during the course of religious travel. Travellers used to travel during the day and take rest during the night. Roadside inns used to accommodate these travellers at nominal prices. Some inns used to cater to people only of a particular nationality. By fourteenth century AD, religious tourism had become a mass phenomenon.

Travel during Middle Age : Religious tours were the dominant activities during this period. Although spiritualism was at its peak during this epoch, yet most of the nations of the world were engaged in wars and battles. India saw the invasion of many a warrior from the central Asian region; they came here to loot the valuable of the country. Some of them like Babur settled here forever. But some others like Ghauri, Abdali, Timur the Lame (Timur Lang) and Ghaznavi plundered the country and went back with large booties. In 1100 AD, the facilities for travel and comfort were almost non-existing. The new rulers of Rome did not promote travel and excursions.

In 1552 AD, an Act was passed in England during the rule of Edward VI for keeping holidays and fasting days. So, the public and semi-public offices of that country used to be closed on certain religious days of the year.

Religious tours were replaced by the curiosity for education, exploration, learning and sightseeing. This age was called Renaissance Age. It was witnessed in Europe, especially in Italy. It was marked by travel to distant places for the purpose of learning, getting new sets of knowledge, exploring the unknown and honing skills in various fields of arts and sciences. Thus this age led to another turning point in the history of travel.

Italy was the economic and cultural leader of Europe during the Renaissance Age. But wars were fought in the Italian soil during this era. These wars played an important role in the spread of the Renaissance thought. This thought ultimately led to the concept of the Grand Tour. The elite and rich people of north-western Europe sent their children to France and Italy, so that they could learn new concepts of arts. Progress in sciences was also one of the reasons for such tours. But only the rich few could afford to take up education of this kind. The Romans visited Greece and the eastern Mediterranean. The English visited Italy from sixteenth century onwards. The Grand Tourist had a closer look at the antiquities, knowledge sets and social structures of the Old World. The Eighteenth century (1763 Ad to 1793 AD) proved to be the golden era of the Grand Tour. The British had gained many colonies around the world. They were rich and curious to know more about the world. So, many British authors and intellectuals visited Italy during this period. The Grand Tour was no longer the exclusive right of the rich few. The bourgeouis had also started traveling to Italy. The grand tourist of those times was more keen to learn the arts and crafts of the Old World. This trend created a platform for tourist activities for the nineteenth and twentieth centuries.

The Europeans also introduced the concept of annual holiday. Under this concept, they took at least nine days off their schedules and visited places that were unknown to them. This period was usually from December 24 up to January 1 every year. They used to celebrate Christmas and the New Year with fervour during these days. This concept had started taking firm roots during the eighteenth century. Thus, the Europeans had ample time to explore the world, thanks to this new trend. Earlier, the concept of holiday was derived from Holy Day, which refers to the period from December 25 to January 31; Jesus Christ was born on December 25 and the world was created by God in seven days. But today, these holidays are not taken as religious days in the strict sense of the word. People travel to far-off places for celebrating Christmas. They also attend Mass in churches on the Christmas day. Later, they enjoy in the environs of a tourist spot or at their homes. With passage of time, these holidays assumed the status of paid holidays and employers started sponsoring the trips and excursions of their employees. This practice is prevalent in Europe and the USA even in the present era. Note that the concept of annual paid holiday is the outcome of the industrial revolution of England. It had a religious hue during the beginning, as already stated. But later, it developed as a chief tool to satisfy or appease the employees of the State or the firm (engaged in industrial production).

Alexander, Christopher Columbus, Selucus, Ferdinand Magellan and many other explorers and warriors discovered new parts of the world, including India, Sri Lanka and the USA, which is called the New World. However, we Indians must be proud of the fact that India was the source of all fascinations and myths during the historic tunes due to her diversity, resources and spiritual finesse. When Alexander arrived in India, he found well-maintained roads in the country that were lined with shady trees. Along the royal highway, which had a length of 1,920 m and breadth of 19 m, he found people travelling on chariots, horses, camels, elephants, palanquins and bullock carts. The State was responsible for the upkeep of these roads. Marco Polo left Venice in 1271. He travelled to Persia, Afghanistan and Tibet. He visited the palace of Kublai Khan and lived in China for more than 20 years. When he set out for home, he visited India, Java, Sumatra, Ceylone (now Sri Lanka). Benjamin of Tudela was the first traveller of the medieval times to travel to the Orient. He travelled to Europe , India and Persia for 13 years. Further, Ibn Batuta left his home (Morocco) in 1325 AD. He visited the countries of west Asia and Africa. He crossed the river Indus in 1333 AD. He covered a distance of more than 17,000 miles and also visited China and Indonesia; out of this distance, he covered 13,000 miles in India, Ceylone (now Sri Lanka) and Maldives. Vasco da Gama visited the coast of Malabar in 1492 AD. He wanted to indulge in trading with the local Indians. He was keen to take spices and other delicacies and specialty items of India along with him.

By 1526, India had a small network of roads. Sher Shah Suri had built the Grand Trunk Road; it still exists. The Mughals also developed roads and kuccha roads to facilitate trade and travel activities. However, travel was not a pleasure game during those times because of the lack of facilities, ill-constructed roads and threats of hooligans en route the destinations.

Haridwar, Puri, Dwarka, Hazratbal, Srinagar, Badrinath, Kedarnath, Harimandir Sahib, Durgyana Mandir, Jwala Ji,

Chintpurni, Vaishno Devi, Red Fort, Qutab Minar, Shirdi, Dargah of Sheikh Salim Chishti, Dargah of Hazrat Nizamuddin, Balaji, Chiragh Dilli, Church of Bom Jesus and other destinations were visited by the masses even during the medieval age. But the transport modes were primitive and people were not safe while they travelled to these places. The rulers of those times did not take pains to develop the infrastructure simply because the country was divided into several kingdoms or states. Note that the mediaeval age was marked by violence and invasions from the north-western frontiers of the country. That is why, people were not very much keen to travel during those times. Thus, the trend of the Renaissance Age of Europe was not observed in India.

Sub voce : People have been travelling to religious destinations in search of spiritual solace. They travel to Mecca, Madina, Karbala, Puri, Dwarka, Badrinath, Kedarnath, Shirdi, the Holy Sepulchre at Jerusalem, the wailing wall of Jerusalem, the Harimandir Sahib at Amritsar and the Cathedrals and churches of Rome, London and Paris. Religious travel was dominant during the medieval age but the modern age did emphasise upon the lighter aspects of life. This shift was witnessed during the early sixties of the last century when the Europeans adopted a policy of "eat, drink and go merry." This policy continues to have its strong footholds in all the parts of the world. True, it is beneficial for the tourism industry. But people are moving away from religion. It is not that they do not undertake religious tours. They do but out of compulsion in many cases. Many of them are forced by their elders to undertake such tours while some others (especially, the elders) do so willingly. The youth do not undertake religious tours, their age being the decisive factor in making their pleasure-oriented tour plans. Executives do not have time to undertake tours. Ladies, especially those in their early forties and fifties, undertake religious tours. However, some young preachers and nomads do undertake religious tours.

Travelling in Modern Age

By the year 1865 AD, major seaside resorts were developed in Britain, France and some other nations of Europe. The industrial revolution had changed the face of Europe. Western Europe and North America were the beneficiaries of the machine-based production units. The incomes of people were rising and thus, their spending power was also increasing. They had time to spare and money to spend. Thus, they used to undertake small trips. The industrial society of the West promoted such activities as could increase the trade with other nations in terms of volume and currency. Thus, travel became essential for a modern industrialist of that era. This represented a shift from the trend prevalent in the Roman society; in Rome, only the rich could indulge in trade and travel but in the West, every industrialist was free to travel and engage in trading activities to enhance his business operations.

During the nineteenth century, many resorts were developed in central Europe, namely, French Riviera, Cannes and Monte Carlo. Until the twenties of the nineteenth century, the Riviera was deemed a winter health resort as the Europeans shunned heat. By the end of the late twenties of the same century, Cannes became a popular resort. The Italian Riviera gained importance later and became popular among the English and French. By the early twentieth century, the Americans arrived at the Riviera; they were bowled by the beauty of Europe.

The First World War took place from 1914 to 1918. It took away the sheen from the world of tourism and travel. Then came the Second World War (1939-45). During these wars, tourism activities were at their abysmal levels. Tourist spots were abandoned and most of them were destroyed, except the beaches that were able to face the wrath of those times. The Second War ended and the Americans took a lead in developing their nation as the most coveted tourist destination of the world. Europe followed Uncle Sam in this process.

Development of Infrastructure

Passengers were carried by rail for the first time in 1830 in England. Organised travel by rail was started in 1841 in England, thanks to Thomas Cook. In India, trains started plying from 1853 onwards. During 1870s, GW Pullman developed and built first class railway coaches. By 1872, 700 railway cars were plying across the Big Apple and covering 30,000 miles. Nearly 150 companies were in contract with Pullman Company during those times. The arrival of rail transport systems changed the face of America, which was a large country by any norm.

In 1950s, Henry Ford developed the car. He was the second in line to develop it, after Carl Benz (Germany). Cars were manufactured on a professional basis. People used to take these cars on long distance tours across the continent. These cars used to guzzle petrol in large quantities. But petrol was cheap; Texas was full of this natural resource and the times were good in economic terms. In 1930s, the Germans developed motorways; so did the British. In America, the economy was given a fillip during the early thirties due to the development of motor-worthy roads and highways. As the number of cars increased in Canada and the United States, so did the number of nicely-laid road tracks and intra-city passages. Buses also started plying within major cities.

In India, the scenario was slightly different, though. Railways were spreading their wings (tracks) but at a slow pace. The British were not very keen to spread this network throughout India due to commercial considerations. Moreover, they had realised that they would have to leave India, sooner or later. Thus, they stopped laying emphasis on rail tracks and developed some road belts. These road belts were connected only to major cities, especially to Delhi. Thus, road network in India had its modest beginning during the days of the British Raj.

Commercial air travel started only after the Second War. After the First War, some companies tried to make commercial ventures in the field of air travel. Thus, the process had started at the end of the First War itself. But air travel started after the Second War. In 1952, two-class travel was started. The larger capacities of new aircraft led to reduction in airfares. Package holiday concepts were sold after 1952. The Americans were keen to try such tours. They also travelled to Europe through such packages. Within Europe, the resorts of the Mediterranean are were developed and visited by people from Europe and the Big Apple. In 1958, jet aircraft was developed. From 1960 onwards, the jet revolution wrote a new history of civil aviation in the skies of the world. But in 1973, due to rise in prices of oil, this revolution received a setback. Several types of fares were offered to woo the tourists of those times, namely, Excursion fare (1948), Coach Fare (1952), Family Fare

(1955), Economy Class Fare (1958), Affinity Group Fare (1963), Group Inclusive Tour fare (1967), Youth Fare (1972) and Apex Fare (1975). As a consequence, airfare per seat mile declined from 1963 to 1975. Concorde, Tupolov, Lockheed, Airbus Industries, Boeing,. McDonnell Douglas and Rolls Royce made wide-bodied aircraft for the travellers and tourists of that era. The sky train concept reduced the fares across the Atlantic.

In 1960, the British railways electrified the London -Manchester service. Trains started moving at a speed of 160 km per hour on this route. In 1970, France started its turbine train service in her northern territory. In 1971, Germany started inter-city services. These trains had modern amenities like telephone, stock quotations, dining car and secretarial services. The tourist was no longer bound by the environs of the train to communicate and complete his important tasks, which he would have otherwise completed had he not been aboard the train. The credit of developing luxury railway systems goes to Europe and Japan. During the early seventies, Amtrak was developed in the United States.

Steam ships were in vogue during the eighteenth century. These were used to carry passengers and cargo. During the nineteenth century, people travelled to Europe and Asia by steamships. By the beginning of the twentieth century, ships and ferries started using diesel as the fuel. The Titanic sank in 1912 and this gave a blow to luxury travel by sea. But times changed after the Second War. Cruise lines came into being during the late seventies. Today, cruise lines are being used only for the purpose of luxury travel. These are the major USPs of many travel agencies of the world. Star Cruises is the leader in the field of luxury travel by sea routes.

Evolution of Travel Agency

The origin of professional travel started in 1841. Thomas Cook was the first man who worked on the idea of organising and selling travel-and services related to it. A Baptist preacher of Derbyshire wanted to hire a train to take his friends of the Temperance Society from Leicester to Loughborough and bring them back. Thomas Cook accepted the challenge. A few weeks later, 570 passengers were transported by the Midland Countries Railway. The propaganda caused a sensation and a second trip had to be arranged.

In 1843, Cook took 3000 children from Leicester to Derby. The Liverpool-Canterbury trip of 1845 was a grand success. Cook thought of all the possibilities regarding fixed accommodation and basic amenities that could be provided to passengers during their journey. He made a preliminary survey of accommodation and facilities and published a handbook of the trip to Liverpool. From 1948 to 1963, Cook conducted circular tours of Scotland with 5,000 tourists a season. By the mid-nineteenth century, it became customary for a larger social group to spend holidays away from home. In 1851, he was offered a great opportunity of conducting excursion trains to the Great Exhibition of 1851. Cook transported 16,500 people to and from the Crystal Palace. In 1856, he organised a great "ground circular tour of the continent." The tour was so successful that he had to repeat it after six weeks.

In 1862, Paris Excursions were the first package tour of Cook in which, transport and accommodation were arranged before hand. In 1863, Cook visited Switzerland where his ideas were welcomed by hotels and railway authorities. After that, he visited Italy and surveyed the tourist attractions and facilities available there. In 1860, Cook introduced a coupon system to acquire railway and hotel facilities. By the 1890s, 1,200 hotels throughout the world accepted his coupons In 1865, he established his first office by the name of Thomas Cook and Son in London., Later, his son took the charge of the London office.

In the year 1880, John Mason Cook came to India and established his office in Bombay (now Mumbai) and then, in Calcutta (now Kolkata). Taking advantage of nineteenth century advances in transport technology and hotel business, Thomas Cook and Sons brought about a revolution in the arena of travel and tourism. It was now an industry. Equipped with Cook's hotel and rail coupons, the tourist could enjoy uniform prices and standards of food and accommodation. The tourist was made comfortable for the first time through a professionally managed organisation. This was new trend!. Earlier, travellers used to decide their tour programmes and suffer. But Cook had taken the burden of planning their trips and executed these plans with an amazing finesse.

In 1898, the management of the company passed on to three sons of John Mason Cook. Three aspects of travel were involved in the business of the Cooks at the time of John Mason Cook's death. These were selling tours, travel and shifting. After the Second World War, the British government took over the company. In 1972, the company was sold to Midland Bank Consortium by the British government. The company has 700 offices around the world at present.

Thus, we can conclude that Thomas Cook was the father of modern travel agency.

Growth of Travel Agencies

Two largest travel agencies, Thomas Cook and Son and the American Express Company started in the same year, 1841. Thomas Cook first persuaded a railway company to carry a train load of passengers while Henry Wells started his freight business in the USA at the same time. Initially, Henry Wells started his business as a shifter; later on, he established the well-known company of America known as Wells Fargo.

Besides selling tours, the company dealt in banking. It deals in traveller's cheques and international currency transactions. It also purchases and sells foreign currencies. The company is also dealing in credit cards (popularly called AMEX). These cards are used all over the world and the CC holder can buy international air tickets, pay hotel bills and buy other things that are of interest to him. The company also gives life insurance and general insurance facilities to its clients.

Scope of the Modern Travel Agency : The scope of the activities of the modern travel agency involves the following :

(a) To give advice to the potential tourist an the merits of alternative destination.

(b) To make necessary arrangements for a chosen package, which involves the booking of accommodation, transport modes, transfers to and from airports, sight-seeing and half-day or full-day excursions in the cities visited by the tourist.

A travel agent can be considered to be a useful intermediary (retailer) as he has accumulated knowledge, expertise and contacts with providers of services (wholesalers).

The functions of travel agency depend upon the scope of activities it is involved in and also, its size and location.

Travel Agency : Varied Function : Some of the major functions of a travel agency are as follows.

Marketing and Promotion of Tour Packages : In order to succeed in the highly competitive markets of today, travel agencies promote themselves through the following methods :

(a) Advertisements in local and regional newspapers, which are read by the prospective clients.

(b) Advertisements in magazines related to the travel trade, namely, Trav talk, Go Now, Where, Travel & Tourism, etc.

(c) Supply of printed material like leaflets and small brochures through newspapers to clients.

(d) Despatch of E-mail messages to the E-mail accounts of clients.

(e) Despatch of SMS and MMS messages to the cellular phones and palm-top notebooks of clients through the Net.

(f) Letters (with specific offers) to those clients who have already availed the services of the travel agency in the past.

(g) Telephonic marketing activities; for such activities, a nice looking well-dressed lady is told to call prospective clients from the office of the agency. If the client is interested, he is called to the office of the travel agency and the tour package is sold to him by a senior marketing executive.

(h) Personal selling efforts; these are undertaken by large travel agencies of the metropolises to sell tour packages to corporate clients, rich businessmen and MNCs.

(i) Participation in fairs related to the travel and tourism industry.

(j) PbP material that is on display in the racks placed at the reception of the office of the travel agency. Prospective clients (and even the existing ones) come to the office, pick the leaflets (which describe various tour packages) and decide after they discuss the modalities with the marketing executive of the travel agency.

Informative Function of Travel Agency : When the client or prospective client arrives in the office of the travel agency, he seeks information that would help him undertake the tour. Travel agencies provide necessary information about travel to their clients. This job is performed at a convenient location like an office where the tourist could get information. The travel agent has knowledge of various travel plans. He must be in a position to give up-to-date and accurate information about travel and tour programmes. The travel agent can also employ a marketing executive for this purpose who knows all the details about the travel trade. The travel agent must be aware of the needs and interests of the tourist and travellers. The knowledge of foreign languages is a must but a marketing executive or sales executive should communicate with the customer in the language of the latter. In order to achieve good results, the communication must be accurate, effective and forceful.

Travel Agents as Service Providers : Travel agents promise to provide services to customers and also, sell these to customers by taking money in lieu of the services provided. They do so on the behalf of service providers because they are not involved in the process of delivering such services. So, the process requires efficient coordination between the travel agent who promises and the service provider who actually provides the promised services. There must be legal contracts between them so that a travel agency may be able to sell the services without any confusion and chaos during the execution stage. Such service providers include transport companies, hotel proprietors, providers of surface transport like taxis or coaches for transfers to and from hotels and firms involved in sightseeing. In a large travel agency with a worldwide presence, the liaison work involves a great deal of coordination with the service providers.

Tours's Planning and Costing : Before planning a tour for his prospective customer, a travel agent must answer the following questions :

(a) Who are the potential buyers and where do they live ?

(b) What are their likes and dislikes ?

(c) What are their travel purposes and interests ?

(d) Where do they prefer to buy ?

(e) What are their transport preferences ?

(f) What are their entertainment preferences ?

(g) Whether they would mix business with excursion ?

(h) What are their budgets ?

(i) What are their special preferences if they are travelling along with their families, elders, children with disabilities, etc ?

(j) Would they be regular clients of the agency ?

(k) When would they like to start their itineraries ?

(l) When they would like to end such itineraries ?

The present-day buyer is whimsical and fussy. A travel agency plans his tour after understanding his needs and budget. According to his needs, a travel agent or executive of the travel agency coordinates with tour operators, transporters, airlines, hotel owners, etc. Then, he makes a plan and performs the costing exercise for the tour. He tries to provide him best facilities at least costs. If the tour to be planned is a foreign tour, the duties of a travel agent are tough. He arranges airline tickets, gets passport stamped for visas, purchases foreign currency on the behalf of his customer and prepares the comprehensive (and an exact) tour itinerary. Therefore, the tour arranged by the travel agency must be well-planned and cost-effective. Plans must be made in such a manner as to deliver the best possible levels of comfort and economy to the traveller.

The executive of the travel agency notes the details of tour on an order booking form. The format of this form has been given earlier. It lists all the details of the tour programme.

Finally, the itinerary is defined and the costs of each part of the tour are calculated. A reasonable service charge is added for each one of the services provided. Travel agencies are entitled to a commission of 8 per cent on the air ticket; this percentage may vary from airline to airline. They also get commission from tourist resorts and hotels. These are predefined terms and the prices of tour packages are inclusive of their commissions. In addition, the tourist may ask the travel agency to get his passport stamped for visas. The travel agency charges Rs 100 to 200 for getting each visa from the embassy or high commission. The final tour cost does not include these sundry costs. The tourist can himself go to the embassy or high commission and get his passport stamped for visa. But that is a tedious process; and he may also be too busy to carry out this task.

Concurrence of Tour Programme : This is the most important part of the operations of the travel agency. It may have to send an executive to the office of the client. It may invite him to come to its office and finalise the tour programme. The client would naturally alter or modify the tentative tour programme made by the agency (and discussed quite often over the telephone). But when the travel agency's executive and the client sit across the table, all the clarifications are obtained from the client in respect of his tour programme. The experienced executive of the travel agency also modifies the tour programme according to the practical problems that the tourist is likely to face during the course of his tour. Some tourists may oppose these suggestions but they should know that the executives of travel agencies are more experienced. So, it is better to accept the pragmatic suggestions given by the executive.

The final package is decided and the client pays some advance amount. Some clarifications may have to be made on a later date. The client is also required to submit his passport so that the same could be got stamped for visas. The dates of departure from the station of origin, stay at destination spots/hotels and return from the tour are decided. The number of days of stay in hotels of various cities is decided according to the special needs (and financial resources) of the client. Once this is done, the client gives a green signal to the executive of the travel agency to take necessary actions.

Purchasing of Ticket

The first action to be taken to execute the tour programme is the purchase of tickets. These could be air tickets, railway tickets, sea cruise tickets or tickets of coaches. Note that the passport of the client cannot be stamped for the grant of visas until and unless he has purchased tickets for travel foreign travel usually involves travel by air. Thus, it is important to purchase air tickets from an IATA approved travel agent or airline. The travel agency performs this function alternatively. If the tourist is experienced, he can purchase air tickets from the airline or travel agency of his choice.

A travel agent must have thorough knowledge of schedules of various modes of transport. Sometimes, two or modes of travel may have to be combined. For this purpose, the tour itinerary would have to be checked and tickets booked accordingly. Ticketing is not an easy job as the range and diversity of international airfares are very complex. Changes in international and local flight schedules are very common. Knowledge of roadways, railways, airlines, steamship companies and taxis is essential in this context.

The Computerised Reservation System (CRS) has lessened the load on travel agents in context of airline ticketing. This system comprises a computer network that can be used by the travel agent to reserve an air ticket as also accommodation in a hotel. Through a worldwide network, confirmation of ticket and hotel reservations can be got done in a matter of seconds. For this purpose, professionally-trained executives of the travel agency help the client. They interact through the CRS and get all the bookings done.

Coordination with Hotels : The travel agency also coordinates with hotels, tourist spots and other places of temporary stay, namely, manors, forts, chateaux, havelis, heritage hotels, etc, in the destination cities/countries. It gets reservations done for their clients for such places. If possible, it also arranges tickets for museums, these parks, zoos and other such places in which the tourist might be interested. In some cases, advance bookings can be done but in many others, on-the-spot bookings are in vogue.

If the travel agency cannot get tickets for these important places due to constraints imposed by rules, then it arranges a person (normally, a tour guide or a local assistant) who gets such tickets for the tourist when he actually arrives at the spot. The reservation procedures and planning processes take a lot of time. Thus, the tourist should start the procedure of getting bookings at least two months prior to the date of his departure from the station of his origin. Stamping of passports takes long time nowadays.

Arrangements for Foreign Commences : It is also an important activity carried out by the travel agency. It arranges foreign currencies for travellers. Some agencies deal exclusively in the provision of foreign currencies, traveller's cheques etc. This is an important facility to its customers as it saves a lot of time and energy of the customer. Once the traveller has taken foreign currency from one travel agency, it cannot take foreign currency from another agency for the same tour. The guidelines of the Reserve bank of India are strict in this context. Further, a travel agency can issue foreign currency equivalent to US $ 10,000 to a traveller who intends to undertake a foreign tour. If he spends only a part of this amount during the tour, he can return it to the travel agency and get back its Rupee equivalent from it. He should preferably go to the same travel agency (for this conversion) from which, he had taken this foreign exchange.

The format of the application through which, the tourist is able to get foreign exchange, has been shown earlier. The authorised money exchanger comes to the office or residence of the client and gives him the exchange in lieu of Indian currency. Alternatively, the client can go to the office of the money exchanger and get the foreign exchange according to his travel needs.

Arrangement for Insurance : The travel agency also makes arrangement for the insurance of the traveller. Insurance companies make insurance for both personal accident risks and theft/damage of baggage. It is also the duty of a travel agent to provide proper guidance regarding insurance. In any case, it would have to sign tie-ups with the leading travel insurance firms to provide such services. The travel agency itself cannot provide insurance.

Preparation of Tour Itinerary : The tour itinerary is prepared by a senior executive of the travel agency. Normally, he or she is a person with lots of experience of eight to ten years in the field of travel agency operations. There are two objectives of preparing this important document, as follows :

(a) The tourist should know about his departure and arrival schedules from the origin as well as from various places, which he is going to visit. He should also know what types of service

Application for Availing Foreign Exchange Under Basic Travel Quota ABC Pvt. Ltd.

A-1/402,

Sector-6 Janakpuri

Delhi

Dear Sir,

Release of Foreign Exchange Under Basic Travel Quota for the Year.........

I/We intend to travel abroad and wish to avail foreign exchange under B.TD for you. My/Our particular are given below :

Passport No./Date of Issue :

Place of Issue :

Nationality :

Country(ies) to be visited :

Currency & Amount :

ATM Already Availed

In The Current (Year) :

In settlement, I/We hereby tender cash by Rs............. / Personal / Banker cheque for Rs................. I further declare that I have not / have availed US$....................... under BT during the current year and the total amount including the amount now requested does not exceed US$ 5000.

I/We further declare that all the statements are true and correct and the transaction will not involve any contravention or evasion of the provision of the Foreign Exchange Act, 1999 or any rule, regulation, notification, direction or order issued thereunder.

Thanking you

Your faithfully

(.......................... ....)

Applicants Signature

Name

Address

Ticket No.

Date of Travel

Applicant's Contact No.

which are called Service Vouchers. These vouchers are also given to the client along with the itinerary. Some of these vouchers are prepaid while some others are not.

(1) Complete tour itinerary with dates of departure, arrival, stay in hotels, breakfast provisions, airport-hotel-airport transfers, etc.

(2) Passport with stamped visas.

(3) Hotel vouchers or service vouchers.

(4) Air tickets.

(5) Carry bags or any other free gifts given by the travel agency or by the airline.

(6) Identification labels or marks, which a tourist must carry, or stick to his dress so that he could be identified at the destination airport.

(7) Foreign exchange demanded by the tourist for which, he has to apply on a prescribed form and get such exchange from a money exchanger (authorised by the Reserve Banks of India). Normally, a travel agency is the money exchanger. But thé travel agency through which, the tourist is travelling, may not be the money exchanger authorised by the Reserve Bank of India. Note that foreign exchange has to be procured only from an RBI-authorised money exchanger.

We would suggest that a tourist do not procure this exchange from unauthorised persons or spurious travel agents.

The format of a tour itinerary has been given in elsewhere in this volume. The same is not being repeated here. The format of a service voucher has also been shown.

Holidays Incentives

Travel Consortium

23, Community Center,

Rohini, New Delhi-85

Phone : 64219227/8/9, 6484384/5, Fax: 6225217

Service Voucher No.: 80;0

Favouring : Mr. Arvind Kumar X 01

Drawn On: Mr. Michael / GTM /0065 - 67324477

Date : 31st Oct '02

File No.: OBD/Nov/02

Kindly provide the following services against this Service Voucher:

-02 nights & 03 days hotel accommodation on Single Occupancy

-Daily Breakfast

-Arrival & departure transfers

-Half-day City tour

-Nice Coach ticket for Sin

-Kul on 8th Nov at 1400 Hrs.

Room: One single

-All hotel taxes & service charges.

Singapore: Tropical 6th Nov to 8th Nov '02

Confirmed by: Ms Megha / GTM / Confirmation No. 3603

Billing Instruction : pre-paid at Delhi Office

for Incentives Holidays

Authorised Signatory

Coordination while Tour : When the tourist leaves the station of origin, the travel agency coordinates with the travel agents of the destination station or its own employees at such a station. It informs these executives that the tourist is on his way to execute the tour. E-mail messages are sent to these executives so that they could receive the tourist at the destination stations. Telephonic conversations may also be resorted to in this context. Once the tourist has arrived at the destination station, the executives (of another travel agency with whom the travel agency of the station of origin has tie-ups or its own employees) receive the tourist and take him to the hotel. They also collect Transfer Vouchers from him. Finally, they also tell him to make payments as and when he arrives at the destination airport, if this is a term mentioned in the tour itinerary. Once the tourist is in safe hands, the travel agency of the station of origin can relax.

The tour programme would be executed according to the previously-defined schedule. It is already mentioned that how the format of a service slip is issued to the representative of the travel agency at the destination airport, coach station or seaport. On the basis of this service slip, the coach driver is able to identify the guest at the destination port. The guest is also told to bear a sign of the travel agency on his person (at the front side of his suit) so that the coach driver or representative of the travel agency could identify him in the departure hall of the airport, coach station or seaport. This identification is important because the tourist and the representative/ driver are not known to each other: The representative or driver receives the tourist and takes him to the hotel where the arrival of the tourist has been preplanned. The service slip mentions the flight details and the name of the hotel where he would be taken by the driver or representative. Note that the tourist has to sign the service slip after he has arrived at the designated hotel.

The original travel agency (of the station of origin) is not involved in this stage. The representatives of this travel agency or its associates perform the tasks related to the itinerary as the travel agency of the station of origin cannot perform these in any case. Naturally, these personnel are responsible for the execution of the tour of the tourist. The system has to be very smooth and efficient.

When the guest has to be taken out on a half-day sight-seeing tour, then another service slip is made that mentions the name of the guest, his passport number, station of origin and other relevant details. The travel agency picks up guests from various hotels and takes there around the city. A tour guide accompanies them so that they are able to know more about the history, polity, buildings and popular spots of that city. These sets of information are collected from transfer vouchers of tourists. E-mail messages are sent in advance so that there may be no confusion during.the execution stage. If need be, telephonic conversations an be done to confirm the bookings. E-mail is exchanged frequently.

Organisation Travel Agency : Structure : We can divide travel agencies into two parts—large and small. A small travel agency depends upon other large travel agencies to prepare and execute tour itineraries of its clients. A large travel agency has its own executives stationed at important tourist spots, which are visited by its clients quite often. A small travel agency can have tie-ups with other small and large travel agencies whereas a large travel agency has its own dedicated staff in major cities of the world. But both the types of travel agencies depend upon producers (like owners/managers of hotels, bars, resorts, beach resorts, forts, palaces, wildlife sanctuaries, etc.) to deliver the entire product and service package to the tourist.

Welcome to Singapore

Arrival

lame :

Hotel :

Date :

Departure

Please be informed that your departure transfer pick-up schedule is

DATE: ——————————————

FLIGHT——————————————

PICK-UP TIME:——————————————

Tours Date

Pick Up Time

O City Tour

O Night Bird Park

O Jurong Bird Park

O Sentosa Tour

O Johor Bharu

O Batam Day Tour

O

O

Note:

* Please be on time at the hotel lobby for your transfer:
* Re-confirmation of pick-up time is not necessary.
* Hotel's check-out time 12:00 noon.

____

Name of Representative

Tel: 6444 797

(24 Hrs Emergency)

Signature of Guest

Service Slip of the Representative of a Travel Agency at the Destination Airport : The organisation structure of a small travel agency is also mentioned above. It is a private limited company in most of the cases. A small travel agency can become a large travel agency with the passage of time.

The organisation structure of a large travel agency is also mentioned above. It is a public limited company or an MNC in most of the cases. A large travel agency may become a producer of tourism services with the passage of time. In that case, it may acquire hotels, motels, resorts, cruise lines, etc. Then, it operates as a producer-cum-distributor.

Tour Package's Marketing : Like all other industries, the tourist industry also faces the problem of formulating and refining the marketing mix. A marketing mix is the formulation of a recipe with marketing elements (sub-mixes) for marketing tourism services in the targeted market niches. The different sub-mixes are

(a) product mix;

(b) promotion mix;

(c) price mix; and

(d) physical distribution mix.

These have been explained in the text that follows.

Concept of Product Mix : The tourism product is intangible, well a large part of it really is. The tourist cannot feel, taste, see or try a package tour. The formulation of a product mix is very important task for marketing the tourism services.

The product mix for the tourism industry includes the following elements -

(a) *Accommodation :* Hotels (five-star deluxe, five-star, four-star, three-star, two-star, one-star, heritage and non-graded, according to the classification made by the Government of India).

(b) *Recreation :* Theatre, pubs, theme parks, children's parks, joy rides, musical shows, meetings, get-together, etc.

(c) *Restaurant:* Western, Chinese, Continental, American and Indian cuisine.

(d) *Attraction :* Natural spots, wildlife sanctuaries, biosphere reserves, historical monuments, man-made spots, socio-cultural heritage of India, zoological parks, lakes, natural and artificial resorts.

(e) *Transportation :* Airways, railways, roadways, seaways, local subways and cable cars.

(f) *Shopping :* Books, handicrafts, handloom items, apparel, gold and jewellery, antique items and figurines, sandalwood items, woollen garments, etc.

Tourists belong to diverse cultural backgrounds. Their needs and requirements are different as they hail from different social and economic strata. The services provided by the tourism business depend considerably upon the extent to which, the marketer is able to understand the precise needs of these customers and deliver products and services according to such needs. As already stated in this volume, the tourism industry cannot cater to the precise needs of each and every customer because of several limitations. But these clients can be segregated into well-defined market niches so that they could be served with efficiency.

Concept of Promotion Mix : The following are various components of the promotion mix.

Advertisements : These are an important component of the promotion mix. Through glossy and creative advertisements, the travel agency can promote and sell tour offers and packages to prospective customers. It can promote the package, with the help of creative slogans and swashbuckling USPs, to its clients.

The media blitzkrieg helps the targeted audience prepare in mental and psychological terms for undertaking tours. In the tourism industry, product includes such elements as recreation, accommodation, attraction, transportation, etc., as already stated in Section 6.7.1. Advertising industry uses three modes to disseminate information related to tourism products and/or services. These are print media (magazines of the trade, general magazines, newspapers, journals of the trade, journals of general interest, etc.), audio-visual media (TV and cable TV advertisements, conferences and seminars, cinema slides, coverage of spots in movies, etc.) and visual media (hoardings etc) and audio media (radio advertisements). We have arrived at the conclusion that travel agencies tend to spend more on the trade-related magazines and newspapers so far as their promotional efforts are concerned. These agencies do not use TV advertisements, cinema advertisements, hoardings and other modes of advertising to attract clients. Further, personal selling matters in the field of tourism advertising; so do personal relations between the travel agency and its clients.

Example : A travel agency can advertise its tour package in a magazine (like Trav Talk or Go Now) by showing main attractions, recreation spots and hotel rooms. It can also give the package costs in a nutshell and inform the prospective clients about the various options within a tour package. The client can enquire about the tour package of his choice. Tour packages of 3 Day/4 Nights (also called 3D/4N for the sake of convenience in the advertisement) are popular among economy-class tourists. So, the travel agency advertises these package costs quite often.

If other attractions like hotel rooms or important tourist spots are also shown in four-colour photographs along with their chief USPs and prices, then the customer is easily hooked on to the deal. Further, many travel agents describe the details related to transport, airport taxes, transfers to and from airports, etc. The prospective client gets a quick idea of what he would have to spend on a particular tour package. Some advertisements are so attractive that the client calls the travel agency over telephone as soon as he comes across the advertisement in the newspaper.

Many prospective tourists cannot read magazines or newspapers but most of them watch TV regularly. Thus, this most sensitive but inexpensive communication mode can help travel agencies promote their businesses. We have not seen any advertisements of reputed travel agencies on cable TV, however.

Clear Publicity

This is an another dimension of the promotion mix. Publicity plays a positive role in attracting tourists and promoting the businesses of travel agencies. A neatly-defined publicity programme includes the following :

(a) Regular publicity stories and photographs in newspapers, travelogues, contact with magazines on stories. It helps in projecting the positive image of tourist organisations since the prospects trust on the news items publicised by the media people. Its main purpose is to inform the people about the activities and vision of a travel agency.

(b) Participation in programmes, seminars and conferences related to travel and tourism also helps. The travel agency has to get a stall booked for this purpose. The prospective clients as well as professionals related to the field of tourism and travel throng the stall in large numbers. They inadvertently disseminate information about the travel agency in question. The senior executive or director of the travel agency may also give lectures related to the travel trade. These activities help the firm build an image in the markets.

(c) Word-of-mouth publicity is the best weapon in the hands of an executive of a travel agency. A satisfied client would bring ten more clients. Thus, it is important to satisfy the existing set of clients and solve the problems of those clients who are on tour.

Sales Promotion : Sales Promotion refers to the promotion of products at the points of sale. Same sales promotion techniques are as follows :

(a) Directed at Employees : The travel agency gives incentives to its employees. Companies pay commission to their employees on the total sales made by them.

(b) Directed at Dealers or Retailers : In case the products are sold through dealers or retailers, a travel agency offers gifts to these dealers or retailers such as flight bags, wallets for tickets, pens and stationery items, ashtrays, diaries, paper weights, calendars, participation in trade exhibitions and joint promotion exercises, etc.

(c) Directed at Consumers : For ultimate consumers (tourists), the pull strategy is used. The travel company offers gifts of various types to its customers such as flight bags, passport covers, wallets for tickets, free airport-hotel transfers etc. The hotels offers a number of facilities like shoe shine, welcome drinks, first aid kit, caps and toys for children, free bakery products, soaps and shampoos. The travel agency passes these benefits on to the consumers. Thus, the travel agency also stands to gain if the hotel gives such sundry items to the tourist.

Personal Selling

Personal selling is a very important component of the promotion mix. It is based on the personal selling skill of an individual. The travel and hotel business depends considerably upon personal selling skills of the top-notch marketing and sales executives. Only well-educated and trained personnel can help the agency develop stable sets of clients. In the tourism industry, personal selling is required to influence the decisions of travellers or tourists. The personnel who attend tourists must be responsible and honest towards their duties. The staff with the tourists come in contact includes travel counselor, marketing executive, sales executive, etc.

The hotel manager, hotel waiters, bar staff, porters, hotel cleaners, coach drivers or airline cabin crew also play vital roles in ensuring that their products satisfy tourists. But they are not doing personal selling jobs in the strict sense of the word; they are just doing their jobs and not selling their products or services to clients. Sales personnel are required to be polite, friendly, empathising and above all, result oriented. We have observed that most of the efficient sales professionals eventually start their own travel agencies.

Concept of Price Mix : As the tourism industry has a multi-segment characteristic, the pricing decisions are crucial. The total cost of a tour includes the expenses incurred on transportation, accommodation, intra-city travel, food, wine/liquor, visits to forts/palaces and other activities of entertainment/excursion. Pricing decisions must be consistent with the policy of the travel agency and the needs of the client. Thus, like all other organisations, travel agencies are also required to take pricing decisions carefully.

A rational pricing policy is must in the tourism industry. The government has allowed the firms in the travel trade to operate under some norms. Within those norms, they can charge fees according to the impact of the market forces. Recession, terrorist attacks, surge in economic activities, closure of tourist spots, political developments, wars, other natural calamities (like the impact of SARS pneumonia on China, Singapore and Hong Kong) and above all, weather affect tourist arrivals into a country. If the number of tourists flying through an airline falls, it has to reduce its fares to keep itself afloat. The American Airways has filed an application for bankruptcy in an American court because it has not been able to cross the red line after the recent events of 9-11 attacks on the WTC towers and the Iraq-US war. Thus, global polity also affects the travel and tourism business. The price mix has to be varied quite often in the context of international travel and tourism. Further, five-star hotels charge high prices from their guests. So, the number of guests remains low if recession strikes the country. But the price mix of a luxury tour remains the same because a reduction in the price component create a feeling in the mind of the tourist that he would not get the five-star luxury at lower prices.

The standards ought to be maintained even if there are less clients for these package tours. We have observed that five-star hotels have also slashed their prices in the wake of rising number of vacant rooms per day of 24 hours in their hotels. But this offer was withdrawn later and these hotels have now started charging normal fees from their guests. In other categories of tours, such trends are not being observed. Package tours attract discounts if the number of tourists is large. A single tourist may not get hefty discounts. He may get some other facilities like free airport-hotel-airport transfers, to quote an example in the context of operations of the modern travel agencies.

Naturally, the client has to pay all the costs before he boards the aircraft at the city of origin, except those that he has to pay when he arrives at the destination station.

Concept of Physical Distribution Mix : In the tourism industry, various services, namely, guided tour, transportation, attractions, accommodation etc, are the parts of a tour package. The product/ service package also includes other facilities like catering, amusement, skiing, roller skating, shopping, etc. These services reach the ultimate users through tour operators (wholesalers) and travel agents (retailers). The method through which, the services reach the client at the destination station is known as Channel of Distribution in context of tourism administration. These middlemen are the link of the tourism industry. Tour operators and transport operators buy services like hotel rooms, seats in aircraft, railway tickets, chartered flights and tickets to resorts, palaces, forts, museums and wildlife sanctuaries. They sell the same to travel agencies or directly to tourists. The former are known as Middlemen. Tour operators are also called Middlemen. Thus, the middleman are engaged in the process of distributing the services/products of tour operators. These middlemen can also sell the services/

products of producers who are hotel owners, resort owners, transporters, airlines, fort/ palace managers (working on behalf of the government) and theme park owners. Note that the client may not buy tickets for such places; he may like to decide as and when he arrives at such tourist spot. The travel agency can give him leeway in this context and give him information regarding that place so that the client may be able to decide at the spot. Example : A travel agency may include the airfare, hotel stay and airport-hotel-airport transfers while making the tour programme of a client to Kathmandu (Nepal). It may also include the airfare to Pokhra. But it may exclude the trip to Chitwan simply because the client may like to be on his own at Chitwan. Such types of variations are common and the choice of the client is deemed supreme, though the travel agency can give suggestions to make his tour comfortable.

Sources of Income of a Travel Agency : Travel agencies generally do not charge anything from their clients (tourists). They earn by providing various services of producers and tour operators. We have observed that each travel agency is commercially associated with a few tour operators, travel agencies and producers. Until or unless the tourist has specific preferences, the travel agency contacts the tour operators and producers with whom it has been dealing with for the past 5 to 10 years.

The sources of income of a travel agency are as follows :

(a) *Commission from Modes of Transport :* Travel agencies get commission from various operators of transport services such as airlines, air-conditioned coaches, cruise lines, ships, etc. These transport companies give commission on as certain percentages to the agency that books the packages for its clients. Normally, this percentage varies from 2 per cent to 20 Per cent.

(b) *Commission from Hotels and Tourist Resorts :* Travel agencies book hotels on behalf of their clients. This way, they market and sell the hotel services and get commission in return. Thus, they get certain fixed percentage on sales effected by them.

(c) *Commission from Tour Operators :* Travel agencies approaches a tour operator for its services on the behalf of its client. It sells the services of a tour operator as a middleman between the tourist and the tour operator. It gets a commission, which is also a part of its income.

(d) *Services Charges :* Travel agencies normally take some service charges when they provide services like visa stamping, traveller's cheques, etc. from their customers (tourists). Such charges are very nominal and vary from Rs 100 to Rs 250 per task. Different firms charge different prices; we have mentioned the real life figures here, which were charged from clients for tours to the Orient.

(e) *Profit from Sale of Own Tours :* Some travel agencies operate as tour operators in limited areas of tourist interest, called Sectors. Thus, they earn profits from the sales of their own tours. We have already stated that some travel agencies graduate themselves to tour operators after some time. It is quite natural if their operations expand in the domestic and international markets.

(f) *Incentives :* Travel agencies also receive incentives from tour operators. If they are able to sell a fixed number of tour packages in a fiscal year, the tour operator gives them turnover incentives. The amounts of such incentives are mutually decided.

8

Travellers' Movement

Travel necessarily means movement of people from one place to another. Mobility is the key factor. A tourist, in order to get to his destination, has to travel and, therefore, some mode of transport is necessary to make possible this travel. In other words, transport is an essential precondition of travel. The growth and development of transport, both public and private, have had a tremendous impact on the growth and direction of organised tourism, especially mass tourism.

The Backdrop

Mechanised transport was invented in the nineteenth century beginning with the introduction of railways. The introduction of railways was a crucial landmark in the annals of the travel history. In fact, the seeds of the modern travel agency system were planted way back in the year 1830 when passengers were first carried by rail in England.

Rail-road Transport : The newly completed railway track between Liverpool and Manchester in England featured special provisions for carrying passengers in addition to freight. However, the birth of organised rail travel came in the year 1841. A Baptist preacher of Derbyshire, England, was on his way to a temperance meeting in Leicester when he was inspired with the idea of engaging a special train to carry the friends of temperance society from Leicester to Loughborough and back to attend a quarterly delegate meeting. The man behind this was Thomas Cook. He broached his idea to his friends. A few weeks later, 570 passengers made the journey by the Midland Countries Railway at a specially reduced fare. This venture was followed by various excursions to beauty spots. In the year 1843,3,000 school children were taken on a trip from Leicester to Derby. From 1848 to 1863 Thomas Cook conducted circular tours of Scotland, with 5,000 tourists a season.

The Liverpool and Manchester railway, opened in the year 1830, encouraged many other countries in Europe to open railway lines. Railway tracks were laid in France, Austria and in Switzerland. Across the Atlantic the tracks were laid in America. This revolution in rail transport technology produced an immediate expansion in European tourism. In the year 1881, the railways carried over 600 million passengers over lines operated by one hundred odd companies. The railways were now keen to stimulate travel and to improve the system. There was also an element of competition and the various railway companies tried to make travel as comfortable as possible. In the early 1870s, first class railway travel was introduced by an American, G.M. Pullman, who developed the Pullman coaches with their luxury furnishing and dining facilities. Long distance travel could now be undertaken in comfort and pleasure. The Pullman cars manufactured in America were imported by some railway companies in England and other countries in Europe. The cars which were very comfortable for long journeys were first introduced in America. The longer distances in America necessitated the ensuring of great comfort for passengers. By the year 1872 the Pullman Company had 700 cars working over 30,000 miles of railway under contract with other 150 different companies.

Rapid Expansion in Europe : Europe was one continent where rail transport developed very fast. In Europe the expansion of rail networks linking different countries within Europe as also outside Europe expanded rapidly. The urge and the motivation to travel within Europe was responsible for the introduction of several new railway lines which were responsible for the introduction of great trains, both of short and long distances. These train and train journeys even today are remembered with nostalgia.

The great Inter-European Express, the Nord Express connecting Paris with Vienna in Austria, the Orient Express from Paris to Vienna and Constantinople, the Trans-Siberian, the Ostend-Vienna and Ostend-Warsaw services, and those from Berlin and Vienna to the Riviera and Italy are all creations of early twentieth century. There were several other services like between Entente countries, the Calais-Brindisi, the express from the Channel ports and Paris to Switzerland and Italy through Basle and Lausanne by the Lotschberg and Simplon, the Paris-Rome-Palermo, the Sud Express from Paris to Madrid, Lisbon, Seville, and even the fast services from Paris to Riviera, Nice and Genoa in Italy.

Important Reasons

The compelling influence of mass individual as well as organised travel in the subsequent years brought in great development in the rail transport not only in Europe but in many other continents. It was, however, in Europe that revolutionary experiments were made and are continued to be made in the area of high speed luxury trains.

The energy crisis in 1974 which resulted in widespread recession and galloping inflation had adversely affected travel by air and by private car. It was becoming increasingly expensive to travel by air and private car and coach. The fuel consumption per passenger per kilometre is two to four times more in automobiles and ten times more in aeroplanes as compared to trains. This factor of increase in oil prices is responsible for the remarkable achievement in recent years in the growth of faster and cheaper rail transport. Besides the cost factor, the railways also have an advantage over the airlines in that the terminal stations are often located in the heart of the cities and the train timings are generally more convenient. To add to this, the growing congestion on highways and airports has given a further impetus to this trend. All the above factors coupled with advanced technology and increasing needs for mobility are leading to a renaissance of the rail transport. The railways which were pioneers in the growth and development of early mass travel and were relegated to a secondary place with the introduction of motor and air transport, are once again assuming an important role. In almost all the European countries, the United States of America, Asia and elsewhere, revolutionary ideas for achieving higher speeds and comfort are being conceived and put into practice.

The trend, however, was discernible before the world was affected by the energy crisis. It was in Europe that designs for faster and comfortable trains were first formulated. In the year 1960 the British Railways electrified its London-Manchester line, a very busy line to achieve the speed of 160 kilometers per hour. The new high-speed trains on this line reduced the running time by a full one hour from the former three hours forty minutes trip. Passenger traffic almost doubled in five years. In Germany, a new inter-city system introduced in 1971 provided a rapid train service at two-hour intervals between major cities in the country and brought over 30 per cent more passengers in the first twelve months. Passengers were provided with extra conveniences like telephones, secretariat services, latest stock quotations and 'a la carte' dining-car service round the clock. Similarly, in France, the 160 kilometers per hour turbine train service, which began in 1970 between Paris and Caen in Northern France cut travel time by almost one-fifth. Passenger loads went up by 25 per cent in the first year. High-speed train services elsewhere in Europe connect Paris and Lyons in France, Rome and Milan in Italy and Moscow and Leningrad in Russia.

High-speed Trains : It was japan which took the epoch-making decision to use the latest technology and convert the rail line between Tokyo and Osaka, covering a distance of 515 kilometers into a high-speed track. This ambitious project was completed in the year 1964. The superfast train known as Hikari Express—'bullet train'—running on the new Tokaido line at a speed of 210 kilometers per hour cutting the journey time to less than three hours against six and a half hours taken earlier—was a revolution in high-speed trains. Encouraged by the success of its bold venture, Japan went further and built the new Sanyo line, 565 kilometers in length on which trains travelled even faster at a maximum speed of 260 kilometers per hour. Elsewhere in Asia, new and faster rail tracks were introduced as the number of passengers carried by rail have been increasing in Malaysia, the Philippines and Thailand.

In France a world record of speed was broken in the year 1981. In September 1981, a new high speed train owned by the State-run SNCF Railroad Company shattered the 26-year-old world record for rail speed by clocking 380 kilometers per hour (236 miles). The record-breaking time was achieved near the central French city of Tonnerre during the test run of the French manufactured 'Train à Grande Vitesse' (TGV) train. It broke the previous record of 331 kilometers per hour (205 miles) that was set earlier. The commercial operations of this high-speed train began in 1981 between Paris and Lyon. The fastest train in the world, TGV, was launched in September 1981 covering the 560 kilometers distance between Paris and Lyon in one hour and 48 minutes. In comfortable, sound-proofed cars the only noise heard is the quiet hiss of air-conditioning. The latter version, the 'TGV Atlantic', reduced an hour off journeys from Paris to main cities in the West of France from Brest to Bordeaux. By mid-1990 the French started running TGVs along half their long distance routes, to bring London, Bordeaux, Rotterdam and Cologne within 3.5 hours from Paris. The 320.0 mph (515.3 km/h) TGV Atlantic today holds the world record in speed.

Several other new rail projects were announced in the European countries. The Italian State Railways inaugurated high-speed runs between Rome and Milan. The nonstop train makes the 393 miles (638 kilometers) trip in four hours and 20 minutes, about an hour less than the standard runs. Sweden improved its four major lines to reduce the travel time between its major cities in the year 1994.

In the United States of America, the railways are coming back into the scene in recent years. Increasing number of railway lines are being built to carry a large number of passengers not only within the suburbs but also long distances. There is a great spurt in the urban rail system construction all over the United States. It is increasingly being felt that as mass transit system, it can reduce congestion in high density towns and that this may reduce the automobile pollution. Long distance trains running on the Amtrak system between New York and San Francisco have been modernised. The Amtrak has also added new double Pullman coaches on the system with a view to encourage more rail travel. High-speed train services now connect highly populated

Washington-Baltimore-Philadelphia-New York-Boston 'Corridor' in the United States.

The concept of high-speed trains has come to USA as well. Amtrak has recently selected the Canadian firm to build its first high-speed train to link Washington and Boston at speeds up to 150 mph. The national passenger railroad Amtrak is planning to procure 18 train sets composed of six cars each, as well as leading and trailing locomotives. Another famous company, GEC-Alsthom NV of France, the maker of the world-famous French high speed train TGV (Train a Grande Vitesse) is also joining to modernise the rail system in USA. The trains would start running in the fall of 1999 and are designed to maintain speeds far faster than the current Amtrak top speed of 125 mph.

The day is not far off when trains will cruise at the speeds of 600 kilometers per hour. The new technology aims at dispensing with conventional rails. It aims at providing an air-cushion to replace the conventional run on a track. The projected aero-trains will not only be fast but also sleek looking, noise free, low pollutant, and above all, will cause no wear and tear on the track because they never touch it. Glimpses of such trains are already available in France, Germany and Japan where many experiments have already been performed successfully.

The Eurostar : The first yellow-nosed Eurostar train, the most recent revolutionary development in the rail transport carrying up to 800 passengers, pulled out of London's international station parked at Gare du Nord Station in Paris in June, 1994. Eurostar, operator of the cross-channel high speed passenger train service between London and Paris and London and Brussels, hopes to capture one-half of the annual air traffic of over 5 nillion passengers on those routes by the end of 1996. About 18 to 22 million passenger journeys will be undertaken on the three-hour London-Paris and Paris-London route by the end of the decade. The channel tunnel marks a new era of European rail travel and follows the development of many more high-speed networks in France, Germany, Italy and Spain. These will be linked up later with the tunnel service and provide good competition for airlines on journeys of over 500-600 kilometers. Airlines have to face a stiff competition as the first class inter-city train travel is much cheaper than flexible airline fares.

According to Gunther Ellwanglr, high-speed director at the Paris-based Union International des Chemins de Fer, "The tunnel marks the advent of a real international high speed network. Until now, we just had the French TGV going to Switzerland or the German ICE train to Zurich. Many more lines will be built by end of the century, notably into Germany, then into Spain and Italy." It is estimated that the volume of rail traffic will be far greater than 3 million passengers on the London-Paris air corridor. The railways expect to absorb over 40 per cent of airline business.

Speed and economy are not the only factors in the futuristic trains; comfort and convenience are the other two major advantages. Many travellers find it more convenient to travel from one city centre to another rather than endure the hassles and extra expenses of getting to and from airports. A three-hour journey on the high-speed Eurorail on London-Brussels or London-Paris route provides an uninterrupted stretch of time in which one can work, read or doze in comfort. Eurostar trains are provided with phones, faxes and meals supplied by a British, French and Belgian consortium. French specialist, Carlson Wagon Lits, provides meals that combine French culinary skills with computer-aided delivery.

The Airways

While rail transport played a crucial role in the growth and development of inter-regional travel, especially within Europe, air transport on the other hand introduced an entirely new dimension in the introduction of mass inter-continental travel. It has certainly been a key factor in the growth of international travel and tourism. Although commercial air travel was introduced before the Second World War on a limited scale, air transport for the masses has essentially been a post-war phenomenon. The principal period of growth was from the late fifties continuing into sixties when overseas holiday became a systematic benefit of society, experiencing rising living standards and resulting in disposable incomes for holidays.

Attempts to introduce commercial airlines were, however, made immediately after World War I in Europe. The war itself had a direct bearing on the development of air transport in a similar way as it had with motor transport. Certain commercial civil air services were inaugurated and developed in this period. Besides Europe, air transport was developed in many other countries during this period. Although international air travel was born at the end of World War I and slowly grew between the two wars, it was only at the end of World War II that it made a tremendous breakthrough. It emerged into a practical mode of transport over long distances only in the late forties when the aircraft industry in America applied the technical and manufacturing resources that it had developed during the war. This period saw the development of large pressurised civil aircrafts like the Douglas DC-6s and the Lockheed Constellations followed by the DC-7s and the Super-Constellations operating at twice the speed and flying altitudes of their predecessor war-planes.

Commercial Mobility

The tremendous speed, safety and comfort provided by the new aircrafts released the long pent-up wanderlust of the people the world over. In the year 1952 the two-class travel was introduced which was made possible by the larger capacity of the new aircrafts, resulting in lowering airfares. The steady fall in the real cost of flying has been chiefly productive in the traffic across the Atlantic and within the USA, stimulated by the introduction of tourist fares in the year 1952. This period also saw the first port-war attempt to build a "package holiday" around air transport, the model for most of today's global tourism. The growing willingness of tourists to take to air travel during this period was responsible for the annual flood of North Americans across the Atlantic to Europe. This trend continues even today. Within Europe, there has been the spectacular explosion of the Mediterranean resorts.

Air traffic between commercial sectors was now growing rapidly. In Europe, before World War II, Swiss-air was already flying the twin-engine Douglas DC-2s carrying as many as 14-16 passengers between Zurich and London. In the year 1920 KLM, the Dutch Airlines, introduced the first commercial service between Amsterdam and London. The journey in two-seater De Havilland DH-9 took about four hours. In the year 1929 KLM inaugurated another service to the Far East to Jakarta and within the next few years it was flying most major West European cities. Travelling in these early commercial flights was more an adventure than a pleasure that it is today. It was only after World War II that commercial air travel started surging ahead. More facilities were added for the passengers and travel was being made more comfortable. The commercial jet air travel, however, was pioneered by Great Britain in the year 1952 with the inauguration of jet flights, by BOAC. Thereafter, Pan American Airlines introduced the Boeing 707 service between Paris and New York in the year 1958. By the year 1968 most of the European carriers had converted totally to jet aircraft.

Introduction of Jet Air Travel : As a result of the introduction of jet air services, there was a tremendous boost of air travel from the year 1958. The most decisive development during this period was, however, the development of the concept of 'inclusive tours' in which travellers were carried on charter flights at rates substantially lower than those on normal scheduled services. Air transport can be considered to be responsible for the introduction of cheaper travel, especially long distance, enabling a large majority of potential travellers to now think of visiting far off countries for the purposes of holidays.

The introduction of 'Jumbo Jets' in the year 1970 heralded the phenomena of mass market international tourism as well as business tourism. The jumbo jets—the Boeing 747s—DC-l0s and L-7077s made air travel convenient, comfortable and luxurious. Luxury air travel was made possible for business as well as non-business travellers. This was possible as the big size of jets gave the airlines space enough to partition off a section of the space for executives who were willing to pay extra for the luxury. Pan Am and Japan Air Lines (JAL) were among the first carriers to offer to its passengers what came to be known as business class travel. The seats in this class were wider, giving more space to stretch and relax in comfort, making the long distance travel less cumbersome.

As the popularity of business class travel grew, more and more airlines introduced the scheme. It became extremely successful on long-haul international flights. As an outcome of the success of business class yet another class known as 'Executive Class' was introduced. As the volume of the number of business travel grew and competition increased, the airlines started to further upgrade their services for their clients. This resulted in the introduction of the 'Executive Class'. It was once again Japan Air Lines which in the year 1975 started an 'Executive Service' lounge in the Imperial Hotel in Tokyo, complete with conference rooms, having all the facilities for organising meetings. Lufthansa opened a lounge at Frankfurt and SAS at Copenhagen airports. Many other airlines such as TWA with Ambassador Club, Singapore with Silver Kris Lounges, Pan Am with Clipper Club, Air France with Le Club, Cathay Pacific with Marco Polo, British Airways with Supper Club and airlines like Qantas, Air India, Air Canada, Singapore Airlines, Swissair, etc., offered additional on-ground facilities to their clients. In addition to facilities like office and a club, these airlines provided various other facilities to its members. These included special check-in counters, priority baggage handling and clearance, free transport to and from airport, free drinks, etc. The membership is open to those who pay a nominal fee or is offered free to travellers who have travelled frequently on the carrier.

Growth in Air Traffic : In spite of ever increasing fuel costs and inflation the air transport industry is able to control successfully fare levels as a result of economies of scale provided by the big wide-bodied aircrafts of modern times. The improved fuel efficiency of the later models of jet engines combined with ingenuity and marketing expertise of airlines, travel agencies and tour operators have made air travel accessible to an increasing number of people. This is also illustrated by the North Atlantic route—the so-called golden route of traffic—which saw the successive introduction of excursion fares in 1948, coach fares in 1952, family fares in 1955, economy class fares in 1958, affinity group in 1963, group inclusive tour fares in 1967, youth fares in 1972 and apex fares in 1975. As a result of these innovations in air travel, fares per seat mile declined in real terms, between 1962 and 1975.

In the recent past great advances have been made in air travel, more particularly for overseas holiday making. Tourism in turn has had a significant impact on the aircraft industry and on the carriers. Factors like comfort, speed, and safety influence the tourists' choice of mode of transport. Now wide-bodied jets such as Boeing 747, the McDonnel-Douglas DC-10, the Airbus A-300,

A-320 and Lockheed Tristar L-1011 are all part of the response to the requirements of the ever-growing travel market. The technical brilliance of the supersonic aircraft like the Concord are remarkable landmarks in the aviation history. The industry has a bright future. As far as the long range international travel in the nineties is concerned, the large majority of the aircrafts used will continue to be of the current wide-bodied generation. In order to achieve further economy in running the aircraft to offset the increase in aviation fuel costs, the subsequent period may make substantial further advance in the form of still larger aircrafts such as the doubledeck-800 seater, derivative of the Boeing 747. This new application of the concept of long distance international travel is likely to stimulate the growth of tourist traffic in the coming years. With a view to meet the competition, the stand-by and budget fares have been introduced by the scheduled airlines on the Atlantic and other routes.

Recent global economic recovery has resulted in increase in overall seating capacity and a marked increase in the number of business travellers. In the year 1994, for example, the total number of passengers on Lufthansa German Airlines—among the world's top five carriers—increased to 29.6 million, up 4.1 per cent over 1993. KLM Royal Dutch Airlines increased its passengers load from 9.5 million in 1993 to more than 11.6 million in 1994, an increase of more than 22 per cent. In Europe, overall, traffic increased nearly 9 per cent and total passenger traffic was expected to double from 500 million in 1994-95 to 1 billion by the year 2010. Air transport, thus, is a single key factor which has largely been responsible for the spurt in travel and tourism, especially modern tourism. The future of air transport is bright and the airlines will continue to play a vital role in the growth of international tourism for a long time to come.

Ocean Transport

Like the railways, ocean transport made a significant contribution to travel during the nineteenth century. While railways were responsible for inland travel, especially in Europe, the steamship crossed the boundaries and made strides in inter-continental travel. The shipping technology made a number of innovations in the nineteenth century. In America a number of sailing ships were built which were considered to be superior to those built in England or elsewhere. The English felt a great need for improved communications across the Atlantic with America for the purpose of trade and passenger transportation. As a result of this there were great strides in the development of deep sea shipping. The history of the Canard Steamship Company in England demonstrates important features in the growth of North Atlantic shipping. A subsidy in the form of an award of the mail contract represented a recurring theme in the development of passenger transportation. With the passage of time toward the last quarter of the nineteenth century, emigrant traffic became an important factor in North Atlantic travel. America was considered at this time the 'new world' full of opportunities and fortunes for people in Europe. A great number of people from the continent started going to America in search of fortune. First Great Britain and later Germany along with other countries became the principal generators of emigrants to the new world. Many travelled as tourists to see the new world. The opening of the Suez Canal in 1869 brought about the possibility of a much shortened route between the West and the East and in turn stimulated the introduction of better steamship carriage to the Far-East.

Liner Passenger Service : Engagement of the ships in the cruising fashion for the charter and operation of cruises on a limited scale dates from the mid-nineteenth century. One of the earliest cruises, perhaps, was that described by Mark Twain in his first book, *The Innocent Abroad,* published in 1869. Cruising, however, did not play a significant part in the world of shipping until the beginning of the twentieth century. The period just before the First World War can be considered the heyday of liner passenger service. It was an era of large and comfortable fast ships operated by a relatively small number of companies in various countries. The glamour of the deep-sea travel was, however, reserved for the wealthy Europeans and Americans. In the luxury liners, a large space reserved for the not-too-wealthy was used by the emigrant traffic. In fact, the bigger volume of trans-Atlantic passenger transport was the emigrant traffic.

In the first half of the twentieth century, the descendants of those migrants must have formed a large part of the trans-Atlantic tourist movement. Transport by water makes a significant contribution to the development of travel on land and by air. Scheduled liner transport, formerly much used for inter-continental travel, has presently almost vanished. The expansion of international tourism has however led to an increasing use of ferry boats by tourists on short sea crossings. Tourist sea transport on the whole does not seem to have a promising future. Long distance sea travel may continue to contract, although there will always be a limited demand for sea cruising, since this leisure and attractive mode of travel has a great appeal. In the recent past one of the most important developments in sea traffic has in fact been that of holiday sea cruises, especially in the Mediterranean and Caribbean and also in South-East Asia.

Introduction of Cruises : The advantage of travel by vessel, however, is the element of relaxation and entertainment of a voyage by sea. This advantage has resulted in the introduction of cruises. Since the beginning of the 1969s, passenger shipping industry has gradually shifted in emphasis from the voyage services to cruises. More and more rich and elderly people initially, promoted cruise as they wanted a holiday in a completely relaxed atmosphere.

Subsequently, many companies discovered the advantages of cruise for their incentive winners. Cruises became increasingly popular to motivate top producers as more and more incentive winners wanted to enjoy the delights of life on the high seas. Cruise lines aim to please as cruises offer everything which is a five-star luxury like gourmet dining, top class entertainment, and excellent service. In addition, it offers fascinating shore visits with unusual shopping opportunities and enough activities to keep most athletic and energetic individuals satisfied.

Cruises had record business in the year 1994 when more than five million holiday muters embarked on the world's over 200 cruise liners and mega-yachts. These cruise liners headed for destinations ranging from the Caribbean to Alaska. The Mediterranean and the Pacific, China and Vietnam are now ports of call. They made it a record year for cruising, the fastest growing sector of the travel market. The reasons for this rapid growth in cruises are numerous. These include new exotic holiday destinations, early booking discounts, built-in airfares to departure points, streamlined facilitation at port, gourmet cuisine, entertainment including champagne breakfast in bed.

Cruising is also acquiring a new image by tapping a younger market. The under-50s now form half the complement on the 120 ships of the New York-based Cruise Lines International Association, serving the North American cruise market. With an extra half-million people taking to the sea every year and the dominant North American market expected to almost double to more than 8 million passengers during the decade, more liners are on order to meet the demand.

Shipyard workers in Papenburg, Germany, for example, are putting the finishing touches on the $296 million, 67,000-ton Oriana, the first cruise liner specifically designed for the British market. This market is expanding by 15 per cent a year, while the much bigger North American market has been growing at 10 per cent a year.

The new generation of ships has not been converted but are custom-made for cruising. The future superliner of Carnival, the market leader, will have 2,600 berths. When the Oriana sailed from South Hampton on its inaugural cruise in April 1995 it marked a new chapter both for the P & O line, which invented cruising in 1848, and for what is now a global phenomenon in travel. The high-tech Oriana has a record deck space, 17 public rooms and capacity for 1,900 passengers. Other new ships include Carnival Cruise Line's 2,200 passenger Fascination, Holland America's 1,266- passenger Ryndam and the 295-passenger Silver Cloud and Silver Wind, part of the new generation of upmarket smaller boats led by France's Club Med II, which caters to Japanese and Asian cruisers in the Pacific. Other newcomers are Radisson's Diamond and Ruby, both luxury catamarans.

The number of cruises transiting the Panama canal has almost doubled in recent years, while the Southern Caribbean is drawing more ships in addition to those visiting island ports farther north. The concept of fly-cruise deals mean that it is cheaper in many cases to fly to the Caribbean from Europe and join a cruise than it is to sail around the Mediterranean.

Passenger sea transport on the other hand has, however, not made much strides compared to railroad and air transport. Because of the advances in air technologies resulting in reduced airfares on most of the routes, especially across the Atlantic, most of the shipping lines were unable to compete, resulting in a decline in their services. Coupled with this, the higher labour costs, prohibitive replacement costs of older and outdated vessels and operating costs resulted in many companies closing their business, specially after the early sixties. During 1960s and 1970s most of the major shipping companies either reduced their services or discontinued their long established routes. Cruising, on the other hand did manage to come up to a point where it was necessary to diversify the product and change the marketing strategy in order to survive.

Short sea voyages or ferry services have managed to withstand competition and are doing well in many areas. Channel crossing between some European countries and England by ferry service or hovercraft has been a profitable business for many ferry companies. This could be attributed to the general growth of tourism in the region, lower prices due to competition as also shorter journey time. Increase in the private car ownership in the region is another very important factor in the success of short sea voyages. However, with the completion of Eurotunnel in the year 1994, ferry companies are having a tough time as did the ocean liners with the introduction of cheaper air transport across the Atlantic in 1960s.

9

Civil Aviation

Sitting in the cozy comfort of a drawing room, one may pick up the phone and call Air India Reservation Office in the town. Tell the girl at the other end of the phone to write a ticket for you from New Delhi to Rio de Janeiro in Brazil and back with stopovers in Bangkok (Thailand), Kuala Lumpur (Malaysia), Jakarta (Indonesia), Tokyo (Japan), San Francisco (USA), Vancouver (Canada), New York (USA), London (UK) and New Delhi. For the purpose of payment, you may quote your American Express Card number. Your itinerary involving a number of international airlines in different countries of the world and lasting four weeks, is confirmed in a matter of minutes. It is just a phone call away, and, you make only one payment. The payment, in due course, is shared by all the airlines you use on the basis of the proportionate mileage travelled on each carrier. Credit cards are slowly but surely supplanting cash as a medium of payment in travel business. According to America's Airlines Reporting Corporation (ARC), seventy-five per cent of the bookings made by travel agents today, are made with credit cards in the USA.

In India, payments through credit cards is relatively new phenomenon. Half the customers pay cash to avoid being caught in the income tax net. The new Government order forcing those travelling overseas to file income tax returns compulsorily, will increase cheque or credit card payments.

It is all part of the present-day tourism mechanism made simple for the convenience of the travellers by agreements/ arrangements, among the international and domestic airlines of the world.

Growth of World Scheduled Air Transport : The world scheduled air transport industry, has grown from an estimated nine million passengers in 1945 to about 1.5 billion passengers in the year 2001.

The volume of freight is up from a few thousand tonnes in 1945 to twenty-five thousand million tonnes today.

About forty per cent of the world manufactured exports are flown by air.

The average consumer of scheduled airlines products is today paying seventy per cent less than what he was paying twenty years ago—thanks to deregulation and competition.

More and more airlines have been de-regulated in the world and most of them have benefited from deregulation.

In 1998, the Air Transport Industry produced at least twenty-eight million jobs for the world work-force.

The gross annual output of the World Air Transport Industry was US$1360 billion—a colossal amount. *Source: IATA*

IATA : The organisation which has made all this possible is called International Air Transport Associations (IATA) with its headquarters in Montreal (Canada). It was established in 1945. Most scheduled airlines, Government-owned or private-owned, are members of IATA and if some of them are not full members, they have joined IATA's revenue sharing system for international air tickets.

The system is called the IATA Clearing House. If the cost of a ticket is Rs 50,000, it is shared on the basis of mileage flown by each airline and the carriers are paid according to the rules governing the distribution of revenue. Since the entire international ticket is issued by the originating carrier, debits and credits often sort themselves out without massive payments. The magnitude of the Clearance House can be imagined from the fact that in the year 2000, payments worth US$20 billion were shared among IATA member airlines.

IATA had two hundred and fifty-one airlines of the world as its members in 2000 including Russia's Aeroflot.

IATA also regulates the prices of tickets on different sectors of travel in the world. A lot of thought and effort is involved in deciding the tariff on a given route. The decisions are taken on a unanimous basis. Once the fare is approved by IATA, every airline including non-members have to apply the same fare. All international fares are decided by IATA except when two sovereign Governments agree to apply a special fare between their countries, on the basis of bilateral agreements. In such cases, IATA respects this fare. IATA governs only international fares and not domestic fares. Domestic fares are the concern of the respective airlines or Governments. Airlines have to run on profits to remain in business. Therefore, considerations of profitability weigh in the determination of air fares on each sector.

The air fares are determined on considerations like density of traffic demand in an area. For instance, the air fares over the Atlantic, between Europe and the USA, are lower in terms of mileage flown compared to, say, the same distance between London and Delhi. The reason is that the density of traffic on the London-Delhi route is not as high as on the London-New York route. The capacity available on a certain route, level of competition on the sector, the cost of operation of that route are the other factors taken into account. All international fares are quoted in US dollars. Similar arrangements exist for determining air cargo tariff.

If you hear that someone bought a ticket for less than the amount written on the ticket, it is due to the increasing practice of discounting done secretly either by the airlines concerned or by the travel agents. These discounts are given under the table and, therefore, it is not easy to police them. If proof is available, the airlines concerned can be technically fined by IATA or if it is not an IATA member, the local Government can take punitive action. During these days of de-regulation, punitive action against an airline, is an exception rather than the rule. And for all practical purposes, the airlines find their own level of pricing to remain in competition.

The Profitability

Buoyed by the economic recovery in Asia in the new millennium, IATA member airlines carried during 2000, about 1.4 billion scheduled passengers—a growth of 3.8 per cent from 1999. IATA has brought only 2000 edition of World Air Transport Statistics (WATS) which deals with all aspects of air travel. An important conclusion is that passenger traffic growth was higher than the growth in capacity.

IATA member airlines carried 27.7 million tonnes of cargo in 1999—up 4.9 per cent.

The airline industry though profitable in 1999, yet profitability on international scheduled services fell, as the average yield declined due to cut-throat competition and higher costs. Of the top fifty airlines ranking for passenger and freight traffic, the top six passenger carrying airlines were American, while the international airlines were dominated by European Airlines.

Source: World Air Transport Statistics (WATS) - 2000

Website - IATA online: www.iataonline.com

(Note: After September 11, 2001 attack on WTC in New York, airlines business was hit badly but is now recovering slowly.)

Organisation for International Civil Aviation : While a stable air fare structure and smooth working of international airlines system is provided by IATA, there is another equally important organisation which ensures the safety of flying. This organisation is called International Civil Aviation Organisation (ICAO) established in 1945, also based in Montreal. This is an inter-governmental organisation which means that only Governments can be its members. It had one hundred and eighty-five member Governments in 2001. The decisions taken by the Organisation are ratified by each Government. To operate a commercial airline from one country to another, the two Governments have to enter into a bilateral agreement regarding the frequency of flights. If Air India, for instance, wants rights to operate ten flights a week to London, the British Government will demand reciprocal or better rights for British Airlines to fly to or through India. And if Air India wants rights to fly and pick up passengers from London to New York, India must give similar rights to British Airways to fly from India to Hong Kong and Singapore, picking up passengers from India. There is a lot of bargaining on rights to fly to a destination and beyond for it is good business. All Governments do it. However, some tourism-receiving countries can offer more generous treatment to countries generating tourism. Tourism helps them earn more foreign exchange.

For special charter flights, prior Government permission is needed.

When you fly across the continents, comfortably seated in a plane and sipping a drink, you are not aware of what is happening on the ground. Hundreds of civil aviation personnel are working twenty-four hours a day for you, to ensure the safety of your plane. The pilot is in touch with air-controllers at the airports enroute to stay on course and weathermen are telling him about the weather conditions ahead. When the plane takes off, scores of ground staff are working to ensure a safe take-off. At the other end of the journey, another set of ground staff is waiting to ensure your happy landing. These services are provided by different countries enroute, according to international agreements between nations. ICAO has been instrumental in drafting these agreements and later getting them ratified by each Government. ICAO has a membership of one hundred and twenty-five nations. The main objective of ICAO is to ensure safety in the air. A few years ago, the ICAO passed a law on punishing hijackers of an aeroplane. The law has already been ratified by most countries of the world. Normally, no sovereign country would allow a foreign plane to overfly its territory. But, under ICAO agreements, commercial planes are allowed to overfly without any hindrance, over countries that may not be even friendly to a carrier's own country, for example, India and Pakistan, USA and Iran.

India is a respected member of the ICAO and a member of its Executive Committee for many years. Till 1991, an Indian, Dr. S.S. Sidhu, was its Secretary General, the first Asian to be elected to this high office.

Imagine how difficult it would be if we did not have organisations like IATA and ICAO. At IATA, airlines thrash out their business problems and differences and at ICAO, Governments sit together to ensure safe-flying and discipline in the skies.

Scheduled and Chartered Airlines : We have used the word scheduled in the case of most airlines. These are called scheduled because these are the airlines flying according to regular schedules or timetables. The non-scheduled airlines are called charter airlines. The charter airlines fly only when there is a demand. Most tourist charters are operated by such carriers. They work out cheaper than scheduled carriers because they operate only if there is very high load factor, preferably hundred per cent, back to back. Scheduled airlines have to fly even if there is hardly any passenger in a flight on a given day. The author recalls a Japan Airlines domestic flight in the mid-seventies where he was the lone passenger in a Jet plane. Charters are an interesting phenomenon. The fast growth of tourism has been made possible due to the inexpensive tour packages provided by charter airlines to popular destinations in Europe like Spain and Portugal. India gets a few charters every year, especially to Goa and Thriuvantapuram. There may be five hundred return trips from Europe to Goa in a given year, everyday one or two groups landing or taking off. In this way, no capacity is wasted and the price per seat works out to be the most economical. Now, it is proposed to encourage charter flights to other places in India.

Crowded Skies

Air traffic has been growing at a fast rate and our skyways are crowded. The Civil Aviation authorities in countries of Europe, the USA and the Pacific are concerned about safety due to the overcrowding in the sky.

The Indian sky is one of the overcrowded routes and the air spaces over Mumbai's international airport are heavily crowded. ICAO is concerned about problems relating to congestion in the sky. Steps are being taken to sort out the problems as the number of flights is increasing from five to ten per cent annually on busy routes. Almost every second minute, a plane takes off from John F. Kennedy Airport, New York, or from Heathrow, the London

Airport. The aviation experts are considering ways and means to overcome the danger to safety posed by overcrowding.

Fare Endorsement

In the early seventies when the 747-Boeing Jumbo Jets came into operation offering some four hundred seats in one plane, the world had a glut of air capacity. The airlines thought of offering cheaper promotional fares to attract more passengers. Important among these fares are:

Short Journey

These are sold on the basis of return journey to individuals and have restrictions of minimum or maximum stay at the other end of the journey. For instance, to avail of an excursion fare, a passenger must spend at least ten days in the country where he is going. The idea of putting these restrictions is to dissuade business travellers from using cheap excursion fares for short business visits. A business traveller may like to visit a country for three to four days, but an excursion fare involves a minimum stay of one week or fourteen days. So, the business traveller cannot use the cheap fare. Such fares are often discounted by twenty to forty per cent to encourage new holiday travellers, who would not have otherwise travelled. A businessman has to travel anyway.

Group Fares

These fares are applicable to groups and are discounted by twenty to forty per cent. Off-season discounts can be even higher. Here again, there are restrictions; for example, a minimum of ten to forty persons must travel together on the same itinerary. A minimum stay is also stipulated. In some cases, the package has to be sold inclusive of the ground arrangements like hotel bookings, sightseeing, etc.

The introduction of such promotional fares brought about a tourism boom in the world. Soon the Jumbos were filled up and there was even shortage of capacity on some popular routes, despite steady augmentation of fleets.

History : The multi-billion dollar airlines industry had a very humble beginning in the early twentieth century. The route to the wide-bodied modern jet planes has been through balloons, gliders and airships followed by the modern flying machines.

Although man has dreamt of flying and there are references to it in Hindu, Greek and the Chinese mythology, the credit for thinking of building a flying machine goes to Leonardo da Vinci, the great artistic genius of the sixteenth century, who lived in Italy. He published a book called *Flight of Birds.* One of his disciples experimented with a flight on a contrivance made by his master. The contrivance failed and his disciple was crippled for life, the first casualty of flying in the world.

In the sixteenth and seventeenth centuries in Europe, the power of the church was so strong that no one could think of flying, because it was considered to be against the laws of the God. Any person attempting it could be tried by the church and sentenced to death. Therefore, no one ventured to make a flying machine.

It was only in the late eighteenth century that two brothers, Joseph and Etienne Montgolfier accidentally discovered the principle of ballooning. They saw smoke rise up from a fire and concluded that hot air must be lighter than the air at normal temperature. Based on this discovery, they constructed a balloon of linen-lined paper with a circumference of a hundred feet and released it on 6 June, 1783, with a sheep, a cock and a duck. The balloon rose to a height of six hundred feet and remained in the air for eight minutes. The passengers returned safely except that the cock was injured by a kick from the sheep.

Thus, man was off the ground and the flying of human beings looked possible. The same year, two other adventurers, Pilatie do Rosier and the Marquis of Arlandes, flew in a balloon over Paris for twenty-five minutes in the presence of the King and Queen of France. Simultaneously, hydrogen was discovered and a Frenchman flew in a big hydrogen balloon. An American, John Wise, tried to cross the Atlantic in a balloon; he failed but he was the first man to fly a distance of one thousand, one hundred and thirty miles at one stretch. The vision of flying was becoming clear and in 1842, Tennyson foretold the shape of things to come, in one of his famous poems:

I dip into the future, far as the human eyes could see,

Saw the vision of the world, all the wonders that would be,

Saw the heavens fill with commerce argosies and magic sails,

Pilots of the purple twilight, dropping down with costly bales

Heard the heavens fill with shouting and there rained a ghastly dew

From the nations' airy navies grappling in the central blue.

How prophetic!

From balloons people moved to airships. On 2 July, 1890, Count Ferdinand Von Zeppelin, a German engineer, flew his airship at a speed of sixteen miles an hour against the winds. The airship was made by joining a number of balloons. The German Government gave Zeppelin a generous subsidy to further develop his machine. During the World War I, hundred Zeppelins were made. Their speed was increased to eighty miles an hour and they could carry up to fifty tons of bombs.

The credit for developing modern aeroplane goes to the Wright Brothers, Willbur and Orville, of the USA. They designed a motor-driven aeroplane, weighing thirty-five kilograms, and made their first flight at Kitty Hawk. The flight lasted twelve seconds and covered a distance of one hundred and twenty feet only. Later, they improved their machines and in 1908 Wilbur flew for two hours and twenty-one minutes, ushering in a new era of civil aviation and flying for pleasure.

Air travel has reached new heights. There are over ten thousand commercial aeroplanes in the world, offering 1.6 million seats everyday. The scheduled airlines fly 1.6 billion passengers a year. Charters fly another four hundred million. The number of passengers travelling by scheduled carriers is increasing at the rate of five per cent annually.

Future Prospects

Airlines business has seen its ups and downs. It was in bad shape in the early eighties due to an economic recession and intense competition. However, it has recovered and the growth in the late eighties was eight to ten per cent per annum. It was stable till the end of 1990, but the brief Gulf War in early 1991 affected the profitability of all major carriers. In 1998, the Airlines Industry provided at least:

- Twenty-eight million jobs for the world's work-force
- US$1,360 billion in gross annual output.

International air transport is still today—one of the fastest growing sectors of the world economy. The passenger and freight traffic are expected to grow at an average annual rate of five per cent between 1999 and 2010, the number of passenger journeys by air could exceed 2.3 billion each year.

In the increasing global society, the economic and social contribution of this industry will continue to expand. By the year 2010, aviation economic growth impact could exceed US$1800 billion and provide over thirty-one million jobs worldwide.

During the next twenty years, airlines are likely to buy sixteen thousand aircrafts worth US$1200 billion. The infrastructure providers— airports and traffic services will spend another US$350 billion to meet the needs of growth in traffic. That is not all—international aviation is the prime engine in travel and tourism industry, presently contributing more than US$3,500 billion to the world economy—nearly twelve per cent of the total. Tourism also generates one hundred and ninety-two million jobs—eight per cent of the total.

Capital investment in travel and tourism at present is estimated to be seven hundred and thirty-three billion US dollars every year—representing eleven per cent of the world's total capital investment.

Profit in the Business

What about profits? The quick answer to this question is—taking all airlines together—the answer is—NO. For the first thirty years after World War II, air transportation was guided by the view held by majority of nations that their air transport services were of overriding importance for economic and strategic reasons and had to be protected. The airlines served foreign policy objectives and defence too. States, therefore, owned their flag carriers and subsidised them to an extent—without caring for profits. Some carriers did make some profit at times, some made a lot of profit and some lost money too. It may be a shocking revelation that in the four years of 1990 - 93, IATA members lost US$15.6 billion on their international scheduled services. That is more than the total profits made by them in the preceding forty-four years—1945-1989.

Liberalisation in Control

Deregulation is a term in aviation referring to the removal of controls on the operation of airlines. It started in the USA, when the US Government decided in 1978 that competition among the airlines should be encouraged and the Government need not regulate tariffs or the flight frequencies of airlines. As a result of this policy, the airlines in the USA were allowed to fix tariffs at will and could operate any number of flights to a city in the USA. The deregulation policy helped the travellers as cheaper fares became available to them and the air traffic increased considerably.

The policy of deregulation is being increasingly applied in countries of Europe, Japan, Australia and Canada. To beat the competition, several European carriers are trying to amalgamate their services with each other. The future trends are towards the elimination of small carriers and the emergence of mega carriers.

This has also led to the privatisation of some Government-owned airlines. For instance, British Airways which was fully owned by the British Government is now a private company, doing better than ever before. Japan Airlines was totally privatised in 1991. So has Air New Zealand and a few others. In India too, private airlines have been permitted. Air India and Indian Airlines too are on their way to disinvestment and control by private partners.

Indian Profile

India was one of the first countries to take to aviation. The earliest recorded flight in India was on 18 February, 1911, when

Henri Piquet flew a Howber bi-plane to carry mail from the Allahabad Exhibition ground to Naini Junction, a distance of eight miles in thirteen minutes. India's strategic location helped the country in becoming an important stopover point for air services. The British, the Dutch and the French, all needed to stop in India on their way to their colonies. The British to Singapore, the Dutch to Indonesia and the French to Indo-China, now called Vietnam. India provided a convenient refuelling stopover in long distance routes.

The first scheduled airlines service in India was started by the Aviation Department of Tatas on 15 October, 1932, later known as Tata Airlines. It was a service connecting Karachi, Ahmedabad, Bombay, Bellary and Madras. The World War in 1945, virtually put an end to these services. After the War, there was an airline boom and as many as twenty-one airlines started operation in India with American war surplus, Dakotas, bought as scrap. In July 1946, Tata Airlines was renamed Air India. The Airline started its nonstop services from Bombay to Delhi, Calcutta and Madras with newly-acquired Viking aircraft. In 1948, Tatas floated Air India International, to start their international operations.

In 1952, the Government of India decided to nationalise air services. All existing airlines were merged to build two national carriers—Air India for international routes and Indian Airlines for domestic air services. The two nationalised airlines started operation in 1953.

Air India : India has two major official national airlines—one, Air India which operates primarily on international routes and two, Indian Airlines which is predominantly a domestic Airline. Apart from these there are a couple of private airlines in the field. Domestically, Air India connects major metropolitan cities— Mumbai, Delhi, Kolkata, Chennai, Thiruananthpuram, Kochi, Kozhkode, Hyderabad, Bangalore, Goa and Ahmedabad—to provide international connections. It has forty-five on-line and sixty off-line stations all over India and the world. It flies to forty-five cities in forty-five countries, in four continents, some on code sharing basis. At present, it does not fly to Australia. It has modern fleet consisting of the latest Boeing 707-4000 and Airbuses. It is now phasing out its old Boeing 707. In recent times, its growth has been retarded due to overstaffing poor management. Currently it has been running in the red.

Presently, Air India is Government-owned carrier with a Board of Directors nominated by the Government—normally headed by a Chairman-cum-Managing Director. Irked by massive losses, the Government has decided to disinvest its equity in the carrier and worldwide tenders have been called for a strategic partner. The Government believes that by bringing in new management and greater investment, Air India will be better operated and also be profitable. Presently, Air India flies some 2.5 million passengers annually—not enough for a country of the size of India. Airlines of much smaller countries like Singapore and Thailand have done better.

Air India runs two subsidiary companies—Air India Charters as well as a hotel company which operates four deluxe hotels in Delhi, Mumbai and Srinagar—the Centaur hotels. It is also proposed that Air India should quit hotel business. And, most of its hotel have been sold.

Air India has come a long way from that far-off day, way back in 1932 when all it had was one palm-thatched hut at Juhu Airport, two single-engined planes—a Puss Moth and a leapord Moth—one full-time pilot and two apprentice mechanics. From its inception, Air India has followed a policy of self-sufficiency. This has been a matter of necessity for the simple reason that Air India is located away from the main centres of air transport activity in the world, and the planes could not be sent out for either maintenance or major checks without disrupting services and subsequent loss of revenue.

This has meant a considerable investment and often expensive facilities, but the major advantage of this policy has been that the airline now possesses one of the most modern and up-to-date engineering bases in the world, capable of handling complete work on the fleet.

Air India has never relied on foreign pilots and over the years, has been able to train its own pilots, engineers and technicians in-house.

The first decade of the twenty-first century will certainly see some momentous changes in the structure, financing and management of Air India.

Indian Airlines : Started in 1953, Indian Airlines is one of the world's largest domestic airlines and Asia's second largest. With a wholly owned subsidiary, Alliance Airlines, it operates two hundred and seventy flights a day, carrying some twenty-three thousand passengers to various domestic and international destinations. It has a fleet of fifty-six aircrafts including thirty airbus A-320s. Indian Airlines connects sixty-three station-cities in India and sixteen abroad—from Kuwait in the west to Singapore in the east. The neighbouring countries connected by Indian Airlines include Pakistan, Bangladesh, Sri Lanka, Thailand, Afghanistan, Myanmar, Malaysia and Sharjah. Indian Airlines is phasing out most of its old aircrafts and trying to induct new ones. Together with its subsidiary, Alliance Air, it carries 7.5 million passengers annually. For the financial year 1999, Indian Airlines had a turnover of US$850 million, profit after tax US$43.2 million and net worth US$22 million. The turnover of its subsidiary for the same period amounted to US$140 million.

It has well-developed infrastructure built over the years to carry out all checks and maintenance of aircrafts. It has a complete set -up for the training of its pilots as well as mechanics. In fact, many of the pilots currently working with private airlines as well as some foreign carriers have been trained by Indian Airlines.

For its own reasons, Indian Airlines charges foreigners dollar fares which are higher than the Indian rupee fares. Being a Government-owned Airline, it has to offer subsidised fares in less developed areas of the country like eastern India. It worked well when the Airline had monopoly over domestic skies but now it makes it a lossmaking proposition. Interestingly, Indian Airlines was the first in Asia to employ woman pilots. Today, it has nineteen women pilots of whom six are commanders.

Besides, Indian Airlines offers fifty per cent discount to students flying to their schools and colleges during holidays and back. Same facility is given to the Armed Forces of India. Senior citizens too get fifty per cent off.

Special Fare Package

Foreign tourists to India get special fares of US$750 for unlimited travel for twenty-one days. Foreigners have special fares for shorter durations. Anyone in the age group between twelve and thirty can avail a twenty-five per cent discount on Economy Class US dollar fares on domestic and Indo-Nepal Sector. Groups travelling together for a common purpose/interest are offered ten per cent off on specified international and connecting domestic services. Offered also on international travel within SAARC countries, Bangladesh, India, Maldives, Nepal, Pakistan and Sri Lanka, if touching a minimum of three countries.

India Wonder Fares : The India Wonder fares consist of four fares, each priced at US $300 which allows unlimited travel for one week within the north, south, east, or west India regions. It gives one year round Economy Class travel between any cities in the region of your choice, provided you don't touch the same point more than once, except for purpose of transfer/connection.

Indian Airlines has modernised its reservation system—providing instant reservation to passengers through its computer terminals. Travel agents too have their computer terminals linked to Indian Airlines. Besides, Indian Airlines is participating in mega CRS Systems like SABRE, GALILEO, ABACUS and GETS, etc. It makes Indian Airlines easily accessible to travel agents as well as consumers all over the world.

Indian Airlines has passed through a difficult period in recent years with the opening up of the Indian skies to domestic competition—its accumulated losses exceed Rs 1000 crore, caused by overstaffing—twenty-two thousand employees, unionisation of the staff and other factors.

The Governments of India has, therefore, decided to dilute its equity in the airlines. A disinvestment programme has been announced—it plans to disinvest twenty-six per cent of its shareholding in the Indian Airlines to a joint venture/strategic partner. In addition, the Government of India proposes to sell twenty-five per cent of its shareholding to the employees, to create a stake for them. Management may also go in the hands of the strategic partner.

It will be interesting to watch the new developments in the Indian Airlines.

Alliance Air : In January 1982, India saw the emergence of a new third-Level Airline—Vayudoot—financed jointly by Indian Airlines and Air India. Its objective mainly was to provide air services in the remote areas of eastern India where the big Indian Airlines planes could not operate economically. The new airline acquired eighteen Dorniers—eighteen seater aircrafts from the former West Germany. Indian Airlines also leased out its Avros, etc.

But, the Vayudoot strayed from its original objectives of providing air services to the remote areas and instead spread its wings to all parts of India, providing as many as hundred stops— surpassing the network of its parent airlines, Indian Airlines which flew to about sixty cities.

The results were on expected lines—it piled up huge losses and had ultimately to be merged in Indian Airlines. Vayudoot is no more now.

But Indian Airlines revived one of its old subsidiaries— Allied Services Ltd—and started operating it under the brand name of Alliance Air. It is a lean, no frill airlines, no hot meals, etc. Its ground requirements including reservations were taken care of by the Indian Airlines, the overheads were negligible. The new airlines got most of the Boeing 737 planes from the Indian Airlines and connects over thirty stations.

Indian Airlines had undergone huge losses because the private airlines had poached as many as one hundred and sixty of its trained pilots—mainly Boeing commanders and the utilisation of Indian Airlines Boeing fleet was reduced to minimal. Now, some of the commanders poached by private airline have returned and more new pilots were trained and paid the best wages in India. Alliance has since become a profitable airline—its fares are the same as that of the Indian Airlines.

The aim in floating a new airline was to improve efficiency by running a lean organisation with less overheads. They have succeeded.

Private Airlines on Boon

In 1990, India declared an 'Open Sky' policy which implied that private parties could launch and operate airlines in the country. But, the 'Open Sky' policy was not so open. Private airlines could not operate as scheduled carriers, as the law provided Indian Airlines the monopoly of the domestic skies. Initially, these airlines operated as Air Taxis Services. Later, some ten airlines were licensed to operate as scheduled carriers. They had a great success as they provided an alternative to the badly bruised Indian Airlines, which lost some thirty per cent of its traffic to private domestic carriers. But, their golden period did not last long as Indian Airlines changed its strategy and the Government forced the private carriers to run also on unprofitable non-trunk routes as Indian Airlines was obliged to do. The new order cut into their profits. Some of them are now passing through a bad patch and have since folded including East-West Airlines, Modi Luft, NEPC Airlines.

Jet Airways : The only profitable private airline functioning since May 1993 is Jet Airways. With a fleet of thirty aircrafts, it has flown ten million passengers during the last eight years. It has about one hundred and ninety-five flights daily to thirty-seven cities in India. It provides world-class service

It also offers discounted dollar fares to foreign passengers.

Sahara Airlines : Sahara Airlines is yet another successful private carrier giving a tough competition to Indian Airlines and Jet Airways. It connects twenty-five destinations with the most modern fleet.

Taking advantage of the liberal policy of the Government of India in domestic aviation, Tata applied for running a domestic airline with forty-nine per cent equity base of Singapore Airlines. The Government of India has not yet cleared the project on the plea that they would not like foreign airlines equity in the aviation sector.

Now, the Tatas are candidates for Indian Airlines take over with their equity more than that of Singapore Airlines.

Airport Authority of India

In 1994, by an Act passed by the Indian Parliament, the Government of India set up an Airport Authority of India (AAI) to manage both the domestic and international airports of the country. There are more than sixty airports in the country.

Earlier, there were two authorities for the management of Indian airports. While the International Airport Authority of India, set up in 1972, managed the international airports— Delhi, Mumbai, Kolkata, Chennai—later Thiruvananthapuram was added—the National Airport Authority managed domestic airports. Prior to 1972, all airports in the country were run by the Department of Civil Aviation—a wing of the Ministry of Civil Aviation.

The International Airport Authority of India, a public sector organisation was highly profitable—but the National Airport Authority of India, also a public sector was starved of funds, as its sources of income were limited. In 1990, the then Minister of Civil Aviation, late Madhavrao Scindia, took a decision to merge the two authorities which sometimes worked at cross-purposes and duplicated each others roles.

The merger took place in 1994 and the profits from international airports are now ploughed back in the development of national airports. In recent years, some of the domestic airports have been upgraded. The new development has also attracted private capital in building the airports as has happened in the case of Kochi, which is already an international airport. It is also proposed to develop a new international airport in Bangalore with private sector investment.

It is estimated that the turnover of the merged authority will exceeds Rs 1400 crore. In the year 2000, the international airports were handling sixteen million international and another sixteen million domestic passengers. Of the one hundred and fifteen domestic airports only fifty are functional—they are handling only sixteen million passengers annually.

The World Bank experts have estimated in 1995 that the Indian airports should handle three hundred million passengers by 2001—a highly exaggerated estimate. The Airport Authority of India has acquired good reputation and has built several airports in different parts of the world.

Future of India's Airports : Although India's international airports have had improvement in standards, facilities and technical equipment, it has been a slow and tardy process, mainly due to financial constraints of the Government. Our international airports are overcrowded and the growth facilities too are not upto the international mark.

India is still not aiming too high for upgradation of its airports, as evident from the speech of the A. H. Jung, Director General, Civil Aviation, Government of India (late 2000). He said, "Our future plans for Indian airports would certainly not make India another Changi (Singapore), but provide basic facilities in an efficient manner."

He disclosed that a major change in the air is privatisation. Ministry of Civil Aviation, will soon invite bids to lease out Delhi, Mumbai, Chennai and Kolkata airports to private investors.

It was proposed to have a second module for the international terminal at Delhi, with an annual handling capacity of 6.6 million passengers sufficient, to meet the requirements till 2015—at the rate of six per cent growth annually.

The Delhi ILS was being upgraded to enable passenger planes to land and take-off during heavy winter fog. Fog virtually disrupts flying in and out of India in December-January every year. The Government was also exploring the idea of augmenting the revenue of airports by making good commercial use of airport space specially in the area of duty-free shopping. In the pacific region, six per cent of the airport revenue comes for non-aeronautical use.

Indian airports handled thirty million passengers during 1999-2000 an increase of five per cent over the previous year. Delhi had the largest share of passengers—twenty-one per cent and handled the largest number of foreign visitors to India.

Department of Civil Aviation : The Civil Aviation Department, a part of the Ministry of Civil Aviation, regulates aviation in India and carries out dialogues with foreign Governments for bilateral rights. The head of this department is called Director General of Civil Aviation. The department issues and renews licences to pilots. It is also entrusted with the safety of aviation in India.

Air India, Indian Airlines, and the Pawan Hans work under the discipline of the Ministry of Civil Aviation, though notionally these are autonomous public sector organisations. Interference by the minister and the bureaucrats is not uncommon as under the present set-up, the minister is supposed to be responsible to the Parliament for the efficient management of these organisations.

The Government has amended the Indian Air Corporation Act, 1953, to prepare the ground for the gradual privatisation of both Air India and Indian Airlines. The monopoly of the national carriers has now ended. Private sector airlines are functioning along with Indian Airlines with equal rights as scheduled carriers.

Domestic Air Travel Exceeds : Domestic Air Travel has been growing in India at a fast rate since liberalisation of Indian economy and opening up of the Indian skies in the continent, to private airlines. After a slower growth in late nineteenth century, it was up by ten per cent in 2000 to 13.2 million. Air cargo capacity in 2000, too has been enhanced up, by about fifteen per cent. On international sector, an additional seventeen thousand seats per week were added in 2000, according to D.G.C.A. sources.

Computerised Reservation System (CRS) : Computerised Reservation System (CRS) means a computerised system containing information about airline schedules, flight availability, fares and related services, i.e., advance seat selection, boarding passes, frequent flier's preferences inventory, field management, departure control, pro- rata calculations, market analysis, etc.

The system helps the airlines and travel agents to make airline reservations and issue tickets to passengers. Computer terminal facilities are made available by the owning airlines to subscribers, like travel agents, airlines and business houses.

In view of the importance of information technology in tourism.

British Airways

From a rapidly deteriorating airline in the early eighties British Airways achieved the distinction of being one of the most successful airlines in the world by 1990. Most major airlines have a similar product, but not necessarily the quality of service or the ability to manage the people it is supposed to serve. Failure in providing service and meeting consumer demands leads to customer apathy. By rational management systems and intensive training of its staff, British Airways has transformed itself into an 'Airline of the Year', perhaps one of the most dynamic and most profitable at present.

Airlines were generally operationally-oriented because of the dramatic rate of technical change. Competition was largely controlled because Governments were, in several cases, the owners of airlines. They could influence the development of routes and negotiated bilateral agreements with other Governments to the advantage of their national carrier. This led to regulation of capacity, frequency and fares. IATA also served as an international control body that regulated the industry and controlled tariff.

However, a number of significant events brought about changes in the airline market in the seventies. Increase in oil prices in 1973 followed by another hike in oil prices by the end of the decade, interrupted the steady rate of growth in the airline industry. Costs increased while the demand for air travel slowed down, bringing less revenue and smaller profits.

At the same time, charter companies expanded their network considerably. With lower overheads, they were able to reduce the price of holiday travel and diverted passengers from scheduled to charter airlines. The emergence of liberalisation policies, first in the USA and later in Europe, only made matters worse.

The deregulation policies of the US Government had a dramatic effect on American domestic carriers in the late seventies. The European Economic Community (EEC) extended support to a similar policy in Europe in 1979 and subsequently reaffirmed it.

The move towards liberalisation led to increased competition allowing more airlines to enter the market, which resulted in lower fares.

As a result of these influences, the air transport market is now different and is trying to free itself of the Government controls which had bugged it in the past.

There are now more airlines competing on the same routes. New airlines are emerging and creating new market opportunities. Customers, on their part, are demanding higher standards of service from the airlines and they get it.

Passengers are more discerning because they now have more experience of air travel. With an increased number of carriers to choose from, they are in a position to expect better service and that too at lower fares.

This means their demands are changing quickly and airlines have to rise to these challenges if they want to market their services successfully. Therefore, airlines must study what success can be achieved by identifying the changing demands correctly and meeting them without upsetting the needs to show profits. That is what British Airways did when it was in a spot due to escalating costs and dwindling profits.

At the beginning of the eighties, British Airways had major problems. Costs were rising faster than yields which, in turn, did not keep pace with inflation. Profitability was low and staff number too many, which often happens in all Government-owned airlines. British Airways, it seemed, was destined to remain a loss-making enterprise. The first step to change course was the British Government's decision to let the airline go private in stages.

At this critical juncture, Sir Colin Marshall took over as the chief executive of British Airways. He brought about a miraculous transformation in the fortunes of the airline, with his immediate concerns being rationalisation of staff strength and change in the attitude of the staff towards customers.

After a thorough analysis of the difficulties, the new management set the corporate goal for British Airways, of developing it into the best airline in the world, because only by aiming for the highest standards could they hope for achieving long-term success.

First, the productivity was improved. The work-force was reduced from fifty-nine thousand to thirty-seven thousand more flexible working conditions were negotiated; old aircrafts were replaced by new ones and aircraft utilisation improved.

This provided a sound base. But, it was essential to set up a new organisation to meet the needs of the market and to serve customers better. This was introduced in July 1983.

The chain of management was shortened, younger people were appointed to senior jobs and changes in management style introduced to improve overall managerial performance. A new pay structure was introduced to link rewards to productivity.

The new organisation made it possible for the airline to move quickly to respond to customer needs in any area of the world. It enabled British Airways to anticipate rather than react to these needs and enabled them to lead the market in the provision of good services. Instead of providing services which they tried to sell, they found their customers designing the services that they wanted to buy.

At the hub of the organisation are the eight mainline market centres, built around the principal geographic areas of the British Airways network and the sources of passenger revenue, and three separate businesses covering cargo, charters and tours. To provide them with the essential support services, a central marketing organisation was established, offering sales and reservation services: planning, advertising and promotion.

All staff of the British Airways were given training in dealing with customers more effectively. The 'Putting People First' courses were introduced which proved successful. These courses helped in changing the attitude of the staff and the image of British Airways changed among the people who fly frequently and it acquired the reputation of a friendly and efficient airline.

The change in the attitude of the staff has helped in gaining the airline numerous awards, including the 'Airline of the Year' award. Refresher courses for putting people first have begun, and 'Managing People First' courses aimed at improving management performance were also organised.

"While changing ourselves, we have changed our whole image with newly-designed aircrafts, shops, tickets, vehicles and uniforms."

"An unprecedented number of new routes have been introduced during the last few years to meet the requirements of passengers and to improve levels of productivity. New products and services have been examined. An additional fleet of quiet, fuel-efficient aircrafts have been acquired to meet the challenge of the 'twenty first century' ", a British Airways spokesman said.

To sum up, improved productivity means better control over costs and increased profits, improved management techniques means better and more sensitivity to the needs of staff and customers.

'Putting People First' implies a better relationship between the staff and customers and, therefore, better service. A market-led organisation leads to a better understanding of what the customer's needs are and a quicker response by way of a better service. The new image of the airline demonstrates most graphically that it has changed.

British Airways has to deal with a much more competitive environment. Now, they have to anticipate rather than react to change. British Airways is now a totally private company with a fair amount of its shares in the hands of the employees, who have a stake in the company.

Soon after the Gulf War in 1991, British Airways was the first to launch a worldwide marketing blitz to assure people that travel was no longer unsafe. They threw a $16 million party in the skies on 18 April, 1990, for about fifty thousand people, all free travellers.

On that day, British Airways gave away complimentary seats on all its flights to and from Great Britain, under what was termed as the greatest publicity blitz in the history of civil aviation in the world. Some six million people worldwide had bid in a British Airways prize draw for twenty-five thousand seats on offer to Great Britain and for twenty-five thousand seats from Britain to places all over the globe. Six thousand people flew out of the USA and seven hundred from India on this free marketing bonanza offered by the airline to the travelling public. It was a fantastic marketing idea for British Airways to instil confidence in the travelling public and it worked.

Although the airline industry was in a bad way in the wake of the Gulf War, British Airways' marketing followed by other airlines' similar attempts, changed the course for the better. Travellers gained confidence.

One is, therefore, not surprised when British Airways bagged the two top US awards at the American Society of Travel Agents (ASTA) World Convention at Taipei in October 1991. The first was the 'Rex Award' from the ASTA Agency Management Magazine for its service to agents and clients—best sales material and support, best toll-free telephones service to agents and clients, and improved relationship with agencies. The second award was from *Travel and Leisure* and *Travel Weekly* magazines combined. The magazines commended the airline for its consistency in honouring reservations and for telling agents of fare changes before informing the public. The runners-up for this particular award were Lufthansa and Swissair, both equally efficient airlines.

Apparently, British Airways has a consistent marketing policy based on quality of service. Their television commercial shown in different parts of the world—"British Airways brings 24 million people together...."—Conveys a message which does not surprise the viewers and is no empty boast.

To attract Indian customers, the British Airways has the maximum number of flights out of India—operating from four metropolitan cities—Delhi, Mumbai, Kolkata and Chennai. It is the only foreign carrier which flies out of the four airports of India. For its flights out of India, British Airways has Hindi-speaking staff and all announcements are made in Hindi. Indian meals are regularly provided as options.

Fast Facts about British Airways

- Destinations served worldwide—one hundred and seventy-four in eighty-three countries.
- Number of passengers carried in 1995—seventy-five million.
- Overall load factor—66.8 per cent.
- Fleet Strength—two hundred and thirty-five, a variety of Boeings, Airbuses, Lockheed Tristars, etc.
- Regularity—98.7 per cent.
- Punctuality—seventy-three per cent.
- Flights in and out of India—Every week: Mumbai-London-Mumbai—seven; Delhi-London-Delhi-seven; Chennai-London-Chennai-two; Kolkata-London-Kolkata seven. Besides, there are seven flights to Hong Kong every week and two flights to Singapore every week. Next to Air India, British Airways have the largest number of flights out of India to the west.

Note: 11 September, 2002 attack on WTC did have an impact on the British Airways and ground realities may have changed somewhat.

Outcoming Airlines

Here is yet another case history of a successful airline which reflects the future trends—bigger and larger airlines—joined together by mergers, networking or code-sharing, etc. The United is, today the worlds' largest airline and profitable too. It carried the largest number of passengers both domestic and international in the year 2000, as you will see from a chart in this chapter.

The following fact-sheet speaks for itself:

Destinations : A total of one hundred and thirty destinations in twenty-six countries and two US territories—Argentina, Australia, Belgium, Brazil, Canada, Chile, Costa Rica, El Salvador, France, Germany, Guatemala, Italy, Japan, Korea, Mexico, the Netherlands, New Zealand, Peoples Republic of China including Hong Kong, Puerto Rico, Singapore, St. Thomas, Taiwan, Thailand, UK, USA, Uruguay, and Venezuela. Soon India too.

Employees : 101,500 including 10,000 pilots.

Average number of passengers carried daily in 1999—226,862

Total number of passengers flown in 1999—125.3 billion

Total cargo carried in 1999—3.1 billion tons.

Size of the fleet—614. (Boeings, Airbuses, McDonnell Douglas)

Average age of the fleet—10.1 years.

Net revenue in 1999—US$18.0 billion.

Net earnings : US$1.24 billion.

But the company has been through thick and thin. One of the oldest Air Transport Company in the USA, it began dabbling in aviation matters since Orville and Wilbur Wright brothers showed the world that it was possible to fly a plane. Its interests intensified soon after World War I in 1918— starting as an airmail carrier in the twenties. A few years later, as the commercial flying started, United became an independent Air Transport Corporation in mid-thirties under a new President William Allen Patterson, who presided over its destiny for twenty-nine years. During World War II in 1939 - 45, it trained thousands of Air Force and Navy personnel in ground handling.

In 1968, UAL Inc. was set up as a holding company with United as wholly owned subsidiary. The next twenty years were a period of turbulence when United even lost money failing to get permission to fly to the Asia Pacific.

However, the scene changed as United prepared itself to move into the new millennium. It provided leadership to the aviation industry by innovative approach. It met the challenge of low-cost carriers and deregulation in the USA in 1978 by introducing its no-frills shuttle services, between the east and west coast in 1994, which was a success. Then followed the Star Alliance Global Partnership with four international carriers—Air Canada, Lufthansa, SAS, Thai—later joined by Varig. It gave United the greatest reach in the world. Next year in 1995, United strengthened its global presence by introducing mainline round—the world service starting from the west coast of the USA through Bangkok, Delhi, London on to the east coast. The service was subsequently suspended.

Another strong point of the United was that in 1994, its new President, Gerald Greenwald, transformed the corporate culture from command and control philosophy, to involving employees as partners and share-holders of the company. Employee's representatives were brought on the Board of Directors of the company—first from among the employees in the USA—and later from the rest of the world. This gave the employees a stake in the company and greater loyalty.

Simultaneously, the company embraced new service ethics—the Customers Satisfaction philosophy. The new philosophy attracted more and more frequent fliers from all parts of the world. This was to be the new global image and the new advertising theme of the United.

United, no doubt, is a high flying and successful world airline in the new millennium—ready to meet new challenges of global airlines. United has announced to that it will soon reintroduce its daily services through the Indian capital—east and west. That may help Indian tourism by overcoming the shortage of seats on international routes and out of India.

A Case Study

***Pan Am** : The world's oldest and most successful commercial carrier —PAN AM—died a quiet death in December 1991 after sixty-four years of operations.*

PAN AM became a victim of bad management decisions. We give below the story of ups and downs of Pan Am to show that the operation of an airline is no glamour business.

Pan Am was founded in 1927 by Juan Trippe. The carrier began flying mail routes. Its first scheduled international flight was between Key West, Florida and Havana, Cuba.

By 1930, it had grown to be the world's largest air transport company.

In the decade that followed, Pan Am was America's flagship carrier and the first with regular service across the Atlantic and the Pacific Oceans. Trippe hired the legendary aviator, Charles Lindbergh, to scout many of Pan Am's early overseas routes.

Pan Am's Clipper flights set industry standards for luxury travel, such as hot meals served on china dishes. Later, Pan Am picneered such fine touches as first-class service and in-flight movies.

Commanding the international skies, Pan Am even built airfields on small Pacific Islands, so its aircraft could refuel on the week-long flights between San Francisco and Manila.

It carried President Franklin D. Roosevelt to Casablanca in 1943, on the first flight by a US President. It ferried the White House press corps, beginning with the Eisenhower administration.

Other Pan Am firsts included: becoming the first US airline to fly a commercial jetliner, the B-707 in 1958. In 1966, founder Tripppe became one of the first to place orders with the Boeing company for the revolutionary new 747 Jumbo Jets.

In 1964, Pan Am even began accepting reservations for flights to the moon—five years before anyone had ever landed on the moon!

As the story goes, an Austrian journalist asked a travel agent in Vienna to book him a seat to the moon. The travel agent suggested Aeroflot and Pan Am. The Soviet carrier responded in jest that its first flight to the moon was full, but Pan Am accepted the reservation. It even went as far as to predict its first flight would depart around the year 2000. By the time Pan Am closed its wait list in 1971, some ninety-three thousand people from more that ninety countries had reserved seats to the moon.

Ever since World War II, it had faced growing competition in the international skies. Its rivals included Trans World Airlines, (TWA), United Airlines and foreign carriers, but Pan Am had a successful run.

After the US airline industry was deregulated in 1978, in an effort to boost competition, Pan Am found itself in need of domestic routes to feed its international system.

It bought National Airlines in 1979 for US$432 million, a price seen by many as too high. The purchase also brought with it a lot of staff that Pan Am could not use. It was the beginning of an end.

In the 1980s, Pan Am began shedding assets to stay aloft. First, it sold its landmark headquarters above bustling Grand Central Terminal in New York in 1980 for US$400 million. In 1981, it sold its Inter-Continental hotel chain for US$500 million. In 1985, its crown jewel, Pacific routes, went to United Airlines for US$750 million.

A deadly blow hit Pan Am on 21 December, 1988, when a terrorist bomb exploded aboard the Pan Am Flight 103 over Lockerbie, Scotland. The tragedy left two hundred and seventy people dead. The airline's public image took a nose-dive.

The asset sales continued. In 1990, Pan Am sold most of its prized routes to London, to United for US$290 million. Pan Am looked around for a buy out or a merger partner, but none was forthcoming. Pan Am was now forced to seek US federal bankruptcy court protection in January 1991. The airline's executives said they were optimistic that Pan Am could keep flying.

But the Gulf War and the recession proved lethal. Leisure and business travel slumped and its earnings slid. In October 1991, Pan Am reached a deal with Delta Airlines that was designed to keep the historic carrier flying. Atlanta-based Delta agreed to provide more than US$400 million in financing in exchange for a forty-five per cent stake in Pam Am.

Under the terms of the deal, Delta won most of Pan Am's European routes and its north-east shuttle connecting Boston, New York and Washington DC. Pan Am, for its part, would slim down into a smaller carrier, based in Miami and serving Latin America, where it had started.

But Delta would not prove to be a good partner. In early December, it quit its end of the refinancing deal.

One day later, Pan Am was no more.

The end came so suddenly that some passengers were seated on board planes waiting take-off. Instead, they were abruptly told to get off. Others were waiting in ticket lines only to learn that Pan Am had no more flights, anywhere, anytime.

Pan Am was a legend. The legend is no more—a major victim of deregulation in the USA. Old timers cannot forget the Pan Am legend.

Jet Airways : Launched in May 1993—Jet Airways has emerged as the most preferred airline for domestic travellers in India. Founded by a young entrepreneur, Naresh Goel, with a long and extensive experience of airlines marketing, it has been giving run for its money to Indian Airlines—the fifty year old Indian domestic carrier in the public sector. Since its inception, the airlines has won some awards of excellence from international bodies.

Among its achievement today the following features stand out :

- Has one of the youngest fleet in the world—average age three years in 2001.
- one hundred and ninety-five flights daily to thirty-seven destinations in 2001.
- An excellent record for on-time performance.
- Friendly, caring in-flight and ground services.
- Good in-flight cuisine during flights. Modern fleet of thirty Boeing 737-400/500/700 and 800.

The world-class frequent flying benefits with tie-ups with British Airways, KLM Royal Dutch Airlines and the Northwest Airlines.

Strategy : The Chairman of the company believes that wherever service is introduced, it has to be a daily flight. The passenger should be in no doubt that he could not fly on a given day. The network of Jet Airways links all the four metres—Delhi, Kolkata, Chennai and Mumbai which had centres and there are more than one flight everyday. Based on its strategy, all the hubs are connected to major tourist and business centres in east, west, north and south. Efficiency in management has established the credit worthiness of Jet Airways. Indian Airlines set up Committees to evaluate the available aeroplane for acquisition—they are evaluating inconclusively. In Jet Airways the decisions are instant, hence they acquired the latest planes in Boeing stable. And, they have never defaulted in payment during their short existence.

Philosophy : The Jet Airways philosophy that "We fly people" not the aircrafts, speaks for itself. And that makes them one of the most customer-friendly airline. To achieve this objective, the Jet Airways sought the help of Speedwings—a subsidiary of the British Airways for training its staff in Customer Service Excellence. British Airways is known for its 'People Come First' philosophy.

For training its pilots and mechanics, the Jet Airways uses the facilities of Ansett—the Australian Airline. To make Jet Airways reservations the most accessible, it tied up with Sabre—the world's largest CRS owned by American Airlines. It is also a participant and is co-hosted by other major CRSs of world airlines. Three months after its launch, Jet Airways became an Associate Member of IATA as well as party to its multilateral agreements. It is also a member of IATA Clearing House for settlement of claims. Jet Airways flies from four hubs—Mumbai, Delhi, Kolkata, and Chennai. It has also introduced day-return flights connecting most metro towns.

Since its commencement nine years ago, Jet has become the largest private sector domestic airline in India. The progress has been fast—from four aircrafts in 1993 - 94 to over thirty aircrafts in January 2002; from twelve destinations in 1993 - 94 to thirty-seven destinations today; from twenty-four daily flights in 1993 - 94 to one hundred and ninety-five flights daily today—it has been the result of hard work and superior service.

Jet Airways emphasis on technology and induction of the newest available planes in the Boeing family, has been a key factor in its success.

It has ambitious plans for further expansion to non-metro towns by the induction of smaller planes.

To summarise, for international travel, flying is the most commonly used mode of transport. Today, over fifteen hundred million people travel annually by scheduled air-services and another five hundred million by non-scheduled services like charters. The airlines have been the fastest growing business in the world with an annual growth of seven per cent—now down to four per cent and even less.

To regulate operation of international airlines, there are two major international organisations: International Air Transport Association (IATA) and International Civil Aviation Organisation (ICAO), both established in 1945 and are based in Montreal (Canada).

IATA is the representative organisation of two hundred and fifty scheduled air-carriers, both international and domestic, while ICAO is an inter-governmental organisation representing over one hundred and fifty Governments. ICAO ensures safety of flying all over the world and frames rules and regulations for smooth flying. The rules are ratified by the member Governments. ICAO has consultative status with United Nations.

IATA helps in establishing uniformity of tariffs on international routes and tries to ensure that both member and non-member airlines do not undercut these tariffs. Through the IATA Clearing House, the airlines get paid for the sectors a passenger flies on an airline during his long journey, when he travels on several airlines with only one ticket issued by the originating carrier. Due to the policy of deregulation, and many Governments are allowing their national carriers to privatise, the IATAs disciplinary role has dwindled.

Before 1953, India had more than twenty small private carriers providing poor and indifferent service. The Government nationalised them in 1953 to create two national carriers: one for international operations and the other for domestic flying. India has two national carriers: Air India which normally flies on international routes and Indian Airlines which flies on domestic routes and a few international routes to neighbouring countries. Both the airlines are Government-owned and are managed by a Board of Directors each headed by a Chairman-cum-Managing Director.

Both the carriers have not grown according to the potential of a vast country like India. Liberalisation being the key word today, it is proposed to gradually privatise the two carriers by disinvesting part of Government equity. It may enable the two carriers to speed up their growth by mopping up new resources. Both the carriers are now in bad shape but remedial measures are slow due to vested interests. Disinvestment seems to be the only solution as has been the case with British Airways transformation.

India adopted an 'Open Sky' policy in 1990 and allowed private airlines to start operations in domestic sector. The Indian Airlines' monopoly on domestic skies ended with the passing of an act by the Indian Parliament. Now, Indian Airlines and private airlines compete with each other on an equal footing in the country.

Vayudoot, a third level Government-owned carrier has been closed down and an Indian Airlines subsidiary called Alliance Air operates to some thirty cities using Indian Airlines planes. The objective is to run a lean and profitable airline with little overheads. The new airline is not losing money.

There are several private airlines operating in the country. Jet Airways is the most successful which carried about three million passengers in the year 2000. Sahara Airlines, another private domestic carrier, is doing well.

The civil aviation policy is formulated by the Ministry of Civil Aviation, headed by a minister who is responsible to the Parliament. General rules and regulations pertaining to flying and bilateral aviation agreements with foreign Governments are handled by the Department of Civil Aviation, which, too, is part of the Ministry of Civil Aviation.

To manage airports in the country, there is an Airport Authority of India (AAI) established in 1994. It manages some ninety airports in the country including the international airports. A public sector company, it is profitable. It is also proposed to be privatised.

Before 1994, there were two authorities—one to manage international airports and the other to run domestic airports.

But the Government of India decided to merge them to upgrade country's airports. The new authority is headed by a Chairman-cum-Managing Director and functions under the direction of the Ministry of Civil Aviation.

In order to create new holiday traffic, international and domestic airlines offer discounted fares, i.e., excursion fares, group fares, etc. Charter airlines have been instrumental in bringing holidays within the reach of people with limited budgets. Several countries encourage charter flights to increase their tourism. The economy of charter operations is based on more or less hundred per cent load factor to a destination and back.

Deregulation is a new policy followed by several Governments. They would not like to restrict the number of airlines flying to a destination. They are also against IATA enforcing standard tariffs. These Governments led by the USA, are of the opinion that competition among airlines should help determine fares. This is beneficial to travellers. The policy has helped in reducing airfares and improving services in many countries of the world.

The deregulation has led to the elimination of some of the weaker airlines. There is a tendency towards emergence of strong, mega airlines. There is also a trend towards privatisation of airlines from Government-owned airlines. Britain, Japan, Singapore and New Zealand have totally privatised their national carriers.

Automation or Computer Reservation Systems (CRS) is another development which has revolutionised airlines marketing. The CRSs of airlines include information relating to availability of flights on various participating carriers, hotel accommodation all over the world, car rentals and other tourism related facilities.

10

Global Associations

The international organizations provide a platform where ideas are exchanged and problems of mutual interest discussed. The subject specialists of various disciplines—be it arts, science or commerce—meet together on a common platform and discuss areas of mutual interest. This results in growth, development and promotion of the discipline. For any industry or discipline to develop, an organization is an essential prerequisite as it plays a vital role in its proper planning, development and growth. An organization consists of individuals whose primary role is the achievement of the objectives for which it has been set up. The aim of the organization is to deploy staff into working groups, associating those with similar functions or purposes so as to move efficiently to obtain a desired result from their combined effort. In other words, organization means combination of a group of individuals whose main purpose is to achieve through group action the objectives for which it has been set up.

An organization of a particular discipline having affiliation with an international body greatly helps in the promotion and development of a particular discipline. Global tourism development and promotion is influenced by various international agreements and mutually beneficial bilateral agreements. The various international and regional tourism organizations emerged with the objective of developing and promoting tourism. The role of these organizations in strengthening tourism by means of combined efforts is therefore of vital importance.

The increasingly international character of modern tourism and the growing influence of international agencies in various fields are reflected in the growth and development of international cooperation and organization in tourism. Organizers and the providers of various tourist services, whether in private or public sector, come together at various forums at the international level to discuss and share common problems and arrive at certain conclusions. The providers of tourist services sometimes meet as individuals or as individual firms, but more often when their national sectoral organization is a member of a particular international body which has been set up for general or specific purposes.

There are numerous international organizations existing today. Some of these organizations are specifically concerned with development and promotion of tourism at the international level while others deal with the development and promotion of tourism in a particular region. There are other international organizations which do not concern themselves specifically with tourism but with fields indirectly connected with tourism like airlines, travel agents and the hoteliers.

Cooperative Organizations

The history of cooperative endeavour in tourism can be traced back to the year 1908. Three countries—France, Spain and Portugal— felt the need of pooling their resources in the interest of promoting tourism and founded the Franc Hispano Portuguese Federation of Tourist Association. This might perhaps be considered as the first international tourist organization. Although started in a modest way and limited to a small region in Europe, this association made a beginning in cooperative endeavour in the field of tourism and paved the way for future endeavours on a very large scale.

The need for international collaboration in the field of tourism found favour with many countries in the years following World War I. This need found its expression in setting up in 1924 of the

International Union of Official Organizations for Tourist Propaganda. The first congress of the organization was held at The Hague, the Netherlands, in 1925, and was attended by delegates from national tourist organizations of fourteen European countries. The aims of this congress were to exchange information on tourist publicity, to obtain international customs concessions for the export and import of tourist publicity material and to alleviate frontier formalities or other obstacles to free international tourist traffic. This organization functioned with a considerable degree of success until the eve of the last World War. The International Union of Official Organizations for Tourist Propaganda was the forerunner of the International Union of Official Travel Organizations. In 1946, the representatives of various national tourist organizations met in London and the following year, in 1947, the International Union of Official Travel Organizations (IUOTO) was founded.

Although cooperative endeavour in the field of tourism began as early as in the year 1908 and the international organization formed in the year 1924, the vital encouragement, however, came from the United Nations in 1963. The importance of the work of the international organizations in the field of tourism was recognised by the United Nations Conference on International Travel and Tourism held in Rome, in 1963. The conference recommended that the United Nations should consider the International Union of Official Travel Organizations (IUOTO) as its "main instrument for the promotion of tourism". The encouragement given by the United Nations to IUOTO paved the way for greater cooperation at international level in the field of tourism. India's first contact with the international tourism organizations was, however, established in the year 1950 when it joined the International Union of Official Travel Organizations.

International Union of Official Travel Organizations : It was in 1925 that the international cooperation in tourism development had its beginning. The growth of international tourism in the twenties, and the consequent need for cooperation between national tourist bodies, led to the holding of an international conference in 1925 called by the National Tourist Office of Holland. Representatives of fourteen countries took part in the conference.

Further conferences led to the setting up of the International

Union of National Tourist Propaganda Organizations (IUNTPO) at The Hague. This body sought to promote facilitation and overcome the obstacles to free international tourist traffic; such obstacles having come about as a result of the First World War. IUNTPO, whose general aims were more streamlined than its title, established close contact with the economic committee of the then League of Nations.

With the advent of the Second World War, IUNTPO had to discontinue its activities. It was with the object of contributing to post-War reconstruction that one of its members, the Travel Association of Great Britain and Northern Ireland, decided in the spring of 1946 to call a world conference of national tourist organizations to discuss the restoration and reconstruction of travel facilitation destroyed by the War. The conference took place in London in October 1946 and the following year, in 1947, the International Union of Official Travel Organizations (IUOTO) was founded. The organization represented over one hundred national tourist offices of various countries as full members and about eighty-eight national and international organizations, of both public and private sector, as associate members. It was at that time the only organization whose activities related to every aspect of tourism throughout the world. One of its major tasks was the stimulation and coordination of tourism development. The category of full members was restricted to national tourist organizations or other organizations set up to promote the development of tourism established or recognised by the governments of the countries. The category of associate members was confined to international or national organizations, either commercial or non-commercial, representing tourist interest or interested in promotion of tourism.

The IUOTO was the only international organization which grouped together the governmental or official tourist organizations of all parts of the world on the basis of one for each country and territory. The principal aim of the organization was to stimulate and increase the free flow of persons in the interest of economic development and to strengthen social and cultural relations. This

it tried to do byway of resolving the problems arising in the field of tourist movements and in the adoption of a common policy amongst the members for all questions dealing with international travel. The organization tried in various ways to develop the tourist industry in the member countries, and particularly by promoting measures on a national as well as on an international level aimed at reducing travel barriers and stimulating the movement of travellers.

A technical and specialised organization, IUOTO was granted consultative status by the United Nations. The supreme body of the IUOTO was the General Assembly which held its meeting once a year. It had various committees and commissions which were assigned different subjects. The executive committee consisted of full members, while the regional commissions covered specific areas. The technical commissions aimed at examining all problems on a universal scale. The Secretariat General, whose headquarters were located at Geneva in Switzerland, was responsible for ensuring liaison between the members.

General Assembly : The General Assembly, which consisted of full and associate members, was a sovereign body of the IUOTO. It met once a year. It elected the president and the vice president of the IUOTO, the members of the executive committee and the auditors and decided upon the applications for new membership. Laying down general policy of the organization and the actions to be carried out was another important function of the General Assembly.

Executive Committee : The Executive Committee consisted of eighteen full members, representing the various geographical areas and, in an ex-officio capacity, the presidents of the regional and technical commissions. Presided over by the president of the IUOTO and assisted by the vice presidents, the Executive Committee was responsible to the General Assembly for the direction of the affairs of the IUOTO.

Regional Commissions : The following regional commissions were created by the IUOTO:

(a) The Regional Travel Commission for Europe included the countries of western and eastern Europe. The countries of western Europe were also grouped in the European Travel Commission which was an independent body responsible in particular for the collective publicity campaigns carried out in the United States of America.

(b) The African Travel Commission was responsible for tourism in African areas which had vast possibilities for growth.

(c) The Regional Travel Commission for the Pacific and East Asia had members who were also members of the Pacific Area Travel Association (PATA), which had accepted to act as the regional commission for the Pacific and the east Asian areas.

(d) The South Asian Travel Commission was responsible for developing modern travel facilities in a very extensive area which had become travel conscious.

(e) The Middle East Travel Commission was responsible for developing travel facilities in the area. It had also created sub- commissions of the Arab and non-Arab countries.

(f) The Regional Travel Commission for the Americas was created following the acceptance of the Inter-American Travel·Congress to act as regional travel commission of the IUOTO for the American continent as a whole.

Technical Committees : IUOTO had the following technical committees:

(1) The Committee on the Elimination of Travel Barriers was concerned with the easing up of passport and visa requirements, frontier formalities including restrictions on the free circulation of publicity material, health regulations, taxes borne directly or indirectly by the tourists and tourist industry, currency controls and other matters which slow down travel.

(2) The Research Committee was charged with studying international travel statistics as well as carrying out other special studies with the assistance of the Advisory Committee.

(3) The Travel Plant Committee was responsible for studies on hotels as well as motels, hotel accommodation and classification, standardization of hotel guides, state aid to the hotel industry, the training of hotel personnel and additional means of accommodation.

(4) The Committee on Travel Development offered assistance to member countries in the field of travel, counselled national tourist offices on publicity activities, dealt with social tourism and youth and credit travel. The committee also dealt with travel films, which came to be regarded as one of the most important means of tourist publicity.

(5) The Transport Committee was responsible for examining the existing conditions in the field of rail, road, sea and air transportation and suggesting better facilities and improvements. It studied and recommended measures to improve the conditions and facilities available at airports, seaports and land frontier entry points.

Secretariat General : The Secretariat General, which was located in Geneva, was the principal executive body for the decisions of the assembly and the executive committee as well as the presidency. It ensured the liaison between the members of the IUOTO, carried out the studies entrusted to it by the IUOTO members and was charged with the administration. It maintained contact with other international organizations. It produced various IUOTO publications and ensured the functioning of the Tourist Documentation Centre.

IUOTO had closer cooperation with the United Nations Economic and Social Council (ECOSOC), the World Health Organization (WHO), the International Labour Organization (ILO), the International Civil Aviation Organization (ICAO) and the Inter-Governmental Maritime Consultative Organization (IMCO). It also had permanent links with the regional commissions of the United Nations.

The organization was set up with the following objectives:

(i) To promote the economic development of countries through tourism.

(ii) To enhance the social and cultural role of tourism in the life of nations.

(iii) To further the vital contribution of tourism to international trade.

(iv) To foster the steady expansion of international tourist flow.

(v) To supply its members with the results of the permanent tourist market research to enable them to keep abreast of development in this field.

(vi) To protect the interests of tourists and the tourist industry.

(vii) To gain recognition of the value of tourism as a means of promoting international understanding and world peace. In order to achieve its objectives, the organization undertook various activities like monitoring and identifying trends in world tourism, studies on travel demands, market trends, tourist motivation, surveys of environmental effects of travel expansion and formulation of recommendations for the protection of natural and cultural resources. Other activities included acting as clearing house for tourist information, keeping its members informed of tourism development and its economic and social aspects, publication of material, fostering research in the field of tourism, organizing vocational training programmes and promoting the implementation of international agreements.

IUOTO's dynamic activities resulted in countless significant achievements. Some of the achievements were undertaken jointly with other organizations. These included preparation and participation in the United Nations on Customs Facilities and Tourism (1954), initiation, preparation and participation in the United Nations Conference on International Travel and Tourism in Rome (1963) and initiation and realization of International Tourist Year (1967). Besides establishing the Tourist Documentation Centre, the IUOTO has been responsible for organizing various international travel research seminars and workshops. Another significant achievement of IUOTO has been the establishment of the International Centre for Advanced Tourism Studies at Turin, Italy and organization of interdepartmental or specialized seminars on marketing, management, physical planning and promotion. It had also organized correspondence courses for the staff working in the field of tourism. Annual compilation and publication of official international travel statistics is yet another significant achievement of the IUOTO.

The IUOTO was the only non-governmental organization whose activities covered every sector of tourism throughout the world. The organization made a pioneering effort in the stimulation and coordination of tourism development at the international level. This pioneering task of the organization is now being carried out by the World Tourism Organization. The World Tourism Organization came into existence as a result of the transformation of IUOTO on January *2,* 1975. It was called upon to succeed IUOTO.

India joined the International Union of Official Travel Organizations in 1950.

Organization for World Tourism

The World Tourism Organization (WTO), an inter-governmental technical body dealing with all aspects of tourism, began its legal existence on January 2,1975. It was born of the International Union of Official Travel Organizations (IUOTO). The swift expansion of travel had created the need for a world body able to deal with tourism problems at the government level, and this led to the transformation of IUOTO into WTO. Like its predecessor, the WTO has a very emphatic technical character, essentially creative and dynamic, performing a well-defined service for its member states. The aims of the organization, its *raison d'eter*, are defined with clarity in Article 3 of the statute which is divided into three sections:

(i) The fundamental aim of the organization shall be the promotion and development of tourism with a view to contributing to economic development, international understanding, peace, prosperity, and universal respect for, and observance of, human rights and fundamental freedoms for all without distinction to either race, sex, language or religion. The organization shall take all appropriate action to attain this objective.

(ii) In pursuing this aim, the organization shall pay particular attention to the interests of the developing countries in the field of tourism.

(iii) In order to establish its central role in the field of tourism, the organization shall establish and maintain effective collaboration with the appropriate organs of the United Nations and its specialized agencies. In this connection the organization shall seek a cooperative relationship with and participation in the activities of the United Nations Development Programme (UNDP), as a participating and executing agency.

The World Tourism Organization was originally conceived as an inter-governmental organization in a UN General Assembly resolution (Number 2529) on December 5,1969. This resolution called for establishment of WTO to play a "central and decisive role" in the field of tourism and to maintain effective collaboration with the appropriate organs of the United Nations and its specialized agencies.

At Torremolinos (Spain), in June 1977, the second General Assembly of WTO approved an agreement with the United Nations for cooperation and relationships. On December 20,1977 the 32nd General Assembly of the UN approved this agreement which is now in force. In immediate implementation of this agreement, the UN General Assembly in December 1977 also approved a resolution sponsored by the Philippines with 24 co-sponsors, including India, requesting the WTO "to intensify its efforts to promote tourism, particularly in developing countries, through international cooperation and to report to the General Assembly at its 33rd session on action taken". The WTO became an executing agency of the UNDP in May 1976. A few months later, UNDP resident representatives throughout the world became WTO representatives for all matters concerning technical cooperation in the field of tourism. The WTO has already completed its first project in Jordan and is now processing many more requests from member states, including Asian members, for both national and regional assistance programmes and projects.

The Membership : There are three categories of members: full members, associate members, affiliate members. Full members are the sovereign states. Associate members are the territories or groups of territories not responsible for their external relations but whose membership is approved by the state assuming responsibility for their external relations. Affiliate members are international bodies, both inter-governmental and non-governmental, concerned with specialized interests in tourism, as well as commercial and non-commercial bodies and associations whose activities are related to the aims of WTO.

The activities of the organization include:

(i) clearing house for all available information on international and domestic tourism including statistical data, legislation and regulation and special events and its systematic collection, analysis and dissemination;

(ii) making travel easier by reducing and simplifying frontier formalities and removing barriers to the free movement of tourists;

(iii) organizing and convening international conferences, seminars, round tables and technical meetings on all aspects of tourism;

(iv) preparation of draft international agreements on tourism; and

(v) examining vocational training programmes with a view to contributing to the establishment of suitable teaching programmes tailored to specific needs, especially in the developing countries. The permanent activities of WTO include the collection and updating of available information on training needs. Special activities include participation in technical cooperation projects for vocational training.

The Functioning : There are three organs through which WTO functions:

General Assembly: This is the supreme organ and sovereign body of WTO composed of delegates representing full members, associate members and representatives of affiliate members. It meets every two years and may consider any question and make recommendations on any matter within the competence of WTO. The General Assembly has created six regional commissions. The regions covered are Africa, the Americas, Europe, Middle East, the Pacific and East Asia and South Asia. The regional commissions ensure the implementation, within their respective regions, of the decisions and recommendations of the General Assembly and the Executive Council. They function and operate within the framework of the organization. There are the regional secretariats which are an integral part of the WTO Secretariat and help the regional commissions in organizing and covering their conferences and meetings.

Executive Council: It consists of full members elected by the assembly at the ratio of one member for every five full , members of WTO organization with a view to achieving fair and equitable geographical distribution. The Executive Council, among other matters, takes all necessary measures in consultation with the Secretary General, for the implementation of the decisions and recommendations of the assembly, and reports thereon to the assembly. The Council meets at least twice a year.

The Secretariat: The Secretariat consists of the Secretary General and such staff as the organization may require. The Secretary General is responsible for carrying out the general policy and work programme of the organization in accordance with the directions of the General Assembly and Executive Council. The Secretary General ensures the legal representation of the organization. By the decision of the first General Assembly of WTO in May 1975, the headquarters were set up in Madrid (Spain) in January 1976.

The activities of the organization cover all sectors of tourism on a worldwide basis. The WTO works in cooperation with all international organizations, the United Nations in particular, as well as with commercial and non-commercial bodies involved in tourism. The organization is performing extremely useful service of concrete and creative character by facilitating the exchange of technical information; the making of specialized studies, the holding of special seminars adapted to world regional requirements and advanced vocational training courses. The essentially practical nature of its work programme, tailored as it is to regional requirements, takes full cognizance of the problems peculiar to countries and regions in all stages of development, such as investments, financial questions, physical planning and area development, economic analysis, marketing and market surveys— all this not only with a secretarial approach but with a comprehensive concern from the point of view of the state.

The creation of WTO coincided with the universal recognition of tourism as an important instrument of economic and social development and its consequent ascendancy to full government responsibility. An inter-governmental body of tourism officials, the WTO is empowered to act in the name of their governments and speak in terms of the impact of tourism on the balance of payments. The creation of WTO thus is not only a proof that the states are fully conscious of their own responsibilities in the field of tourism, but also of the establishment of tourism to its rightful ranking at international level.

Like its predecessor, the IUOTO, the WTO's activities cover all sectors of tourism on a worldwide basis. It provides an international forum where tourism officials, whether governmental or non-governmental, can discuss problems and exchange ideas. Representatives of the private sector also have access to its membership. WTO works in close cooperation with almost all international organizations, the United Nations' organizations in particular, as well as with commercial and non-commercial bodies involved in tourism.

India is a full member of the World Tourism Organization.

Member States of WHO

The following are the member states of the World Tourism Organization:

1. Afghanistan
2. Algeria
3. Angola
4. Argentina
5. Australia
6. Austria
7. Bahrain
8. Bangladesh
9. Belgium
10. Benin
11. Bolivia
12. Brazil
13. Bulgaria
14. Burkina
15. Burundi
16. Cameroon
17. Canada
18. Chad
19. Chile
20. China
21. Columbia
22. Cuba
23. Cyprus
24. Czech Republic
25. Dominican Republic
26. Ecuador
27. Egypt
28. Ethiopia

29. Finland
30. France
31. Gabon
32. Gambia
33. Germany
34. Ghana
35. Greece
36. Grenada
37. Guinea-Bissau
38. Haiti
39. Hungary
40. India
41. Indonesia
42. Iran
43. Islamic Republic of Iraq
44. Israel
45. Italy
46. Ivory Coast
47. Jamahiriya
48. Jamaica
49. Japan
50. Jordan
51. Kenya
52. Korea
53. Republic of (South Korea)
54. Kuwait
55. Laos
56. Lebanon
57. Lesotho
58. Libya
59. Malawi
60. Malaysia
61. Maldives, the
62. Mali
63. Malta
64. Mauritania
65. Mauritius
66. Mexico
67. Mongolia
68. Morocco
69. Nepal
70. Netherlands, the
71. Nicaragua
72. Niger
73. Nigeria
74. Pakistan
75. Panama
76. Peru
77. Philippines
78. Poland
79. Portugal
80. Rwanda
81. San Marino
82. Senegal
83. Seychelles
84. Sierra Leone
85. Spain

86. Sri Lanka
87. Sudan
88. Switzerland
89. Syria
90. Tanzania
91. Thailand
92. Togo
93. Tunisia
94. Turkey
95. Uganda
96. United Arab Emirates
97. United States of America
98. Uruguay
99. Venezuela
100. Vietnam
101. Yemen Arab Republic
102. Zaire
103. Zambia
104. Zimbabwe

Associate Members : Besides the member states, WTO has four associate members, namely,

1. Amba
2. Macau
3. Netherlands Antilles
4. Puerto Rico

Affiliate Members : The WTO has 170 affiliate members that represent the following bodies and sectors of tourism activity:

- Teaching and Vocational Training
- Accommodation and Catering
- Travel Agencies and Organizations
- Transport
- Financial Institutes
- Research Centres and Advisory Bodies
- Development Agencies
- Promotion
- Press and Information
- Social and Leisure Tourism
- Professional Association, Unions, Permanent Observer

The WTO also has Holy Sea as permanent observer to the organization.

General Programme of Work : The World Tourism Organization (WTO) is the only worldwide organization focusing upon all aspects of tourism. It is a leading inter-governmental organization in tourism. It provides a vital forum for governments and the industry to meet and address issues of common interest and concern. The WTO's general programme of work covers six broad areas:

Cooperation for Development: Advice and assistance to governments on a wide range of tourism issues including master plans and feasibility studies, investment needs and technology transfer to marketing and promotion.

Education and Training: A strategic framework for the organization of tourism education and training including courses on educating educators, short term and distance-learning courses and a growing network of WTO education and training centres.

Statistics and Market Research: WTO functions as the foremost centre for the collection, analysis and dissemination of tourism data from over 180 countries and territories. It continuously monitors and analyses trends around the world. A comprehensive series of publications is produced for members and the industry.

Environment and Planning: WTO is working for sustainable tourism development and the translation of environmental concerns into practical measures. It participates in forums and summits concerning global issues on environment.

Communication and Documentation: WTO's communication and documentation work relates to publication and distribution of several books, monographs, technical papers, and news and information bulletins such as *Yearbook of Tourism Statistics, Compendium of Tourism Statistics, Forecasts of Tourism Trends, World Directory of Tourism Education, National and Regional Planning and Sustainable Tourism Guides,* etc. The communication and documentation section of WTO also works as press contact point for the organization.

Quality of Tourism Services: Liberalization, health and safety reflect the broad and interconnected range of issues related to improving the quality of tourism services. WTO is working towards the removal of barriers to tourism and is encouraging the liberalization of trade and tourism services. Additional activities in this area include measures for improving health and food safety and making tourism more accessible to the handicapped.

Travel Association for Pacific Asia

The Pacific Asia Travel Association (PATA) was founded in the year 1951 as a non-profit corporation to stimulate interest in the Pacific region as a vacation land, and to develop, promote and facilitate travel to and among the many Pacific destinations. The association had 44 founder members. The founder, Lorrin Thurston, a leading newspaper publisher in Honolulu, had an idea to organize all travel from the Occident to the Pacific area in a consistent, cohesive and systematic manner so as to ensure maximum benefit from existing opportunities and the creation of fresh opportunities through multimedia publicity. PATA's first conference was held in January 1952 in Honolulu and its headquarters established in San Francisco, USA in 1953. PATA has its own director for Europe who is based in London and works to promote traffic from the European markets into the Pacific region. PATA's first Asian office was opened in Manila, Philippines in 1976.

PATA is a non-profit organization set up with the objective of developing, promoting and facilitating travel to and within the Pacific area and South-East Asian region including India. It primarily operates in the United States market which is the world's biggest travel market. The organization provides the meeting point for the people involved in all aspects of the travel trade from a large number of countries. It focuses attention on travel opportunities in member countries and builds up awareness and specific contacts among the travel trade in countries from where the tourists originate. The underlying philosophy of PATA is that the entire travel industry must work together to develop an ever-increasing flow of pleasure travel from which each member will derive a fair share of the total business.

The activities of PATA include assisting small and up and coming destinations to develop their infrastructure, providing expertise, planning group travel schemes, destinations, hotels operations and discounts. It provides up-to-date information and practical and theoretical experience in the field of tourism. The annual conferences of PATA and its workshops provide greater scope to its members to share their ideas and exchange views about promotion of tourism in their respective regions. PATA staff are outstanding experts in their respective fields of marketing and research and regularly exchange information with others on latest techniques and practices in their respective areas. All members benefit directly or indirectly from the continuing programmes of PATA, which include travel research, marketing, training programmes, and the development of visitor plants and services.

Promotion occupies a major portion of PATA's total effort. The PATA publication, *Pacific Travel News,* is relied upon by wholesale and retail travel agents as an important source of authoritative material on the Pacific. Recently, PATA has produced the first edition of the *Pacific Area Destination Handbook* which compiles in a single volume all the data that are required for the planning and sale of travel. It is the world's most audioritative and comprehensive handbook on 31 Pacific destinations. PATA also publishes its *Hotel Directory and Travel Guide* listing the hotels, resorts and travel services in the Pacific area.

PATA Membership : PATA has nine categories of membership: active government, associate government, active carrier, associate carrier, active industry, allied, affiliated allied, associate and sustaining. *Active government* members consist of the primary official organization designated by the government of any nation, territory, or political division, wholly or partly in the Pacific area. *Associate government* members consist of any organization charged with the responsibility of the domestic or overseas promotion of tourism as designated by the government of any nation, territory, or political division either situated outside or within the Pacific area but not being the primary official organization designated for the overseas promotion of travel, or not meeting other criteria as might be required for active government membership. *Active carrier* members consist of any government recognised, registered or certified air or steamship line operating vehicles having individual passenger capacity in excess of twelve passengers and providing regular scheduled common carriage passenger service to and within the Pacific area. *Associate carrier* members consist of any government-recognised passenger-carrier operating vehicles (a) each having a passenger capacity of twelve or fewer passengers and providing regular scheduled common carriage passenger service or (b) having a passenger capacity in excess of twelve passengers but not providing passenger service in the regular common carriage basis as prescribed for active carrier members. *Active industry* members consist of hotel organization having management authority as distinguished from mere sales, advertising reservations direction, over one or more hotels with a total of one thousand or more guest rooms in one or more Pacific areas, tour operator organizations excluding air or ship transportation. *Allied members* consist of travel agencies, tour operators, hotel representatives and firms serving as general agents of or representing various segments of the Pacific travel industry. *Affiliated allied* members consist of branch offices of an allied member travel agency or tour operator. *Associate members* consist of individual operating organizations and firms such as communication media, media representatives, advertising, public relations and research agencies having definite interest in Pacific travel. *Sustaining members* consist of those organizations, firms or individuals whose commercial or cultural interests, in the judgement of the board of directors, will further contribute to the aims of the association.

The control of PATA is vested in the active government, carrier and industry members. The organizations qualifying for active government or active carrier membership have the right to membership. They require no sponsorship and are requested merely to provide the board of directors with certain pertinent information. Membership in all other categories is at the discretion of the board of directors, and requires not only that the organization comply with certain guidelines for eligibility, but also that certain categories of PATA members must sponsor the new applicant and vouch for its stability and professionalism.

Presently PATA has a membership drawn from over 50 countries. Besides it has over 50 state and local tourism bodies, 65 airlines and cruise lines, and more than 2,000 travel industry companies. PATA'S chapter membership includes over 17,000 travel professionals in 79 PATA chapters located throughout the world.

India, which was an associate member of PATA since 1957, became a full-fledged active member in 1964.

List of Active Members

Active Governments

1. American Samoa Office of Tourism
2. Australian Tourist Commission
3. Bangladesh Parjatan Corporation
4. Tourism Bureau of the Republic of China
5. Cook Islands Tourist Authority
6. Fiji Visitors Bureau
7. Guam Visitors Bureau
8. Hawaii, Department of Planning and Economic Development
9. Hong Kong Tourist Association
10. India, Department of Tourism
11. Indonesia, Directorate General of Tourism
12. Japan National Tourist Organization
13. Kiribati, Ministry of Natural Resource Development
14. Korea National Tourism Corporation
15. Macau, Department of Information and Tourism
16. Tourist Development Corporation of Malaysia
17. Mexican National Tourist Council
18. Micronesia, Department of Development Services
19. Nepal, Department of Tourism
20. New Caledonia, Office du Tourisme
21. New Zealand Government Tourist and Publicity Department
22. Pakistan, Ministry of Culture and Tourism
23. Papua New Guinea, Office of Tourism
24. Philippines, Ministry of Tourism
25. Singapore Tourist Promotion Board
26. Solomon Islands Tourist Authority

27. Sri Lanka Tourist Board
28. Tahiti Tourist Development Board
29. Thailand, Tourism Authority Tonga Visitors Bureau
30. United States Travel Service
31. Russia Intourist
32. Vanuatu Tourist Information Bureau
33. Western Samoa, Department of Economic Development

Active Industry

1. American Express Company
2. Hilton International
3. Hotel Indonesia International Corporation Ltd.
4. Unitours

Active Carriers

1. Aeronaves de Mexico
2. Air-India
3. Air-Lanka
4. Air Nauru
5. Air New Zealand
6. Air Niugini
7. Air Pacific
8. All Nippon Airways
9. Aloha Airlines
10. American Airlines
11. Ansett Airlines of Australia Air Lines
12. Bangladesh Biman
13. Bouraq Indonesia Air Lines
14. British Caledonian Airways Ltd.
15. CP Air
16. Cathay Pacific Airways

17. China Air Lines
18. Condor Flugdienst
19. Continental Air Lines
20. Delta Steamship Lines
21. Deutsche Lufthansa
22. Finnair
23. Garuda Indonesian Airways
24. Gulf Air Company
25. Hawaiian Air
26. Indian Airlines
27. Japan Air Lines
28. KLM Royal Dutch Airlines
29. Korean Air
30. Malaysian Airlines System
31. Merpati Nusantara Airlines
32. Mexicana Airlines
33. North-west Orient Airlines
34. Pakistan International Airlines
35. Pan American World Airways
36. Philippine Airlines
37. Qantas Airways Ltd.
38. Royal Nepal Airlines
39. Royal Viking Line
40. Scandinavian Airlines System
41. Singapore Airlines Ltd.
42. Sitmar Cruises
43. Thai Airways International
44. Transamerica Airlines
45. Trans-Australia Airlines

46. Trans World Airlines
47. UTA French Airlines
48. United Airlines
49. Western Airlines
50. World Airways

Associate Carriers

1. Ansett-Pioneer Road Passenger Group
2. Japanese National Railways
3. Mid Pacific Air

Associate Governments

1. Anaheim Visitor and Convention Bureau
2. Australian Standing Committee of Tourism
3. Bali Government Tourism Office
4. California Office of Tourism
5. Canberra Tourist Bureau (Australia)
6. Central Java Provincial Tourist Office
7. East Java Regional Tourist Development Bureau
8. Gangweon-do Provincial Government (Korea)
9. Hawaii Visitors Bureau
10. India Tourism Development Corporation
11. Jakarta Metropolitan Tourism Board
12. Kementerian Tenaga Rakyat (Malaysia)
13. Long Beach Convention and Tourism Bureau
14. Korea Bureau of Tourism, Ministry of Transportation
15. Marianas Visitors Bureau
16. Melbourne Tourism Authority
17. New South Wales Department of Tourism
18. New Zealand National Travel Association
19. Northern Territory Tourist Commission

20. Pahang State Development Corporation (Malaysia)
21. Pehang State Government
22. Philippine Convention Bureau
23. Philippine Tourism Authority
24. Queensland Tourist and Travel Corporation
25. Sabah Tourism Promotion Corporation
26. Sarawak Tourist Development Commission
27. Seoul Metropolitan Government
28. Travel Alberta
29. Victoria Government Travel Authority
30. West Java Regional Tourism Office

PATA Chapters : To assist in the fulfilment of the objectives of the Pacific Asia Travel Association, the board of directors is empowered to encourage and authorise establishment of PATA Chapters at any place in the world. The chapters concept implemented in the year 1960 is unique with PATA among travel organizations. The primary purpose of a chapter is to conduct continuing education programmes to keep PATA members abreast of the changes in Pacific travel. The chapters also do considerable promotional work, and stage social events for the members. The specific objectives of the chapters are as follows:

(i) To bring together representatives of PATA members at regular intervals to develop a closer working relationship and a better understanding of travel matters relating to the Pacific area,

(ii) To obtain uniformity and combined action by members in pursuing national and local policies within the framework of PATA.

(iii) To implement specific PATA objectives and projects.

(iv) To pass to appropriate government and official organizations such matters approved by PATA, and to obtain action thereon as and when required.

(v) To process generally and to obtain opinions of members of the chapters on any PATA requirement or objective.

(vi) To provide a forum which will enable the individual chapter members to conduct their various assigned responsibilities for selling travel, and providing services to visitors to the Pacific in a more effective manner.

There are two types of chapters, namely, (i) area chapters and (ii) promotional chapters. Area chapters were conceived as of the 8th Annual PATA Conference (1959) by a number of allied and associate members as a means of keeping PATA members and their representatives in the Pacific better informed on happenings throughout the Pacific travel industry and on association activities. Some of these chapter activities include programmes involving matters of facilitation, staff training, improving visitor plants and services, and promotions aimed at developing regional tourist traffic and other marketing activities.

Promotional chapters were authorised by the 9th Annual PATA Conference (1960) as a means of furthering the promotion of visitors from priority market areas to Pacific destinations. Activities of these Chapters are all designed to increase the sale of travel to the Pacific Asia and include regular meetings of the PATA membership/travel trade with programmes on various Pacific destinations, providing up-to-date information on new developments, facilities, services, tours, educational seminars for travel trade, sales personnel and cooperation with PATA in the overall marketing programme, promotions and other PATA activities.

The chapters are, however, not the branch offices of PATA. They are rather like local civic clubs working for the benefit of their respective communities. A chapter is composed of the highest level of executives representing the local tourism industry who volunteer their services and their expertise to develop a constantly expanding overall business. Presently, PATA has as many as 80 active chapters. Two to three new chapters are organized yearly to help more and more people keep abreast of the changes in Pacific travel.

Finances of the Association : The administration and programmes of the association are financed by way of membership dues and the marketing assessments paid by all members. The amount of dues, however, varies with the category of membership.

The marketing assessments of governments and carriers are calculated in accordance with a Stanford Research Institute formula. This formula takes into account, among other things, the growth in visitor arrivals and expenditures at member areas, and the growth in traffic volume of carrier members The association's financial position is reviewed by the board of directors at their monthly meetings, and an annual audit is made by an outside accounting agency. In addition to membership dues and the marketing assessment amounts, there are additional revenues which come from allied and associate members, a portion of which is applied to various marketing programmes.

Functions of PATA : The Pacific Asia Travel Association performs a variety of junctions. These include:

Pacific Travel Conference and Workshop: During the first four months of each year, PATA sponsors and organizes a conference of its members with the objectives of reviewing the progress, exchanging ideas and planning for future programmes. These meetings are held at different areas. The annual conferences attract a large number of delegates from all over the world. The conference also serves as a unique promotional tool for the host government providing it an opportunity to show to the travel industry from abroad what it has to offer in terms of tourist attractions and tourism plant to the foreign visitor.

Marketing: A long-range marketing programme coordinates all the promotional functions of PATA for a maximum impact in the consumer market and also among sales agents. The marketing programme includes:

(a) advertising, publicity and promotion

(b) research and development.

An extensive advertising programme schedule is carried in leading national magazines of North America with a view to increase interest in the Pacific region as a major travel area. The association prepares and distributes a wide selection of sales aids and sales promotion materials to travel agents and tour operators throughout the world. A strong trade advertising programme is directed towards travel agents in order to merchandise PATA's consumer advertising and sales promotion efforts. Weekly news releases, special feature stories and photographs are provided to the various newspapers, magazines and radio and television networks by the associations Pacific news service.

Members were allowed to use the association's various materials including photographs for their own publicity purposes. So far as research and development is concerned, the association's research programme is designed to provide it with the marketing information needed to formulate its own marketing programme as well as to provide its members with information which will assist them in designing their own programmes. The association organizes research seminars, research presentations and technical assistance programmes for its members. Another important facet of the research programme includes the collection, analysis and dissemination of Pacific travel statistics—an effort designed to constantly improve and standardise the tourism statistics of the Pacific region.

PATA and India : India was admitted as an associate government member of Pacific Asia Travel Association in 1957. It was at the specific request of the government that the constitution of the PATA was amended suitably to enable India and other South Asian countries to become associate government members. However, it was only in the year 1964 at Jakarta, Indonesia that India became an active member of the association. Basically, PATA was formed to promote traffic to Pacific countries only. However, the definition of PATA was somewhat enlarged to enable some of the countries bordering on the Pacific to join PATA. India was the first country to enter PATA from among the countries which bordered on the Pacific but were not in the Pacific region. Subsequently, a few other countries also joined the association from this region. Among these countries were Sri Lanka, Nepal and later, Pakistan and Bangladesh.

It was not long before India realised the manifold benefits which this organization had for promotion of tourism. India realised that PATA was one of the most active travel promotional organizations and that the country's association with it would not only benefit her from getting a share of the world's increasing tourist flow but also from the point of view of exposing it to the modern techniques of tourism marketing and promotion. During the 1964 annual conference at Sydney in Australia, PATA agreed to hold its annual convention in India in 1966. Again, during the 1965 conference in Korea, India's invitation to host the annual convention in 1966 was reaffirmed and accepted by the general body of the PATA.

The Conventions

The decision regarding the venue of the conference is generally made three years in advance.

PATA's 1966 conference was the 15th annual conference of the association. The five-day conference and workshop which met in New Delhi was attended by over 500 delegates from a number of countries. India at that time was emerging as a new tourist destination with very little exposure in American and Pacific areas of its tourist attractions. The main objective in inviting PATA conference to Delhi was to expose the facilities to a large segment of foreign tour operators, travel writers, airline executives, etc. The conference was a big success as it resulted in a steady rise in tourist traffic to India during subsequent years. India enjoyed a continuous and uninterrupted growth till 1973 when the steep rise in oil prices followed by initiation in potential tourism markets led to a slight decline in the growth of tourist arrivals. However, during subsequent years the tourist arrivals increased. India after PATA '66 Conference is now a full-fledged member.

India was awarded yet another conference when it was unanimously chosen as the venue of the 1978 conference at the Sydney PATA Conference in 1975. The theme of the conference "Challenge of Change" became particularly significant in view of the fact that tourism was passing into a phase where there were no limits to its growth. The objective of hosting another PATA conference in India after a period of twelve years was to expose tourist facilities to a large segment of tour operators, travel writers, airline executives, etc. The conference was attended by over 1,500 delegates and was the largest conference in the history of PATA. The large number of delegates from all over the world provided an opportunity to India to expose its tourist plant to the international travel world. The conference was responsible for projecting India's image not only as a great tourist destination but also as a great host country. India will host yet another conference in the year 2002.

The PATA (India) Chapter was organized in the year 1969 as one of the area chapters. This chapter has over 130 members with representation from government (Ministry of Tourism), India Tourism Development Corporation, Indian Airlines, Air India and other international carriers, leading travel agencies in India, hotels tour operators, advertising agencies, etc. The chapter undertakes promotional work specifically for promoting India.

Today, PATA provides it members with an array of programmes and events created to promote the region as the preferred international destination. These activities also aim to develop a sustainable future for the travel industry and to assist members with professional development in a number of fields. Originally oriented towards sending visitors to the Pacific Asia region, PATA has grown to encompass the changing market place and now incorporates intra-regional tourism within the PATA geographic boundaries.

The PATA annual conference draws together the top decision makers in the region. The PATA Trade Mart focus on marketing opportunities by matching the buyers and sellers of the region's tourism products. PATA's special-interest marketing seminars and marts are held regularly to help members target new business opportunities and learn the successful techniques for development. PATA also keeps its members up- to- date on relevant industry trends via the strategic information centre, which provides the members with timely research and market intelligence for business planning, product development and marketing.

PATA's office of Environment and Culture and the PATA Foundation coordinate programmes to preserve the region's environmental, heritage and cultural resources. Through targeted marketing and promotional programmes, business networking opportunities, and support and resources services, PATA provides a partnership for their members professional and personal growth.

PATA's mission is to enhance the growth, value and quality of Pacific Asia travel and tourism for the benefit of its membership. PATA has long been an advocate of balancing growth with conservation measures.

In recent years there has been rapid and continuous development of both national and international tourism. The international tourism organizations have played and are continuing to play a key role in the tourism development, both national as well as international. India has regularly participated actively in the deliberations of international bodies which afford an opportunity to establish new contacts and renew old ties with persons from all over the world connected with tourism. These organizations also help the member countries to determine the general travel trends for proper channelisation of promotional activities. India's association with these bodies has definitely encouraged the flow of tourist traffic from international tourist generating markets to India.

Organization for Economic Co-operation and Development: The Organization for Economic Cooperation and Development (OECD) was founded in the year 1961 to foster economic growth and development for the member countries. The headquarters of the organization are located in Paris (France). OECD has 24 member countries.

OECD has a tourism committee composed of tourism officials drawn from all the member countries. Through its tourism committee OECD carries out most of its work related to tourism. The tourism committee produces regular reports and technical papers comprising statistical data on tourism development to and within these countries. Over the years, the members of the OECD have made concerted efforts to advance people's freedom to travel across borders with minimum barriers. The members influence their respective governments about the nature and direction which tourism should take in major industrial countries. One of the important publications of OECD is the report *"Tourism Policy and International Tourism in OECD Member Countries"* which is published every year. This report reviews current tourism issues and the trends in tourism activity for each country. The review is done on a yearly basis and serves as an important document for policy makers.

European Travel Commission (ETC) European Travel Commission (ETC) was established in the year 1948 as a non-profit making body by the national tourism organizations (NTO) of various European countries. The objectives of the ETC are

- To foster international tourism cooperation in Europe
- To exchange information on tourism development projects and marketing techniques
- To undertake/commission appropriate travel research concerning various issues related to travel and tourism
- To promote tourism within and to Europe from other parts of the world particularly from North America and Europe.

The commission's functions include research, marketing and a range of allied tourism policy issues. The activities of the European Travel Commission are supported by the European Commission, which considers tourism as an industry of great potential and of great economic and social significance within the community.

Tourism Organization for Indian Ocean : Founded in 1995, the Indian Ocean Tourism Organizations mission is to enhance regional cooperation and understanding through sustainable tourism.

IOTO has stated in its vision statement that every country in the Indian Ocean region has its own unique tourism product, image, strategies and structure and these are tourism issues of common interest and mutual benefit within the region. The vision for the region is that every country around the Indian Ocean Rim will optimise its own potential in a sustainable manner for the benefit of all of its people.

The approach of IOTO is to complement and add value to the strategies and activities of public and private sector tourism organizations around the Indian Ocean Rim by:

- Positioning and marketing the Indian Ocean region as a unique tourism destination area.

- Facilitating cooperation and coordination among IOTO destinations and members.
- Promoting the expansion of appropriate transportation services and facilities to and within the Indian Ocean region.
- Liaising on behalf of its members with governments and authorities towards reducing barriers to travel.
- Encouraging improved service standards and the quality of the visitor experience throughout the destination area.
- Encouraging all members to support sound environmental tourism practices for the long-term benefit of their communities.
- Facilitating information dissemination and skills interchange throughout the region.

The membership of IOTO includes governments, tourism organizations, carriers, major hotel and resort groups, major tour operators and tourism industry entities from the 25 IOTO core countries. The core countries of the IOTO are as follows:

1. Australia
2. Bangladesh
3. Christmas Island
4. Cocos Island, the
5. Comoros
6. India
7. Indonesia
8. Kenya
9. Madagascar
10. Malaysia
11. Maldives, the
12. Mauritius
13. Mozambique
14. Myanmar
15. Oman
16. Pakistan
17. Reunion
18. Seychelles
19. Singapore
20. Somalia
21. South Africa
22. Sri Lanka
23. Tanzania
24. Thailand
25. Yemen

The Indian Ocean Tourism Organization secretariat is located at Perth, Australia.

UN Organizations

United Nations Environment Programme (UNEP), C.P. 30552

Nairobi, Kenya. United Nations Development Programme (UNDP), 1 United Nations Plaza, New York, N Y10017, USA..

United Nations Conference on Trade and Development (UNCTAD), Palais des Nations, 1211 Geneva 10, Switzerland.

Department of Economic and Social Affairs, Statistical Office, Centre for Housing, Building and Planning, 1 United Nations, New York, N Y10017, USA..

UN Economic Commissions

Economic Commission for Europe (ECE), Palais des Nations, 1211 Geneva 10, Switzerland.

Economic and Social Commission for Asia and the Pacific (ESCAP), United Nations Building, Rajdamern Avenue, Bangkok, Thailand.

Economic Commission for Africa (ECA), P.O. Box 300, Addis Ababa, Ethiopia.

Specialized Agencies

International Labour Organization (ILO), 4, route des Morillons, 1211, Geneve 22, Switzerland.

International Bank for Reconstruction and Development (IBRD), 1818 H. Street, N.W. Washington, D.C. 20431, USA..

International Monetary Fund (IMF), 700 19th Street, N.W. Washington, D.C, 20431, USA..

International Development Association (IDA), 1818 H Street, N.W. Washington, D.C, 20431, USA.

International" Finance Corporation (IFC), 1818 H Street, N.W. Washington, D.C., 20431 U.S.A.

Food and Agriculture Organization (FAO), Via delle Terme di Caracalla, 00100, Rome, Italy. United Nations Educational, Scientific and Cultural Organization (UNESCO), 7, Place de Fontenoy 75700 Paris, France.

World Health Organization (WHO), 1211 Geneva, Switzerland. Inter-Governmental Maritime Consultative Organization (IMCO), 101-104 Picadilly, London, WIY UAE, England.

International Civil Aviation Organization (ICAO), 1000 Sherbrooke Street, West Montreal, Quebec, Canada.

Non-governmental Organizations

International Air Transport Association (IATA), 800 Place Victoria, P. O. Box 113 Montreal, Quebec, Canada, H 42 IMI, E-mail: atdi@iata.org

American Society of Travel Agents (ASTA), 711 Fifth Avenue, New York, N Y10017, USA.

Universal Federation of Travel Agents Association (UFTAA), 30, Avenue Marnix, 1050 Brussels, Belgium.

Conference of Government Tourism Organizations and Travel Agencies, 01 Litewska 200-581, Warsaw, Poland. International Federation of Tour Operators (IFTO), Amaliegade 37,2 TR, 1256, Copenhagen K, Denmark.

International Congress and Convention Association (ICCA), 15, rue de L' Arcade, 75008 Paris, France. www.icca.nl.

International Centre for Conservation (ICC), 13 Via di San Michele 00153, Rome, Italy.

International Youth Hostel Federation (IYHF), Midland Bank Chambers, Howardsgate, Welwyn, Garden City, Hertfordshire, England.

International Association of Convention and Visitors Bureaus, 1390 Market Street, San Francisco, California 94102 USA..

Pacific Asia Travel Association (PATA), 228 Grant Avenue, San Francisco, California 94108, USA.The Travel Research Association (TRA), P.O. Box 8066, Foothill Station, Salt Lake City, Utah 84108, USA.

International Federation of Tourism Journalists and Writers (IFTJR), rue de L'Autumne 32,1050, Brussels, Belgium.

International Social Travel Federation, 99-101 rue de la Loi, 1040, Brussels, Belgium. Inter-American Federation of Journalists and Writers in the Tourist Trade, Calle Rivadavia 755, Buenos Aires, Argentina.

International Federation of Tourist Centres, Schrutkagassell, 1130 Vienna, Austria.

International Federation of Camping and Caravaning, rue d'Arenberg, 44-B.P. 955, Brussels, Belgium.

Federation of International Youth Travel Organizations (FIYTO), 81 Islande Brygge 2300, Copenhagen 5, Denmark.

European Travel Commission (ETC), P.O. Box 536, Dublin, Ireland.

East Asia Travel Association, 2-10-1 Yurakucho, Chiyodaku Tokyo, Japan.

American Hotel and Motel Association (AHMA), 888 Seventh Avenue, NY 10010, USA.

International Bureau of Social Tourism, 7, Boulevard de l'Imperatrice, Gare Centrale, Brussels 1, Belgium.

International Bureau for Tourism and Youth Exchanges, P.O. Box 147,1389 Budapest, Hungary.

World Association for Professional Training in Tourism, 105 rue St. Lazare 75009 Paris, France.

International Association of Scientific Experts in Tourism (AIEST), C.P. 2728, 3001 Berne, Switzerland.

International Academy of Tourism, 4 rule des Iris, Monte Carlo, Monaco.

International Touring Alliance (ITA), 2, Quai Gustave Ador 1207, Geneva, Switzerland. International Union for Conservation of Nature and Natural Resources, 1110 Morges, Switzerland.

World Association of Travel Agencies (WATA), 37 Quai Wilson 1211, Geneva 1, Switzerland.

World Tourism Organization (WTO), Calle Captain Haya, 42, Madrid-20, Spain.

International Centre for Advanced Tourism Studies (CIEST), Coronel Porfirio Diqz, 50 San Jeronimo Lidice, Mexico 20 D.F.Mexico.

Discover America Travel Organization (DATO): 1899 L Street, N.W. Washington, D.C. 20036, USA.

International Airline Passenger Association (IAPA), www.iapa.com International Hotel and Restaurant Association (IH&RA)

www.ih-ra.com

American Society of Travel Agents (ASTA), www.asta.com

World Travel and Tourism Council (WTTC), 20, Grosvenor Place, London SWIX 7TT, United Kingdom, www.wttc.org.

Universal Federation of Travel Agent's Association (UFTAA), www.uftaa.com

Bibliography

Ainaduraj, S.G.: *A Review of Research on Spices and Cashewnuts in India*, ICAR, New Delhi,

Alastair, M. Morrison : *Hospitality and Travel Marketing,* Delemar, New York, 1989.

Aldous, T. : *Battle for the Environment,* Collins, London, 1972.

Anderson, N. : *Work and Leisure,* Routledge and Kegan Faul, London, 1961.

Andrew Vladimir : *The Complete Travel Marketing Handbook,* NTC Business Book, Lincolnwood, USA, 1989.

Andrews, S.: *Food and Beverage Science*, Tata McGraw Hill, Publishing Co. Ltd., New Delhi, 1980.

——: *Demand Forecasting in Tourism,* University of Wales Press, Cardiff, 1974.

Ashworth, G. : *Recreation and Tourism,* Bell and Hyman, London, 1984.

—— : *Recreation and Tourism,* Bell and Hyman, London, 1984.

Austin, A. and A. Ram : *Studies on Chapati-Making Quality of Wheat,* Indian Council of Agricultural Research, New Delhi, 1971.

Awill, R. : *Man and Environment,* Penguin, London, 1967.

Baker, Michael J. : *The Marketing Book,* Heinemann, London, 1985.

Balsdon, J.P.V.D. : *Life and Leisure in Ancient Rome,* Bodley Head, London, 1966.

Baron, Raphael Raymond, V.: *Seasonalty in Tourism: A Guide to Seasonality and Trends for Policy-making*, The Economist Intelligence Unit, 1975.

Barrow, G.M.: *Physical Chemistry for Life Science*, McGraw-Hill Book Company, New York, 1992

Beaver, Allan : *Retail Travel Practice,* Allan Beaver and Gordon Wharton Landtours Ltd., 1975.

Beazely, E. : *Designed for Recreation,* Faber, London, 1970.

Bhatia, A. K. : *International Tourism : Fundamentals and Practices,* Sterling, New Delhi, 1991.

—— : *Tourism in India : History and Development,* Sterling, New Delhi, 1978.

Boniface, B. and Cooper, C. : *The Geography of Travel and Tourism* Heinemann, London, 1987.

Boniface, Brain G. : *The Geography of Travel and Tourism,* Butterworth-Heinmann, Oxford, 1991.

Bryden John M. : *Tourism and Development,* Cambridge University Press, Cambridge, 1973.

Bull, A. : *The Economics of Travel and Tourism,* Pitman, London, 1991.

Calder, N. : *The Environment Game,* Panther, London, 1969.

Charley, H.: *Food Science*, John Wiley and Sons Inc., New York. 1982.

Checchi and Co. : *The Future of Tourism in the Far East* (1961).

Cherry, G.E. : *Town Planning and its Social Context,* Hill, London, 1970.

Cherry, J.P.: *Protein Functionality in Foods,* American Chemical Society, Washington D.C., 1981.

Choudhury, B. : *Vegetables*, National Book Trust, New Delhi, 1977.

Chuck, Y. Gee : *The Travel Industry,* Van Nostrand Reinhold, New York, 1989.

Clare A.J. Gunn : *Taylor and Francis, Tourism Planning*, Taylor and Francis, New York, 1988.

Coltman, Michael M. : *Introduction of Travel and Tourism*, Van Nostrand Reinhold, New York, 1989.

Coltman, Michael M. : *Introduction to Travel and Tourism—An International Approach,* Van Nostrand Reinhold, New York, 1989.

Cooper, C. : *Tourism Principles and Practices,* Pitman, London, 1993.

Dale, E. : *Management Theory and Practice*, McGraw Hill, New York, 1983.

David Off, Phillips and Doris : *Sales and Marketing for Travel and Tourism*, Blackhill, USA, 1990.

Davidson, Rob : *Tourism in Europe*, Pitman Techniplus, London, 1992.

Dick, D.A.T. : *Cell Water,* Butterworth, Washington, 1966.

Dickerson, R.E. and I. Geiss : *Proteins: Structure, Function and Evolution*, Menlo Park, California, 1983.

Douglas Pearce : *Tourism Today: A Geographical-Analysis,* Longman, New York, 1987.

Ed Gell, D. L. : *International Tourism Policy,* Van Nostrand Reinhold, New York, 1990.

Eisenberg, D. and H. Kauzmann : *The Structure and Properties of Water,* Clarendon, Oxford, 1969.

Fennema, O.R.: *Food Chemistry,* Marcell Dekker Inc., New York, 1976.

Fersht, A. : *Enzyme Structure and Mechanism*, W.H. Freeman & Co., 1977.

Forrest, J.C., E.D. Aberle, H.B. Hedrick, M.D. Judge and R.A Merkel : *Principles of Meat Science*, W.H. Freeman and Co., San Francisco, 1975.

Frank, R.E. : *Market Segmentation,* Prentice-Hall, New Jersey, 1972.

Furia, T.E.: *Hand Book of Food Additives*, C.R.C. Press, T.C. Ohio, 1977.

Galbraith, John C. : *The New Industrial State,* Signet, New York 1986.

Gearing Charles, E. : *Planning or Tourism Development,* Praeger Publishers, New York, 1976.

Gottlieb, Edward and Klarnet Philip : *Successful Publicity,* Crosset and Dunlop, New York, 1964.

Gould, R.F. : *Flavour Chemistry*, American Chemical Society, Washington, D.C., 1966.

Gunn, C. : *Tourism Planning,* Taylor and Francis, New York, 1988.

Gunstone, F.D.: *An Introduction to the Chemistry and Biochemistry of Fatty Acids and their Glycerides*, Chapman and Hall, London, 1967.

Gurr, M.E. and A.T. James : *Lipid Biochemistry—An Introduction*, Cornell, Ithaca, New York, 1975.

Harrison, S.G., G.B. Masefield and M. Wallis: *The Oxford Book of Food Plants*, Oxford University Press, London, 1975.

Hascherneyer, R. and A.H. Haschemeyer : *Proteins: A Guide to Study of Physical and Chemical Methods*, John Wiley & Sons, New York, 1973.

Hawkin, Donald, A. Elwood Shafer and James Rovelstad : *Tourism Planning and Development Issues,* George Washington University Press, Washington D.C., 1980.

Hibbert, Christopher : *The Grand Tour,* Weidenfel and Nicolson, London, 1969.

Hodyson, A. : *The Travel and Tourism Industry,* Pergamon, Oxford, 1987.

Hollander, S. : *Passenger Transportation,* Michigan State University, Michigan, 1968.

Hunt, P. : *Fruit and Vegetables,* Ward Lock Ltd., London, 1972.

Hunziker, W. : *Social Tourism, its Nature and Problems,* Aliance International de Turisme, Geneva, 1951.

Hurdman, L.E. : *Tourism: A Shrinking World,* Wiley, New York, 1980.

Jafferson, Alan and Lickorish, Leonard : *Marketing Tourism,* Longman, UK, 1983.

Jarari, J. : *Role of Tourism in Socio-Economic Transformation of Developing Countries*, 1973.

Jasscler, D.K. and M.A. Joslyn : *Fruit and Vegetables Juice,* The AVI Publishing Co., Connecticut, 1971.

Jull, M.A.: *Poultry Husbandry,* Tata McGraw-Hill Publishing Co. Ltd., New Delhi, 1977.

Kent, N.L.: *Technology of Cereals*, Pergamon Press, New York, 1978.

Kernan, J. B. : *Promotion,* McGraw-Hill, New York, 1970.

Kotler Philip : *Principles of Marketing Practices,* Prentice Hall of India, New Delhi, 1985.

Lennarz, W.J. : *The Biochemistry of Glycoproteins and Proteoglycans*, Plenum, New York, 1980.

Less, R. and E.B. Jackson : *Sugar Confectionery and Chocolate Manufacture*, Leonard Hill Books, An Intertext Publisher, Burks, 1973.

Lewis Robert C : *Marketing Leadership in Hospitality*, Van Nostrand, New York, 1989.

Lickorish, L. J. : *The Travel Trade,* London Practical Press, 1974.

Lickorish, L.J. & Kershaw A.G. : *The Travel Trade*, Practical Press Ltd., London, 1988.

Lloydryall, A. and W.T. Pendzer: *Handling Transportation and Storage of Fruits and Vegetables: Fruits and Peanuts,* The AVI Publishing Co., Connecticut, 1974.

Marks, J., A : *Guide to the Vitamins: Their Role in Health and Disease*, University Park Press, Baltimore, 1975.

Mate, S. A.: *Cookie and Craker Technology*, The AVI Publishing Co., Connecticut, 1978.

Mcwilliams, M.: *Food Fundamentals,* John Wiley & Sons Inç., New York, 1979.

Medlik, S. : *Economic Importance of Tourism,* University of Surrey, Surrey, 1972.

Medlik, S. : *Profile of the Hotel and Catering Industry,* Heinemann, London, 1972.

Meredith George : *Incentives in Marketing,* NPSEE Education Fund, New Jersey, 1977.

Meridith, George and Fried, Robert P. : *Incentives in Marketing,* NPSC Education Fund Union, New Jersey, 1977.

Meyer, L.H. : *Food Chemistry*, Reinhold Publishing Corporation, New York, 1961.

Murthy, R.B.: *Breeding Procedures in Pearl Millet*, ICAR, New Delhi, 1977.

Nagy, S., P.E. Shaw and M.K. Veldhnis : *Citrus Science and Technology*, The AVI Publishing Co., Connecticut, 1977.

Nath, P. : *Vegetables for the Tropical Region*, Indian Council of Agricultural Research, New Delhi, 1976.

Ogilvie, F.W. : *The Tourist Movement: An Economic Study,* Staples Press, London, 1933.

Page, S. : *Urban Tourism,* Routledge, London, 1995.

Palmer, T.: *Understanding Enzymes*, John Wiley & Sons, New York, 1981.

Pamela, V.P. : *Directory of Wines and Spirits*, North Wood Publication, London, 1974.

Patmore, J. A. : *Land and Leisure,* David and Charles, London, 1970.

Patric Lavery : *Travel and Tourism*, Elem Publications, London, 1990.

Pearce, D. : *Tourism Today,* Longman, Harlow, 1987.

Pearce, Sales, J. : *Travel and Tourism Encyclopedia,* Blandford, London, 1959.

Peterson, M.S. and A.H. Johnson : *Encyclopedia of Food Science*, The AVI Publishing Co., Connecticut, 1978.

Peterson, M.S. and D.K. Tressler : *Food Technology the World Over*, The AVI Publishing Co., Connecticut, 1963.

Raymond, R. : *Ecological Principles for Economic Development,* John Wiley, London, 1978.

Reilly, R. T. : *Travel and Tourism Marketing Techniques,* Delmar, New York, 1988.

Roberts, D.V. : *Enzyme Kinetics*, Cambridge University Press, 1977.

Roberts, K. : *Leisure,* Longman, London, 1970.

Robinson, G.W.S. : *"The Recreation Geography of South Asia,"* Geographical Review, (October 1972).

Rosenow, John E. : *Tourism — the Good, the Bad and the Ugly*, Century Three Press, London, 1979.

Ross, G. F. : *The Psychology of Tourism,* Hospitality Press, Melbourne, 1994.

Rothfield, Crampon, Wahab : *Tourism Marketing,* Tourism International Press, London, 1975.

Russell Williams : *The Nutrition and Health,* Discovery CBS Publishers, New Delhi.

Ryan, C. : *Recreational Tourism :A Social Science Perspective,* Routledge, London, 1991.

Sakumaran, P.S. : *Perental Involvement in the Education of Mentally Handicapped Children,*Discovery Publishers, New Delhi, 2000.

Shreedevi, V. : *Nutrition Education,* Discovery Publishing House, New Delhi, 1997.

Sigaux, G. : *History of Tourism,* Leisure Arts, London, 1966.

Singh, B., : *Races of Maize*, ICAR, New Delhi, 1975.

Smartt, J.: *Tropical Pulses*, Longman Group Ltd., London, 1976.

Smith, S. : *Recreation Geography,* Longman, Harlow, 1983.

Sri Aurobindo : *The Upanishads,* Sri Aurobindo Ashram, Pondicherry, 1977.

Sutton, Geoffrey : *How to Sell Travel ?,* Travel Topics, London, 1959.

Sutton, W.A. : *"Travel and Understanding Notes on the Social Structure of Touring",* International Journal of Comparative Sociology, 1967.

Swern, D, : *Bailey's Industrial Oil and Fat Products*, Interscience Publishers Division, John Wiley & Sons, New York, 1964.

Tandon, H.P.: *Egg and its Care*, Ministry of Agriculture, Govt. of India, New Delhi, 1973.

Turner, Louis and Ash John : *The Golden Hordes-International Tourism and the Pleasure Periphery,* Constable and Company, London, 1975.

Turner, Louis and John Ash : *The Golden Hordes,* London, Constable, 1975.

Underwood, E.J: *Trace Elements in Human and Animal Nutrition*, Academic Press, New York, 1977.

Wahab Salah : *Tourism Management,* Tourism International Press, London, 1975.

Weiss.T. J.: *Food Oils and their Uses*, The AVI Publishing Inc., Connecticut, 1970.

Whistler, R.L. and J.N. BeMiller : *Industrial Gums*, Academic Press, New York, 1972.

White, J. : *History of Tourism,* Leisure Art, London, 1967.

Whiteley, P.P. : *Biscuit Manufacture*, Elsevier Publishing Co. Ltd., London, 1971.

Zeithaml, V.A. : *Services Marketing,* McGraw-Hill, London, 1996.